Framing Friction

FRAMING FRICTION

Media and Social Conflict

Edited by Mary S. Mander

University of Illinois Press
Urbana and Chicago

© 1999 by the Board of Trustees of the University of Illinois
Manufactured in the United States of America
1 2 3 4 5 C P 5 4 3 2 1

This book is printed on acid-free paper.

Library of Congress Cataloging-in-Publication Data
Framing friction : media and social conflict / edited by Mary
S. Mander.
    p.   cm.
Includes bibliographical references and index.
ISBN 0-252-02426-5 (cloth : acid-free paper)
ISBN 0-252-06733-9 (pbk. : acid-free paper)
1. Social conflict in mass media. 2. Mass media—
Audiences. I. Mander, Mary S., 1945–
P96.S63F73   1999
302.23—ddc21   98-9006
CIP

Contents

Introduction

Mary S. Mander

Communications scholars today live in an intellectual pluriverse, rather than a universe. This collection of essays reflects that pluriverse, the current scholarly cosmos in communications.

This book can be read in three ways. First, it can be read in terms of content. This kind of reading focuses on the media themselves, their fare, the effects of their fare, how they operate institutionally, and so on. Reading for content involves a search for the meaning of terms and the findings of research on the media. This reading seeks the answer to the question, What is the relationship between the media and the social order in times of social conflict? Some of the key terms we will discuss here have to do with media audiences, ideology and objectivity, representation and narrative, and everyday life and everyday practices (indigenous knowledge).

The second way to read this book is to read it for form; that is, to look at the structure of the research itself as well as what the French sociologist Pierre Bourdieu called the "universe of the undiscussed."[1] This universe includes all the assumptions that researchers make about the social order, about what being a human being entails, about how social change takes place, or about the relationship of the state to media, to media audiences, and to publics. This book identifies three research traditions, or paradigms of study, which are treated in succession.[2] Positivistic studies are followed by critical studies, which in turn are followed by hermeneutic studies.

The third, and by far the most difficult, way to read this book is to look for the linkages between form and content. Each of us chooses a particular research universe in which to live and work. Besides implying a set of beliefs about the social world, each research tradition also works within the limits of the methods thought to be suitable for that type of social inquiry. There are limits to what can be said about the process and effects of communication, given the research tradition within which one works. Whether we acknowledge it or not, each research tradition is influenced by the others. This influence works most often at the level of explanatory concepts, such as "ideology" or "media dependency." Sometimes, it works at the level of the taken for granted, but this occurs infrequently.[3]

It is not necessary to read this book in more than one way. However, it is my hope and my intention to provide a text that allows the reader both to raise the question, What is the relationship between the media and social conflict? and to explore the limits of our respective research traditions. I do so not to suggest that one tradition is wrong or that "those people" are blind to certain things. Rather, this book is arranged in such a way as to reveal the vitality and pluralism in the field of communications research today. Its premise can be furthered only if and when we get at the roots anchoring theory to phenomena. These root systems are implied in any study of media practices. The inclusion of multiple viewpoints in this book reflects my own approach to media studies as a hermeneutic social scientist.

The reader will not find situations across the research traditions that can be easily compared. This is because each research tradition has its own system of assumptions and practices. Social conflict is conceptualized in a variety of ways in the book because there are a variety of assumptions being made about the social animal, about what communication is, and about the social order. Audiences and publics are thought of and treated in different ways also. What is valuable about our research traditions is this diversity, rather than some form of agreement or similarity fashioned in a desperate search for universal traits or universal understanding. If the 1990s have witnessed anything of import, surely it is the demise of universals as compelling explanations of contemporary experience or values.

Focus on Social Conflict

The topical focus of this book is social conflict. I chose social conflict for two reasons. First, social conflict plays an important part in our everyday (commonsense) world in that it dominates media content and media forms. Second, social conflict has been relatively neglected among communications scholars. Critical scholars focus on social conflict but do few empirical studies of it. Until recently, their work has been rooted in Marx, who saw social conflict as a function of class membership. Thus, both critical scholars and positivists have treated conflict in negative terms. This book presupposes that social conflict is functional rather than dysfunctional.

Social Conflict in the Commonsense World

In the commonsense world—as compared to the social scientific one—we negotiate the conflict we meet daily in our homes and workplaces. We also learn about social conflict on a larger scale through the media. Periods of heightened social conflict and crisis profoundly transmute individual and collective realities. Conflict as it is experienced appears to be episodic or even dysfunctional. In recent history, terrorism, civil wars, the dissolution of political units, and civil protest have affected the parameters of social change at both the national and international levels. Social conflict casts long shadows. It displaces people from their homes and haunts generations to come. It alters diplomatic relations. It shapes foreign policy among nation states.

During times of conflict, the social arena becomes a field, a set of interlocking power lines, wherein men and women seek to control, maximize, or minimize the development and consequences of events. This struggle spontaneously sparks new relationships, problems, coalitions, and configurations of connectedness or power, or both. These in turn affect social choices and the disposition of human consciousness and conscience.

The world around us is in constant modification. Reality, or the empirically observable instances to which we lend coherence as we move through our days and nights, is transfigured. Our perception of it undergoes metamorphosis. In other words, what people experience as true about their relationships to others, to institutions, and to events is transformed, sometimes in fundamental ways. To recognize that change is essential to human experience is to recognize that human beings in essence grow. It is change, not stability, that characterizes human ontology.

Whether we are speaking of war or disagreement over environmental issues, social conflict often is not directly and personally experienced by individuals or communities. Instead, conflict's tenor, urgency, and immediacy are brought home to us by the media. Social conflicts often are inaccessible to us except in narrative and/or expository form. In fact, I would argue that it is because events in the phenomenal world are translated into events in reportorial forms that participants experience disjuncture when they come across media accounts of the very course of affairs in which they played a role.

Media forms become tools for translating the unknown into the known, the abstruse into the understood, and the strange into the familiar. Media forms resonate in what Fredric Jameson called the political unconscious.[4] Media are not the *only* tools, but they are significant ones in the building of our commonsense comprehension of what the world around us is up to.

Social Conflict and the World of Scholarship

In the world of scholarship—as compared to the world of common sense— thousands of studies have been done of media and their effects in social life. Most of these studies have conceived of society in terms of *unity.* There are important exceptions,[5] but most communications scholars interested in media have been more influenced by Talcott Parsons, who argued that the social world was characterized by systemic features to be captured by parallel concepts,[6] than by Georg Simmel. Believing conflict to be dysfunctional, even pathological in some cases, researchers have tended to approach empirical questions in terms of social mobility. When deviance and change were discussed they were made to seem residual.[7] In some ways this belief that conflict is dysfunctional is "borrowed" from our commonsense world experience. In other ways this situation reflects a commitment to social solidarity and a belief that the best way to ensure social solidarity is through social mobility.[8]

Early studies of communications tended to conceive of the social world as more or less stable, or in a state of Parsonian equilibrium. Lazarsfeld argued, for instance, that voters tended to vote as they always had.[9] His principal thesis was that media do not change political ideas, values, or beliefs, but reinforce them. This view was given further credence in the work of critical Marxist scholars several decades later, who were to argue that media are agents of social control. This was ironic, given these scholars' response to positivism.

What would happen if we set this view of conflict (as dysfunctional and pathological) aside and treated conflict instead as a prerequisite for individual autonomy, as the site for identity building for the individual within the social or for the micro group as situated in the macro group? What could we say about conflict and the media if we began our inquiry thinking that communities cannot have harmony *without* disagreement? This question has been raised by Simmel, who understood that conflict is an important vehicle in establishing social relations. He believed that conflict is not just operative *before* union takes place, social harmony is "shot through with elements of divergence."[10]

For this and other reasons, it is important that we move beyond a model in which conflict tears down what harmony has built up. Conflict is the site of identity construction, the place where we, as individuals and as communities, come to know how we differ and what makes us unique. We constitute ourselves collectively and individually in the act of disagreeing. Even if the causes of hostility—for example, income inequities, discrimination in voting rights, or spousal inequities—were present, one's identity would never be found if the feeling and expression of hostility and enmity were not also present.[11]

Opposition makes a relationship reciprocal, rather than dominant, even when disagreement remains unspoken. Relationships in the individual and social order cannot function without conflict because relationships consist of conflict. Some conflict creates a space called *aversion,* which performs an important service for us. It gives us a buffer zone, allowing us to carry on with our business.[12] All conflict involves an understanding of *intent.* As John Dewey pointed out, "Under conditions of resistance and conflict, aspects and elements of the self and the world that are implicated in this interaction qualify experience with emotions and ideas so that conscious intent emerges."[13] This intent makes clear to us how it is we are alike and how it is we differ.

Social unity, then, is composed of both inclination and disinclination, sympathy and aversion, serenity and hostility. When the element of unrestraint is introduced, however, this necessary balance goes up in flames, leaving behind the ashes of reciprocity. As Simmel put it, "when men do not at least restrain themselves from assassination, from treachery, from instigation of treason, they thereby destroy that confidence in the mental processes of the enemy, which is the *one necessary condition* to make possible a conclusion of peace."[14]

In assessing social conflict it is important to keep in mind the element of reciprocity. Social conflict *is* the manifestation of the individual's or group's desire to act *in relationship* with others. Hostility, in this sense, is part of a greater human impulse: the impulse to form unions or relationships with others.[15]

In summary, social conflict is the topical focus of this book for a number of reasons. The media bring us stories of conflict every day, making social conflict part of our daily cultural diet. Nevertheless, communications scholars have not devoted a great deal of study to it, preferring instead the Parsonian world of equilibrium and stasis. This collection addresses that lacuna.

Although social conflict is the focus of the book, several key concepts, thought to be explanatory in the field today, are implicitly or explicitly treated in the chapters to follow. These include audience and public; power, ideology, and hegemony; representation and narrative; and everyday practices in everyday life.

Recurring Motifs

Media Audiences

One set of concerns found in this book centers on the audience. In communications studies the audience wears many different costumes. Very early studies
in the positive research tradition conceived of the audience as homogenous
yet made up of isolated individuals. With the emergence of the limited-effects
tradition of the 1940s, the individual was reconceptualized and treated as a
member of many groups, some of which acted as a screening mechanism af-
fecting the individual's media experience.[16] Within this research tradition, this
was the first step toward the perception that reality is socially constructed. At
the same time, uses and gratifications scholars argued persuasively that the
audience is made up of active, goal-seeking individuals who use media (among
other resources) to satisfy certain needs that are social in origin.

In the eighties, two significant developments in conceptualizing the audience occurred. First, positive research began to move away from seeing the
audience as *either* passive or active. Instead, it came to treat these qualities as
intervening or dependent variables.[17] However, at bottom, whether conceiv-
ing the audience as active or passive, positive studies always assume that a more
or less rational animal attends the media. While activity is no longer treated
as a description, the focus on intention or attention to explain motivational
differences among viewers or readers presupposes that a conscious, rational
process is in play during media attendance. It is this process that researchers
attempt to understand.

In addition, because the positivist is less interested in situations than in
categories of understanding, this research tradition generally treats the audience in terms of transcendence. That is to say, whatever is demonstrated to
be true of an audience in one study is said likely to be true of audiences of
similar samples. The principle of *generalizability* implies that this is the case.[18]

In the seventies, the field of critical studies largely ignored the audience.
Although it gave wide reference to the media audience, it did not make the
audience itself a subject of research. Rather, it focused on texts or on institutional records and more or less implied that the members of an audience were
the puppets of capitalist elites. This tradition goes back to the Frankfurt
school. In *One Dimensional Man,* a key text for U.S. college students in the
sixties, Herbert Marcuse evokes this kind of audience member. There he argues that media are a new form of totalitarianism that relies not on terror for

its force—as Stalin did—but on assimilating potentially critical classes by creating false needs for entertainment and consumption.

This crude picture changed in the eighties when scholars began to realize that the audience did not necessarily "get" the meaning inscribed in media fare. Stuart Hall and other members of the Birmingham tradition argued that meaning is negotiated and can be oppositional at times. David Morley's empirical investigations of the audience for the British television program "Nationwide" verified Hall's critical theory about the audience.[19]

More recently, critical studies has been looking at the *implied* audience. This development was influenced by reader response theory, which focuses on the different ways in which a reader relates to a text. In contradistinction to formal theories of literature or art, reader response theory argues that the reader (or viewer) makes a contribution to the text in interpreting it. This interpretation is a product of the reading or viewing community, rather than of individuals. Since this sort of study examines texts rather than the people who read them, the reader is said to be implied by the discourse found there.

What is notable about critical studies is its privileging of commitment, unlike positivism, which privileges certainty. This commitment fundamentally works itself out in its political agenda, that is, the liberation of individuals from powerful forces working to subvert their economic, social, and cultural well-being. When critical scholars examine current institutions, they have in mind this fundamental liberation. Consequently all critical studies are teleological in nature.

Like positivists, critical scholars presuppose rationality, although one that is shot through with Freudian or Lacanian traits. This is true whether one speaks of Habermas, the most recent spokesperson in the tradition of the Frankfurt school of sociology, the British cultural tradition at Birmingham, or political economists following the work of Smythe and Schiller. This combination of Marx and Freud should not surprise us, for these men were nineteenth-century bedfellows. Both sought a social cure. For Marx, the cure was revolution; for Freud, it was psychoanalysis.

While positivists and critical scholars were rethinking the audience, hermeneutic media studies offered an entirely different view of the audience. Since hermeneutics, or postmodern scholarship, privileges experience, the audience is conceptualized as ever emergent. This view is reinforced by the principal method employed by empirical hermeneutic research: ethnography. In this sort of work, the audience is always a situated one. The meaning statements made in reference to the audience's experience are always situation bound.

This liberates the audience from a static conception, hidebound by time and space. By this I mean that an audience arises whenever and wherever people talk about media fare. It does not refer only to those who go to a film or watch a televised debate. This audience includes a whole range and variety of cohesive, ever-emergent social groups, some members of which may or may not have actually attended the media fare being discussed.

One's conception of the public is implied by one's conception of the audience. If a research tradition conceptualizes the audience as made up of more or less rational beings, the public will be defined accordingly. Conversely, as long as the public sphere is defined in terms of rational debate, the audience will be so defined. An absence of rational deliberation, then, would indicate an absence of a public sphere. In fact, both positivists and critical scholars in the Habermas tradition conceptualize the public within the old classical liberal outlines. It is thought to be distinct from the private sphere. It is conceived as the sphere of civic discourse about the common good. It is centered on the Durkheimian sense of shared values.

Once the audience is redefined as ever emergent, as having experiences that are characterized by continuity, vitality, and connectedness to community, then the public likewise is reconceived in those terms. Community is no longer defined in terms of common values, but in terms of a common conversation.[20]

Both Peter Dahlgren and Svein Østerud treat the audience and public in this way. For Dahlgren, the act of viewing television news invokes an interface between the private and the public spheres. He argues that the public is embedded in the private. Østerud approaches the same sort of situation (television viewing) as Dahlgren. However, unlike Dahlgren, Østerud takes into account both the implied audience, the one implied by the text, and the extratextual audience, whose interpretive codes he garnered through structured interviews. He argues that in the Reagan-Gorbachev 1988 summit there were points at which a fusion between the public and the private spheres takes place.

The categories of analysis in modernity (human nature, the state, the transcendent) do not tell us much about ourselves, or much that we want to know, in the viewpoint of hermeneutic social scientists. For them the operative words are *self* and *community*. For most of them, there is no transcendent order. I do not go as far as this; I would argue that there is a transcendent, but it is not universal. The transcendent has an autobiography. Both Dahlgren and Østerud, on the other hand, invoke the universal transcendent and so reveal their critical roots. Connie Fletcher, however, does not treat the transcendent in any way because her focus is on the everyday experience of her subjects—as is all empirical hermeneutic research. No one of us as situated-in-the-everyday thinks much about or invokes the transcendent. However, the everyday world stands in an ongoing, if tacit, relationship to the autobiographical transcendent.

Power, Ideology, and Hegemony

Studies in the field of communications today often concern power, ideology, and hegemony. Power relations have occupied center stage in the work of critical and cultural studies scholars. In fact, concern with power is so commonly evoked that in my view it has become something of a fetish, in the classical Marxist sense. In volume 1 of *Capital,* Marx notes that a fetish is such because it takes on a life of its own.[21] In my view, power needs to be reconceptualized in the field and there are some signs that this is happening.

Critical theorists tend to explain power relations in terms of class and suggest that social problems can be traced to differential power relations among classes. Largely because they focus on institutional power, critical theorists do not conceive of power as appropriate or good. Once a heuristic concept is treated in rigid black-and-white terms, it loses its usefulness. The truth is, power, including institutional power, is sometimes legitimate. The dean of a college, for example, has more power than other faculty because he or she is responsible for meeting the goals of the institution. Parents and teachers have more power than children or students because they are charged with guiding them and helping them to reach their goals.

J. B. Thompson agrees that some power is legitimate, but he goes too far in the other direction. He notes that "the exercise of power is not necessarily repressive, for the objectives may be commonly shared by the parties concerned."[22]

Unfortunately, all parties involved may share oppressive goals. If we look, for example, at the patriarchal family, we can see that in some cases—not altogether unusual—assault is a way of life. The battered spouse syndrome describes the pathology of the assaulted, who are unable to separate from the perpetrator and who repeatedly act as the perpetrator's support system by remaining in an abusive situation. This syndrome cannot be viewed as the exception because experts have shown that many of the adult women in the United States, for example, have been assaulted before they reached the age of eighteen. Everyone in the patriarchal family works to keep the family together no matter what the cost. They all have the same goal; they share commitment to an end, preservation of the family—and it is a repressive goal and a terribly misguided commitment.

Thompson's theory assumes everyone has autonomy. Instead of shared goals, the test for legitimate exercise of power might be twofold: vitality and cost. In a situation where power is exercised appropriately, the powerless will exhibit varying degrees of vitality. The power holders will also pay a price. All power appropriately exercised costs the powerful something in time and other resources. This is because when power is legitimately exercised, the powerful act for the benefit of the powerless. The presence of power without vitality and cost would indicate the misuse of power. A theory of power that does not recognize its legitimate exercise is a repressive theory itself in the sense that it cannot "afford" to see that power, under some circumstances, is appropriately administered.

Another sense of power found in studies of media is the power of movement. For example, a film or a song may move us in ways that cannot be explained in words. Some cultural artifacts teach, some entertain, but others move us. Critical scholars likely will identify a hidden agenda in these sorts of media fare. It is the hiddenness itself that renders a film or song powerful. Other scholars, especially those in the hermeneutic tradition (e.g., Østerud and Fletcher), will identify the persuasive dimension of communications. They examine the process whereby members of the audience are invited to share another's point of view.

What is largely absent in current literature is an examination of the power of presence. I do not refer here to the metaphysics of presence that concerned Derrida, who called into question the departing point for all Western philosophy. I refer instead to personal power, which carries with it an autonomy not found in other forms of power. This kind of power can be felt when we are in the presence of one, human or beast, who *commands* respect. A crucial part of this phenomenon is the recognition of *otherness*.

John Dewey, one of the founders of hermeneutics, treats the relation of self to other as *other,* as central to his ontology. In this context, the experience of the power of presence casts into relief the codetermining aspect of human understanding. It is likely the hermeneutic research tradition that will look at this sort of experience, precisely because hermeneutics privileges experience.

The question of power is tied in fundamental ways to the question of ideology, another concept receiving a great deal of attention in the last thirty years.[23] Historically, "ideology" has had a number of different meanings. The term was coined during the Enlightenment, although subsequent scholarship treated it as tangential to the era. In the context of the eighteenth century, ideology was a tool used to make distinctions from older metaphysical and often religious concepts. The term privileged science, a science of the mind, and so was inextricably linked to questions of epistemology, rather than to questions of meaning.[24] The significance of this is that for centuries theorists focused on knowing rather than on meaning. This relative neglect has been corrected by Dewey.

Even if we were to treat only the contemporary meaning of the term "ideology," it is clear that the phenomena the term is thought to capture are complex. Popular usage today reflects Marx's understanding, in the sense that "ideology" usually is taken to mean distortion. In political analysis, for example, it identifies an obsession on the right or left, which is thought to be dangerous for modern political systems. The implication is that these extremists will bollix up everything if allowed to go unchecked.[25] This is often the way our students understand the term in our classrooms.

Critical scholars have been the most influential in teasing out the ideological implications of events, ideas, and media fare. Marx himself sought to relate ideology to a range of political, economic, and social relations. Early in his career he characterized it as an inversion, making it thus dependent for its meaning on a manifest phenomenon. He had read Fuerbach's observation ("'God made man' is an inversion of 'man makes God'"). Later he used this idea of inversion to critique Hegel's philosophy, the starting point of which was consciousness, rather than the material conditions of existence. Marx used the term "ideology" restrictively; he did not mean it to describe all errors or distortions. Rather, it designated distortions that conceal contradictions favoring some interests over others.

In the *Grundrisse*, he uses the concept to describe a world of the manifest that hides certain patterns. For example, the ideology of freedom and equality that democracies adhere to, he would argue, obscures the fundamental process of exchange wherein equality is dissolved by virtue of the uneven distribution of resources. He, along with Nietzsche and Freud, pulled the mask off the bandit by pointing out the hidden dimensions of power in social life.

In the seventies and eighties, Louis Althusser was one of the most influential writers on this subject. He offered a structuralist interpretation.[26] He argued that ideology is an imaginary relationship to the real. It is what people imagine is their relation to the social and existential order. The idea is that what is *imagined* disguises the real process of social interaction in which the interests of the few are favored over the interests of the many. For Althusser, the function of ideology is to secure cohesion in society.[27]

Antonio Gramsci, like Althusser, used the term all-inclusively to refer to a conception of the world that is implicit in cultures, from art to law, in economic activities, and in virtually all manifestations of collective and individual life. In his *Prison Notebooks,* he calls ideology the terrain on which men and women acquire consciousness of their position. Ideology provides the rules for proceeding through one's social terrain.[28] Nevertheless, Gramsci seems to have thought that ideology can be transcended. For example, in a comment on Bukharin, he notes, "One should examine the way in which the author of the *Popular Manual* has remained trapped in Ideology; whereas the philosophy of praxis represents a distinct advance and historically is precisely in opposition to Ideology."[29]

It is worth noting that Marx, Althusser, and Gramsci were outsiders. Marx was in political exile, Gramsci was a political hostage, and Althusser was a prisoner of physical deformities. I point this out to indicate the link between theory and autobiography and to suggest that outsidership is a condition for seeing something anew.

Unlike Marx, Althusser and Gramsci do not see distortion as central to ideology. In this way they resemble Lenin, who saw ideology simply as political consciousness linked to class interests.[30]

More recently, the work of Jürgen Habermas has played a significant role in modifying our understanding of ideology and its manifestations. Habermas integrates a whole range of philosophies and social theories, some more successfully than others.[31] He returns the ideological to a more restrictive unit than Althusser or Gramsci used. He argues that the locus of ideology is language. However, he sees language as only one of several dimensions of life. Additionally, language has several functions, only one of which is to legitimate relations of power. Language becomes ideological to the extent that these legitimations of power remain hidden. Not all language is ideological.[32]

Both ideology and hegemony are central concepts in Hall's thought. Hall identifies ideology as chains of discursive links. Like Habermas, he locates the ideological in language, but Hall treats it as an all-inclusive phenomenon, whereas Habermas restricts ideology to language that hides its own interests. With Gramsci, Hall argues that hegemony is a process involving consensus and leadership, rather than simply force. Some members of society are colonized, as it were, by others. This colonization can be found, he argues, in what passes for common sense.

Hall's most sophisticated analysis of ideology and hegemony as a process with particular effects can be found in the essay he wrote for *Critical Studies in Mass Communication.* Here again he gives language primacy in the formation of the subject. Individuals are positioned in language via unconscious processes in the early stages of their formation. These early positions profoundly affect the ways in which individuals situate themselves subsequently. Hall proposes that later-life positions in ideology are not merely the recapitulation of early-life positions. Instead, individuals are positioned in ideology "by discursive formations of specific social formations."[33] We are open to being "positioned and situated" in different ways at different times in the history of our experience. Each of these positions or situations includes a set of social relations.[34] In chapters 5 and 6, respectively, Peter Moss and Peter Dahlgren indicate how media serve to reproduce hegemony. Any research that uses such explanatory devices as ritual, hegemony, cultivation, or culture tends to emphasize social stability. Hence, research in this vein is hard put to account for social change, beyond simply averring that such change takes place.

In the remaining chapters, hegemony is only implied. Ideology, however, is often explicitly treated, in a number of different ways. Peter Moss's sense of ideology is a classically critical one: a framework for understanding the social world and one's place in it. Moss argues that television plays a crucial role in constructing the ideological framework. It produces, distributes, and promotes a particular definition of the world (an ethos of consumption, for example). However, Moss follows Hall when he cautions against any monolithic understanding of ideology, since any given individual's social and private life is continually undergoing change.

Ronald Bettig's work is rooted in classical Marxist philosophy. However, he does not use Marx's sense of ideology. He links language to ideology but does not make the two coextensive. Instead he views ideology as Hunt and Sherman do, that is, as "ideas and beliefs that tend to provide moral justification for society's social and economic relationships. Most members of society internalize the ideology and thus believe that their functional role as well as those of others is morally correct and the method by which society divides its produce is fair."[35]

Svein Østerud liberates the act of viewing television from the ideological. He does so in order to release the subject or viewer from the kind of structural determinacy that, he says, is highlighted in the work of Althusser and Hall. He uses *habitus*, a term central to the thought of Pierre Bourdieu,[36] because, he argues, viewing television is behavioral. Habitus, insofar as it is tracked in empirically observable instances, involves a practical logic. In focusing on behavior, Østerud restores the subject to the scene as a moral agent. In this way Østerud and Bettig treat ideology similarly.

What is significant about these positions is that the moral order is thought to be intrinsically connected to ideology. For Bettig, the moral justifies the ideological. For Østerud, the moral is internalized and linked to self-identity and felt in terms of behavioral procedures. This clearly indicates that the authors are in the critical tradition of the Enlightenment. I say this because the Enlightenment proffered a concept of human nature that recognized morality as the foundation of all human behavior.

Representation and Narrative

A third theme in this book is representation and narrative. In recent years the problem of representation has taken the form of a debate about narrative. Originally representation had to do with representativeness—a concept of importance in statistical studies today. The term "represent" was a political one meaning to present oneself to a person of authority. This meaning can be found as early as the fourteenth century and was accompanied by another meaning: to symbolize. According to Raymond Williams, many early political uses of the term had this sense, "to symbolize," rather than "to stand for." In this way the use of the term assumed that a particular condition was represented by a particular institution. The representative quality came from the whole state and emanated outward. It did not refer to scattered and diverse opinions brought together and *represented*. That more modern understanding arrived in the seventeenth century.[37]

Interestingly, the use of the term in literature and art appears in the eighteenth century and referred to characters or situations that were typical. It is not until the nineteenth century that representation is taken to mean realism or naturalism. In fact, realism as a mode of interpreting outside-the-skin instances took up residence in virtually all institutions in the West at this time. More important, it ceased to be recognized *as* a convention,[38] one among many possible ways of interpreting the phenomenal world. Once a perspective is thought to be coextensive with the natural order, its ability to move, to shape, to mold, to beget is enormous.

In communications studies, when scholars examine representation in the narrative sense, they are looking at the consequences of taking events in the social world and translating them into events in the order of a story. It is in these sorts of analyses that the recognition that form has consequences for content is most apparent. This recognition goes back at least as far as the nineteenth century when theologians began to explore the Bible as narrative. In more recent times, the significance of the medium was highlighted in the works produced by the Toronto school of communication,[39] whose members asked the question, What can we learn about the social world if we take communications technologies and treat them as central to the story of the development of Western society, rather than as peripheral? Their work cannot be reduced to a set of simple ideas, but a central argument that emerges from this body of research is that media have important consequences for social organization (media mediate social interaction) and for human imagination (media provide an environment that encourages certain ways of thinking and perceiving). In essence these scholars substitute the means and modes of communications for Marx's means and modes of production. Thus media, in this frame of analysis, are transformative. At the same time, no one of these scholars would argue that the complexity of social life can be reduced to its communications systems. Rather, they point out that if changes occur in the communications environment, changes in the social order are likely to be occurring also, and in ways that are connected essentially to the new communications environment.

Peter Dahlgren examines the media as form. He looks at the narrative dimensions of television news.[40] Dahlgren suggests that the force or power of narrative form in news rests largely on the prime narrator. This term refers to a whole range of television conventions and actors (reporters and anchors). All together they convey meaning to viewers. At the same time, watching television news reports is a part of the viewer's everyday routine. The viewer's sensemaking practices, Dahlgren argues, involve a dialectic between what that person takes for granted and what he or she questions.

Connie Fletcher's work also addresses questions of form. Her study of the Chicago police sheds light on the degree to which social actors invoke drama as a frame for understanding what they are doing. Police consciously dismantled the media script as they wrote a script of their own. This suggests, among other things, that media form is more potent in its consequences than media content, a conclusion that was reached by both Dahlgren and Moss in quite different contexts.

Everyday Practices in Everyday Life

Everyday practice is explicitly referred to in much of this book and implied in the last three chapters. In these chapters form takes on an importance not found in the others. Probably the familiar understanding we have of form is captured in the well-known axiom, "Form follows function." This accurately captures the relationship between form and content in positivist studies. Once a method is decided, what you can and cannot find out is also decided.

However, form is also a revelation of content.[41] Dahlgren gets to this issue when he notes that television viewers gleaned content from form—and consequently missed the intended message of the news. Hermeneutic media scholars are more likely than others to treat issues of form and content, for two reasons. First, the self in this paradigm is conceived of as relational and in terms of horizon experiences. The horizon experience is to the self what the drone in chants is to Amerindian dance. It provides a pulse underlying it all. Another way of explaining this is to say that the horizon experience is to the self what the eye is to the painter. Without a painter's healthy eye a painting has no horizon and thus no meaning. Parenthetically, it is this phenomenon that is at work in Warhol's art, not what Jameson calls dead objects hanging in space.[42] Everyday practices are the sites of horizon experience.

A second reason why hermeneutic scholars are more likely than others to approach questions of form and content is that experience and theory are always in mutual development. Grounded theory is theory that is in interplay with the data collected. This has many implications. One is that *verification* is done throughout the course of the research—unlike positivism, wherein verification is done through follow-up studies.[43] Moreover, the implication is that researchers understand a particular experience (the subject's) not only in terms of the experience's relational field, but also in terms of a theory horizon and its relational field.

What is manifest about everyday practices is the felt experience of what Gerard Manley Hopkins would call an inscape. He was referring to an intrinsic pattern. Here I am suggesting that everyday practices are experienced as actions, events, objects, and relations with intrinsic pattern. As the term "intrinsic" connotes, this pattern is one of connectedness in and of itself. Beyond that, the experience of pattern refers to a connectedness among a whole range of situated experiences. In everyday practices this experience can be conscious, unconscious, or taken for granted. At times, it involves moments when we actually recognize what we perceive. In these moments we are often brought to speech. This is the condition of *poiesis.* Hermeneutics recognizes that communicative experience is poetic in addition to being politic. Poetic in this sense gets to the heart of the original meaning of *poiesis,* an embodiment, a bodied experience. Such an experience can bring us to speech, but it is equally likely to leave us standing "open-mouthed in the temple of life."[44]

In reporting on their findings, empirical hermeneutic scholars are aware of the form of the report. In fact, one of the most significant issues in this area is that one is representing the other and in so doing has ethical and political responsibilities to be an advocate for the group studied. These groups represent a whole range of peoples. They are not restricted to an "oppressed class."[45]

The first act of advocacy is to represent a multiplicity of voices in one's report. However, good empirical hermeneutics also recognizes the reciprocity of perspectives. The epistemology of hermeneutic ethnography, for example, rests on the principle of interaction between all social actors, including the researcher.[46] This is what separates the positive ethnographer from the hermeneutic one. In positivist ethnography the disparate experiences among the subjects of study are brought under one dominant narrative. The researcher's is the privileged point of view. Rather than engaging in observation, taking a spectator stance, the hermeneutic scholar enters into a dialogue, engages in interaction, and joins in the everyday practices being studied.[47]

The Arrangement of the Book

Although its topical focus is social conflict, this book is organized according to the research traditions within which the authors are working. A number of thematic motifs recur in various chapters, and these allow us to make useful comparisons across those traditions. By using this arrangement, I implicitly raise the question, What would we gain in understanding the relationship between media and social life if we treated the field of media studies as one made up of three distinct paradigms?

One thing we would learn is that the birth of a new approach does not mean mature research traditions are obsolete, unimportant, or out of date. Mature approaches to the study of media continue to evolve. Many times the most implicit or tacit assumptions made by researchers are brought to light by new approaches, forcing them to review what previously was undebatable or what occupied Bourdieu's "universe of the undiscussed."

Second, we would learn that the new approach is not able to answer certain questions, ones that the older school of thought can assess. When epistemological consensus broke asunder among physicists in the twenties, Newtonian physics did not become obsolete. Some aspects of the world, for example, refrigeration, still are best explained by Newtonian physics. Likewise, when critical studies challenged positivist research, the latter did not become an anachronism. Positivism is better able to raise questions concerning public policy, precisely because determining public opinion at the national level requires statistical methods of measurement.

On the other hand, critical scholars are able conceptually to interrogate public issues in ways that challenge received wisdom and force us all to be more politically vigilant. Thus the importance of dialogue between critical scholars and positivists, so that the concerns of the former regarding public life can enter the arena where public policy is determined.

Third, in the context of media studies, we could see that both positivist and critical approaches are progeny of the Enlightenment and modernity. Hermeneutic (or interpretive) media studies are children of postmodernity.

Given the limitations of space here and the vast literature on postmodernity, I am unable to set forth my position in the detail necessary to invite the reader to share my point of view. Briefly, "postmodern" refers to theoretical inquiry that breaks fundamentally with the Enlightenment. Suffice it to say that this break involves a different set of categories of thought and analysis comprising the taken-for-granted aspects of study. For example, human nature is set aside precisely because it implies an absolute standpoint outside all contexts to which comparison might be made. In hermeneutic media studies, "the self," "the audience," "the community," and "the public" are the relevant terms of analysis. Each entity, furthermore, is treated as ever emergent. That is, what each of these terms describes is the condition of experience; this sharply distinguishes a hermeneutic approach from the others.

Fourth, in putting the research traditions side by side, we are able to see the value of multiple viewpoints. Because all research traditions are represented in this book, the reader will encounter a spectrum of methods, a variety of levels of analysis, and a number of conceptual nuggets—all implying a social theory. The reader has the opportunity to make explicit the implicit distinctions among them, as well as to consider what ways each tradition might benefit the others. To reduce the field to one approach by recognizing only those who agree with us does not serve the ends of disinterested inquiry, much less the goals we share in the commonwealth of public life.

Finally, we cannot understand social life if we do not examine our theories about it. All theory is limited and therefore problematic. As long as we think that theory is a straightforward matter of developing hypotheses and testing them, or a transparent process of exposing hidden causes, structures and contradiction, or a simple matter of grounding ideas in lived practices— as long as we believe these things, we close our eyes to certain questions that are necessary and good to ask. To explore the parameters of social life in contemporary society, it is important to dig out the roots, the taken-for-granted aspects of research traditions. It is in this root system that one finds the social foundations of inquiry. This book takes a step in that direction.

Summary of the Chapters in the Book

Phillip Tichenor, George Donohue, and Clarice Olien were the first media scholars to question the social scientific view that conflict is a symptom of social disorganization and deviancy. In chapter 1 they test the knowledge gap hypothesis: the higher the level of perceived conflict about issues in community life, the higher the level of knowledge about those issues. As social conflict escalates, interpersonal communication about issues takes place at increasing rates. This results in a broadening of familiarity with an issue.

One of the most interesting and most important aspects of this study is its account of the dynamics of social conflict. In the process of engaging in conflict, traditional norms and values (the work ethic, the importance of the nuclear family, law and order politics) are articulated again and revitalized. Sometimes they are modified to accommodate new norms (ecology ethics, women's rights, racial diversity). Conflict allows for the revitalization of old norms and values and the emergence and articulation of new ones. The significance of this point is that Tichenor et al. are able to account for social change *and* social cohesion and social stability.

Another important aspect of this work is its suggestion that social scientists are wrong when they view misinformation about an issue as *a problem*. Instead, the authors maintain, misinformation is an important component of conflict. Conflict involves social groups who have varying values and different interpretations about what is at stake. The advantage here is that treating misinformation as part of the process takes into account the social construction of reality. It acknowledges the constructedness of our everyday worlds without reducing them to that constructedness.

In chapter 2 Susan Strohm focuses on life-endangering conflict: riots. The Los Angeles Watts riots of the 1960s have been examined by a number of social scientists who have tried to explain their causes and consequences. Strohm analyzes the content of the coverage of the riots in a black-owned-and-operated newspaper, the *Los Angeles Sentinel.* Unlike peaceful conflict, riots occur outside organized social and institutional channels, amplifying the need for media to "make sense" of daily developments. Strohm agrees with Tichenor et al. that media roles in conflict vary with the situation. At the same time, she argues that media mirror the conditions of social power in the community. She uses the mirroring process to explain her data: the *Sentinel's* coverage of the riots reflects the needs of the black power structure to maintain its power position vis-à-vis the black community and vis-à-vis the power structure of the larger social unit.

In his study of perceptions of mediated social conflict Robert Baukus (chapter 3) assumes that conflict is an intrinsic and dramatic component of the social world, making it ideal for media portrayal. He is interested in audience belief structures concerning media and social conflict. He asks whether beliefs about social conflict vary according to the type of medium a person depends on, and whether the level of involvement influences a person's perception of a medium.

Baukus's complex research design reflects the current trend in positive research toward theory convergence. As many researchers are now doing, he combines dependency theory with uses and gratifications. This convergence allows him to treat members of the audience as both active and constrained in their media choices and media experiences.

Baukus argues that a person's dispositional beliefs are shaped by previous experience with a medium. These experiences lead a person to opt for a particular medium over another. Beliefs about a medium have significant effects on how a person will relate to a range of media options and will have consequences for how a person processes media content. While uses and dependency provide a rationale for explaining the variety of belief structures among media audience members, other factors such as the attributes of the media themselves or the level of involvement influence the kind of media experience people have. Consequently, Baukus argues that knowledge about beliefs concerning social conflict and media will shed light on media dependency.[48]

Ronald Bettig (chapter 4) is not very far apart from Susan Strohm in his thinking about the consequences of media in social life. Strohm's argument about the black power structure certainly points to the sister relationship between positivism and critical studies. Both Strohm and Bettig see the media as agents of social control. However, whereas Strohm implies an ideological substratum at work in media representations, Bettig explicitly focuses on the ideological.

Using the analytical tools of political economy, Bettig takes as his subject matter the institutional conflict between media companies and the U.S. government over who should be allowed to own and syndicate prime-time television programming. Rooted in capitalist state theory, the chapter begins with a review of the theoretical framework guiding the ensuing analysis: critical theory combined with radical state theories. Within that context, Bettig examines the history of network broadcasting and government regulation. A case study follows involving the networks' efforts to push the Federal Communications Commission toward deregulation by repealing the Financial Interest and Syndication Rules.

In chapter 5, Peter Moss's case study of Australian news stems from the critical tradition. He treats conflict as part of the content of media reports and as a part of news form. He argues that stories about social conflict are structured in such a way as to "pose a threat" and then "come to resolution." In highlighting the ritual dimension of television news, Moss demonstrates its rhythmic coding and its appeal to the human desire for experience structured by threat and resolution.

The final three chapters in the book are examples of hermeneutic media studies. Peter Dahlgren and Svein Østerud both work from the viewpoint of critical hermeneutics, whereas Connie Fletcher's study of the Chicago police is an empirical hermeneutic study.

In chapter 6, Dahlgren examines media as form. He focuses on the narrative dimension of news. His treatment of conflict is related to viewers' everyday practices, their assimilation of news of social conflict. He argues that on the everyday terrain of viewing, members of the audience come face to face with social conflict and in doing so find their own place in the social order.

Dahlgren treats viewing as embedded in the horizon of everyday life. This embeddedness is the hallmark of the hermeneutic process and the condition for the interpretive process to take place. Moreover, as he suggests, this embeddedness links the viewer to a public sphere of politics and social issues. Media productions interface with audience sensemaking; the private sphere interfaces with the public sphere. This double relationship evokes the mythic domain, in which the media make the social concrete, in which the viewer celebrates the structure and function of the social order and sees him- or herself as part of the whole. This engagement with the mythic serves to maintain and reproduce the social order, even as it explores current social conflicts. This view of the media as vehicles of social order even in the midst of reporting conflict comes out of Dahlgren's roots in critical theory and that theory's emphasis on media as agents of social control. It is a hermeneutic that he speaks of, but a critical one none the less.

Chapter 7 is likewise a critical hermeneutic, but one in which audience data is collected and analyzed. Svein Østerud examines the Norwegian viewer's reception of television coverage of the 1988 Moscow summit meeting between Reagan and Gorbachev. The news coverage of this event implies that the relationship of the two superpower leaders was adversarial. The political conflict involved in the cold war has been with us since the mid-twentieth century, foregrounding the viewer's understanding of current events. News coverage of the summits plunged the viewer into a protracted state of suspense over the outcome of the meetings.

Østerud draws on several research strands, but the most important are those of Pierre Bourdieu and Roman Jakobson. As noted earlier, he borrows from Bourdieu the concept of *habitus,* which he defines as a moral code that is internalized in the agent and is closely connected to his or her self-esteem. That is, habitus is not so much a moral obligation as it is a logic of practice or behavior. Østerud invokes Bourdieu's comparison of habitus to Aristotle's *hexis,* which is defined as an embodied political mythos that becomes a du-

rable manner of speaking, thinking, and feeling. Habitus provides the sche-
mata that enable us to generate thoughts and actions. These thoughts and
actions are rendered visible in cultural capital.

In testing the viability of Bourdieu's concepts, Østerud goes beyond the
work of David Morley and attempts to bridge the gap between the kind of
research that examines texts and interpretations and the kind that examines
the uses to which people put media fare. For him, "reading a text" involves
the interplay between the "text's" potentialities and the capacities of the "reader." His research examines both aspects of this interplay. Thus he conflates
the "reading of a text" by a viewer with the uses to which it is put. A reading
is an actualization of the function that it serves.

In addition, Østerud draws on Roman Jakobson's analysis of communicative acts, specifically the functional characteristics of language. It is these
categories that he uses to analyze the television coverage of the meeting between the two heads of state.

This chapter offers a clear example of critical hermeneutics in that it demonstrates the degree to which theory is given a privileged position in interpreting audience data. The emphasis is on the general and the theoretical
rather than the lived specificities of an experience horizon. Østerud, like
Dahlgren, sheds light on the ways in which conflict appearing on television
is mediated by complex viewer media practices.

In contrast to these examples of critical hermeneutics, the work of Connie Fletcher, in the last chapter of the book, offers a grounded empirical
hermeneutic. Fletcher looks at the Chicago Police Department's handling of
hostage situations. In this chapter, conflict occurs in an arena that excludes
media. At the same time, the hostage situation and its resolution both rely
on media scripts and oppose them. They rely on media scripts because it is
these scripts that hostage takers depend on in the acting out of the drama.
They oppose them because the police, the exercisers of legitimate violence
for the state, have recognized the need to substitute their own script for the
media-induced one.

Fletcher's work is an ethnography, but a hermeneutic one rather than a
positivist one—or a critical one. A positive ethnography is one in which the
data provided by the subjects is subsumed under a single master narrative.
All empirical hermeneutic inquiry introduces point of view into the study in
a way not done in other research paradigms. Here Fletcher lets the police speak
for themselves.

Besides the subject's account of a situation, Fletcher also provides the social scientist's account by relating the words and acts of the subjects to high-

er-order concepts, not within the experience, purview, or interest of the subject, but of importance in understanding meaning and order in social life. In this case, she utilizes Kenneth Burke's work, specifically the "scene-act ratio," to interpret the social meaning of hostage situations and the media's role in it from the point of view of the police.

There are many interesting things about Fletcher's work, not the least of which is the light it sheds on the media's impact on events outside the viewing situation. Police had to substitute a different script for the one most people, both hostage-takers and hostages, take with them into the hostage situation, in order to deal successfully with it. This script is the media-induced one, one that is deeply ingrained in most viewers before they reach the age of majority. In its place the police use a script based on identification, which is meant to lead to resolution without harm coming to anyone.

In the course of examining media and social conflict, the authors of these essays treat many concepts currently circulating in the field. The chapters are arranged in terms of the paradigm in which each author works, an arrangement that can depoliticize our view of media research traditions. More is gained than lost when we approach research with respect and civility.

Notes

1. See Bourdieu's *Outline of a Theory of Practice,* trans. Richard Nice (Cambridge: Cambridge University Press, 1977). See also Nicholas Garnham and Raymond Williams, "Pierre Bourdieu and the Sociology of Culture," *Media, Culture and Society* 2 (1980), 209–23; and Mary S. Mander, "Bourdieu, the Sociology of Culture, and Cultural Studies: A Critique," *European Journal of Communication* 2 (1987), 427–53.

2. Some readers may quibble with my description of the field as made up of paradigms. In a strictly formal sense, *paradigm* may be aptly applied only to a discipline, e.g., history or physics. However, when one takes a research tradition, such as positivism or critical studies, and treats it as if it were unified (in terms of ideas, methods, and assumptions), one is able to see things not otherwise noticed. The value in treating research traditions as paradigms is that it allows us to examine the taken-for-granted aspects of social inquiry. Further, the word "paradigm" is routinely used by contemporary scholars of communication to explore differences between research traditions. For examples, see: Everett M. Rogers and D. Lawrence Kincaid, *Communication Networks: Toward a New Paradigm for Research* (New York: Free Press, 1981); Karl Erik Rosengren, "Communication Research: One Paradigm, or Four?" *Journal of Communication* 33 (Summer 1983), 185–207; Robert White, "Mass Communication and Culture: Transition to a New Paradigm," *Journal of Communication* 33 (Summer 1983), 297–301; James R. Beniger, "Toward an Old New Paradigm: The Half-

Century Flirtation with Mass Society," *Public Opinion Quarterly* 51 (1987), S46–66; Brenda Dervin et al., eds., *Rethinking Communication,* 2 vols. (Beverly Hills, Calif.: Sage, 1989); and Egon G. Guba, ed., *The Paradigm Dialog* (Newbury Park, Calif.: Sage, 1990).

3. For example, the emergence of hermeneutics influenced positivists to look at the question of context. The "new contextualism" argues in part that the results of a measure applied to a sample will depend on the context of the study. See, for example: Marianthi Georgoudi and Ralph L. Rosnow, "The Emergence of Contextualism," *Journal of Communication* 35 (Winter 1985), 76–88; and David K. Perry, "Implications of a Contextualist Approach to Media-Effects Research," *Communication Research* 15:3 (June 1988), 246–64. Georgoudi and Rosnow link the emergence of contextualism to wider trends than I do; Perry links it to gestalt psychology as well as to hermeneutics.

4. Fredric Jameson, *The Political Unconscious* (Ithaca: Cornell University Press, 1981), 35; see also Jonathan Loesberg, "The Ideology of Narrative Form in Sensation Fiction," *Representations* 13 (Winter 1986), 116.

5. See, for example, Phillip Tichenor, George A. Donohue, and Clarice N. Olien, *Community Conflict and the Press* (Beverly Hills, Calif.: Sage, 1980); William Adams, ed., *Television Coverage of the Middle East* (Norfolk: Ablex, 1982), and *Television Coverage of International Affairs* (Norfolk: Ablex, 1982); Akiba Cohen, *Social Conflict and Television News* (Newbury Park, Calif.: Sage, 1990).

6. Jonathan Turner, *The Structure of Sociological Theory* (Homewood, N.J.: Dorsey Press, 1992), 40. Besides Georg Simmel, Karl Marx offered a theory of conflict, one that influenced media studies. However, in terms of percentages, the majority of research done in the field has not been informed by conflict theory.

7. Ibid., 60.

8. Leola Johnson, my friend and colleague, pointed this out to me.

9. Paul Lazarsfeld, *The People's Choice* (New York: Columbia University Press [1944], 1968).

10. Georg Simmel, "The Sociology of Conflict," *American Journal of Sociology* 9:4 (January 1904), 490–91. This is the first of three articles by Simmel appearing in AJS. Neither I nor any of my research assistants could find the fourth article.

11. Ibid., 492.

12. Ibid., 494.

13. John Dewey, *Art as Experience* (New York: Putnam, [1934] 1958), 35.

14. Simmel, 499; italics added.

15. Ibid., 505–6.

16. See Gerald Kline's account in *Current Perspectives in Mass Communication Research* (Beverly Hills, Calif.: Sage, 1972).

17. See Alan Rubin, "Media Uses and Effects: A Uses and Gratifications Perspective," 417–36, in *Media Effects: Advances in Theory and Research* (Hillsdale: Lawrence Erlbaum, 1994), 424.

18. See James Anderson's treatment of the audience in "The Pragmatics of Audience in Research and Theory," in *The Audience and Its Landscapes,* ed. James Hay, Lawrence Grossberg, and Ellen Wartella (Boulder: Westview, 1996), 75–93. His analysis is thoughtful, but his understanding of the emergent audience is a cynical one.

19. See David Morley, *The "Nationwide" Audience* (London: British Film Institute, 1980). Morley's more recent work comments on the scholarly criticism of this important study; see *Television, Audiences, and Cultural Studies* (London: Routledge, 1992).

20. See Daniel C. Hallin and Paolo Mancini, "Summits and the Constitution of an International Public Sphere," *Communication* 12 (1991), 249–65.

21. See the section in *Capital* entitled "Fetishism of Commodities and the Secret Thereof."

22. See Thompson's *Critical Hermeneutics: A Study of the Thought of Paul Ricoeur and Jürgen Habermas* (Cambridge: Cambridge University Press, 1983), 147.

23. There are numerous studies of ideology. I recommend the following to students beginning study in this area: Raymond Williams, *Keywords* (Oxford: Oxford University Press, 1976); Terry Eagleton, *Criticism and Ideology* (London: Verso, 1976); Patrick Brantlinger, *Crusoe's Footsteps: Cultural Studies in Britain and America* (New York: Routledge, 1990), esp. chap. 3; John B. Thompson, *Ideology and Modern Culture: Critical Social Theory in the Era of Mass Communication* (Stanford: Stanford University Press, 1990); see also Thompson's *Critical Hermeneutics,* and Hanno Hardt, *Critical Communication Studies: Communication, History and Theory in America* (New York: Routledge, 1992), esp. chap. 4. James Kavanaugh gives us one of the most clearly stated accounts, accessible to undergraduate students. He comes to the question from literary studies, however, rather than from communications and so tends to focus on representation. See Kavanaugh, "Ideology," in *Critical Terms for Literary Study,* ed. Frank Lentricchia and Thomas McLaughlin (Chicago: University of Chicago Press, 1990), 306–20. A summary of how the term "ideology" has evolved in critical studies can be found in David J. Sholle's "Critical Studies: From the Theory of Ideology to Power/Knowledge," *Critical Studies in Mass Communication* 5 (1988), 16–41. Some postmodernists, as Tom Lindlof has pointed out, argue that "ideology" is no longer a useful term. See Lindlof's *Qualitative Communication Research Methods* (Thousand Oaks, Calif.: Sage, 1995).

24. Kavanaugh, 306–7.

25. Ibid.

26. Structuralism was a school of thought that centered on linguistics and language, signs and signification. Its most important contributors were Saussure, who distinguished between *langue* (language) and *parole* (speech or utterance); the American Pierce, who developed the science of semiotics; Lévi-Strauss, who examined structures of kinship; Barthes, who treated language as a social practice; and Roman Jakobson, who worked out a theory of binary opposition in the structure of language. Althusser's work privileged structure over experience and argued that the subject is

spoken by the structure. In other words, language, institutions, and social class contruct who we are as persons. Subsequent to the development of this line of thought, the death of the unified subject was announced, as well as the death of the author.

27. Louis Althusser, *Lenin and Philosophy and Other Essays* (London: New Left Books, 1971).

28. Antonio Gramsci, *Selections from the Prison Notebooks* (New York: International Publishers, 1971), 375–77.

29. Ibid., 376.

30. See Sam Becker's account, "Marxist Approaches to Media Studies," *Critical Studies in Mass Communication* 1 (March 1984), 66–80.

31. For example, he draws from important work in psychology. In addition to seeing the human being as a toolmaker in the traditional Marxian way, he also recognizes that men and women are drive-inhibited. Yet, a close inspection of his work shows that his reference to psychology is largely analogical. He says, for instance, that critical theory is to the social order what psychoanalysis is to the individual order (see *Knowledge and Human Interests* [London: Heineman, 1972]).

32. See J. B. Thompson's useful account, *Critical Hermeneutics,* 82ff.

33. Stuart Hall, "Signification, Representation, Ideology: Althusser and Post-Structuralist Debates," *Critical Studies in Mass Communication* 2 (1985), 91–114; quote, 106.

34. Ibid., 106.

35. E. K. Hunt and H. Sherman, *Economics: An Introduction to Traditional and Radical Views* (New York: Harper and Row, 1986), 2.

36. Habitus is treated throughout Bourdieu's work; for its links to popular culture see his *Distinction: A Social Critique of the Judgement of Taste,* trans. Richard Nice (Cambridge, Mass.: Harvard University Press, 1984). For its links to education, see Pierre Bourdieu and Jean-Claude Passeron, *Reproduction: In Education, Society and Culture,* trans. Richard Nice (Beverly Hills, Calif.: Sage, 1977).

37. Williams, 266–67.

38. See John Tagg's interesting account, "Power and Photography," *Screen Education,* no. 36 (Autumn 1980), 17–55, and no. 37 (Winter 1980), 17–54.

39. This school includes Harold Adams Innis, Marshall McLuhan, and Eric Havelock. James W. Carey formulated his own approach to cultural studies based on the works of these and other scholars, especially Geertz and Dewey. Because Carey's work is rooted in that of Dewey, what he proposes goes beyond cultural studies, in particular the cultural studies proposed by the British. It goes to another continent of thought, what Richard Rorty called a philosophy without mirrors.

40. Other notable studies of media and narrative include: Ted Glasser and James Ettema, "When Facts Don't Speak for Themselves," *Critical Studies in Mass Communication* 10 (1993), 322–38; Barbie Zelizar, "Achieving Journalistic Authority through Narrative," *Critical Studies in Mass Communication* 7 (1990), 366–76; Mary S. Mander, "Narrative Dimensions of News: Omniscience, Prophecy, and Morali-

ty," *Communications* 10 (1987), 51–70; and Michael Schudson, "The Politics of Narrative Form: The Emergence of News Conventions in Print and Television," *Daedalus* 111:4 (1982), 97–112.

41. Here I am drawing on the thoughtful essays of Denise Levertov in *New and Selected Essays* (New York: New Directions, 1992). For her insights on form, see 67–73.

42. See Jameson's "The Postmodern Condition," *New Left Review* 146, 53–92.

43. See Anselm Strauss and Juliet Corbin, "Grounded Theory Methodology," in *Handbook of Qualitative Research,* ed. Norman K. Denzin and Yvonna S. Lincoln (Thousand Oaks, Calif.: Sage, 1994), 274.

44. This is Levertov's phrase. However, she is using it in a different way than I am here. See Levertov, 68.

45. Strauss and Corbin, 253.

46. Ibid., 255–56.

47. Ibid., 256.

48. Baukus's work may be less accessible to undergraduates than other essays in the book. In the undergraduate classroom, students may wish to skim the material on measures and methods. If the students skim it, the instructor can explain the difference between social science and journalism, where the former is required to demonstrate in the report the proof of validity of interpretation, while journalistic validity resides in a set of extra-report practices.

1

Community Conflict and Citizen Knowledge

Phillip J. Tichenor, George A. Donohue,
and Clarice N. Olien

Whenever there is a communitywide debate, whether it is about a nuclear power plant, an urban renewal project, or location of a chemical waste disposal site, the question arises about whose ox is being gored. Such events usually produce social conflict, which results in groups considering their interests as being sacrificed for the greater good. They then struggle to redefine priorities in society at large. The issue, as Lippmann pointed out, creates the relevant publics.[1] When a nuclear power plant is proposed as a way of solving societywide energy needs, groups form to participate in the decision to accept or reject the proposed solution or redefinition of the problem. Many argue that an even greater societal interest lies in protecting individual rights and local control over the community or region's future. The style of life implied in the local autonomy perspective includes these interests as well as needs for energy or possible alterations of lifestyle resulting from lack of sufficient energy.

If a group lacks numbers, it must organize as a minority and use effective techniques to get its case before the public. The group must anticipate that speaking out with a collective voice will trigger answers from the established agencies proposing the facility. This sets the stage for a possible conflict situation. Information such as scientific evidence about nuclear fallout and its effects on health becomes important not because of abstract concern about public understanding, but because information is a vital resource in the struggle for public support. Armed with whatever information and expertise they can marshal, groups seek to enlist the attention and/or open support of mass media in waging the struggle.

These debates raise important questions about the consequences of conflict and conflict strategies. Among them is the question about the consequences of heated controversy for citizen knowledge, for example, the cherished belief that communication does not lead to greater understanding between source and audience in a conflict situation. Longstanding statements appear in academic literature that conflict inevitably leads to "communication breakdowns" and to general confusion.[2] Whenever a public disagreement about interpretation of scientific evidence occurs as in, say, the question about banning cyclamates, specialists in relevant research disciplines frequently decry the "misinformation" on the issue. According to these views, conflict arouses high levels of emotion, leading people neither to communicate rationally nor to understand well what others may have said. Selective distortion, both in sending and receiving messages, is thought to increase in proportion to the intensity of the conflict. Such reasoning is akin to the view in some social science literature that conflict is a symptom of social disorganization and pathological deviancy. Although the disorganization perspective has been challenged,[3] social programs often cite some version of it as a basis for confining participation in public decisionmaking to a minimal number of groups, therefore limiting the potential for controversy. This perspective may have limited validity as regards general social stability, but it is a rationale for maintenance of the power elite as primary decision makers.

Data from several phases of the Minnesota community research program provide a basis for testing the hypothesis that the higher the level of perceived conflict about an issue in a community, the higher the level of knowledge about that issue. This hypothesis assumes that conflict is a regular, predictable outcome of organization among countervailing groups participating in social action and that conflict is a stimulator of communication and interest in the issue. So as conflict and communication rise, there should be a resultant increase in familiarity with the issue in question and with knowledge about various facets of the issue.

This "conflict-knowledge" hypothesis is based upon a variety of considerations associated with the conflict theory school of thought. Several scholars in this tradition have referred to the role of conflict in arousing and maintaining citizen involvement.[4] Conflict in this perspective is a basic social process that stimulates a wide range of communicative and other activity.

One kind of stimulation from conflict, in a social system, is a revitalization of old norms.[5] Community struggles over language, sexual references, and other cultural and religious symbols in textbooks frequently draw renewed attention to such fundamental norms as family solidarity, the work ethic, and community identity. Confrontations between segregationists and school boards over racial mixing of school populations often gave new focus to traditional values such as maintaining social order and "observing the law of the land."[6] Clashes over so-called antisubversive activity in several U.S. communities during the decade immediately following World War II often led to renewed attention to basic notions of fair play and due process in the American system.

A second kind of stimulation possible from conflict, according to Coser, can lead to a redefinition of old norms or the emergence of new ones. Labor conflict between teachers and school boards may produce a redefinition of the rights of public employees and of the negotiation process in a given community. When urban-trained educators actively and publicly justified avant-garde reading materials, the textbook controversies cited above may have drawn increased attention to alternative lifestyles and norms of personal conduct. Also, conflict over employment practices, such as that generated by affirmative action regulations and statutes, has to some extent led to a redefinition of the process of filling a wide range of occupational positions.

Third, conflict theorists frequently point to the consequences for building and strengthening internal cohesion, within a group or larger community. A town struggling to keep its main industry alive despite strong federal and state environmental agency pressure to close it may witness a growing "we-feeling" as citizens band together to achieve a common purpose. Recent concern over outside land speculation in at least one Canadian community led to a previously unlikely coalition between Hutterite and non-Hutterite farmers, in the form of a joint petition for protectionist provincial laws.[7] As recently as a few decades ago, the same two groups had been locked in often bitter disputes over the Hutterites' land-owning and communal farming practices.

The Conflict-Knowledge Hypothesis

According to a conflict theory perspective, then, conflict may be seen as a necessary process but not a sufficient condition for maximum diffusion of information about social problems. If conflict leads to renewed emphasis on traditional norms, to the emergence of new ones, or to new levels of social cohesion, a change or increase in communication is implied. Such communication may occur at primary levels or at secondary levels including newspapers and other mass media channels.

Communication and conflict intensity are often related in a reciprocal way. Dissemination of information by a newspaper or other mass medium can

quickly lead to acceleration of an issue through creation of widespread awareness of a potential or acknowledged conflict situation. Moreover, the existence of an organized basis for conflict often produces new and accumulative
forms of communication through a variety of channels, including both primary and secondary contacts.[8] The diffusion literature would lead to the
expectation that the primary, interpersonal communication stimulated by
conflict intensity would be a principal mechanism in producing higher levels of information.[9]

The conflict-knowledge hypothesis, then, is that the higher the level of
perceived conflict about an issue in a community, the higher the level of
knowledge about that issue. This hypothesis assumes reciprocal links among
mass media coverage, perception of conflict, and primary communication,
with conflict as the basic factor. As conflict and communication rise, an increase in familiarity with the issue in question and with knowledge about
various facets of the issue should result.

Measures Used to Test the Conflict-Knowledge Analysis

In addition to the measures of knowledge and familiarity described in our
book, the analysis involved a measure of media coverage. Community mass
media coverage for each issue was estimated according to content in locally
circulated newspapers. This estimate, called the newspaper coverage index,
is a weighted total of all articles about a topic appearing in newspapers that
circulate in the community during the six-month period preceding the survey. The number of articles about an issue in a given newspaper was multi-
plied by the proportion of persons in the sample who reported reading the
newspaper in which those articles appeared. Values on the index ranged from
a low of zero for the mercury issue in community Q to a high of 57.29 for an
environmental issue in community J.

Findings and the Conflict-Knowledge Hypothesis

One part of the conflict-knowledge hypothesis is the expectation that higher
levels of publicity are correlated with a greater degree of perceived conflict
about an issue. Data are supportive of that expectation (rank correlation =
.58, p<.01), although the array of issues in the scatter diagram suggests that
the differences are by type of issue as well as by amount of coverage (fig. 1.1),
a finding which supports the interactive aspects of the hypothesis. The cases
in the upper-right corner of the scatter are very similar issues. All had received

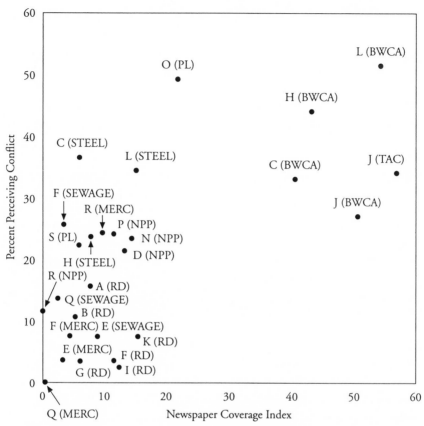

Figure 1.1. Newspaper Coverage Index and Perceived Conflict for Twenty-seven Community Issue Comparisons. (Key to issues: BWCA = Boundary Waters Canoe Area; TAC = taconite; RD = regional development; NPP = nuclear power plant; MERC = mercury pollution; SEWAGE = sewage control; PL = power line; STEEL = steel plant)

heavy statewide coverage and all involved differences between environmentalist groups, largely from metropolitan areas, and local groups. These environmental issues developed in the late 1960s and early 1970s, when ecology was a highly popular topic and tensions between environmental concerns and local prerogatives were first becoming apparent. Four of these cases, for example, concern the questions of whether mining should be permitted in or near a large wilderness area, most of which was reserved for nonmotorized recreational use.

A second aspect of the conflict-knowledge hypothesis is that the higher the perceived conflict about an issue, the more interpersonal communication about that issue within the community. This expectation is based upon the stimulation that conflict produces for everyday life and conversation. Once definition of a conflict is developed, it becomes a part of the agenda for interpersonal discourse. Conflict is cumulative in nature, continuing until an accommodation among the conflicting groups is reached.

Data on perception of conflict (an open-end measure) support this part of the hypothesis. The rank correlation across community issues between community levels of perception of conflict and community levels of discussion is .50 (p<.01). The scattergram for the relationship is in figure 1.2.

A next question is whether interpersonal communication is linked to knowledge. Data support the hypothesis that the two are related (fig. 1.3). For the twenty-four comparisons for which relevant measures are available, the rank difference correlation between amount of interpersonal communication and familiarity with the issue is .84 (p<.01). The relationship is strong and fairly straightforward, quite in line with a diffusion model, in that primary conversation tends to widen topic familiarity. Again, issues cluster somewhat, with regional development topics in the lower-left part of the scatter diagram. Even within that topical area, however, there is a tendency for higher levels of discussion to be associated with higher familiarity.

A direct relationship exists between perception of conflict and familiarity (fig. 1.4). Again, the higher the conflict, the higher the familiarity, although the relationship is not as strong as between interpersonal communication and familiarity (.51, p<.01, versus .84).

While these data do not lend themselves to a multiple regression analysis, the pattern of rank correlations is consistent with the view that newspaper coverage is correlated with high levels of conflict which in turn is associated with higher levels of awareness. The rank-order correlation coefficients, when arranged as in table 1.1, tend to increase from left to right, with the stronger links between conflict and interpersonal communication and between interpersonal communication and familiarity. Newspaper coverage is linked to development of conflict but is only weakly linked (.09) to familiarity. These results suggest that when data across communities are examined on topics such as these, the effect of newspaper publicity on increasing awareness and familiarity with an issue is largely indirect. It is the general level of conflict, in which newspapers play a reciprocal role, that appears basic to stimulating citizens to learn about an issue.

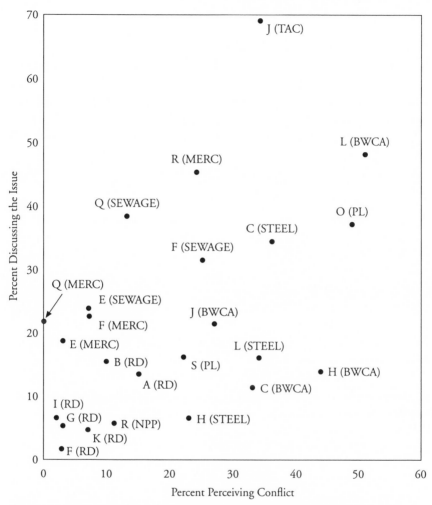

Figure 1.2. Perception of Conflict in the Issue and Interpersonal Communication for Twenty-four Community Issue Comparisons. (Key to issues: BWCA = Boundary Waters Canoe Area; TAC = taconite; RD = regional development; NPP = nuclear power plant; MERC = mercury pollution; SEWAGE = sewage control; PL = power line; STEEL = steel plant)

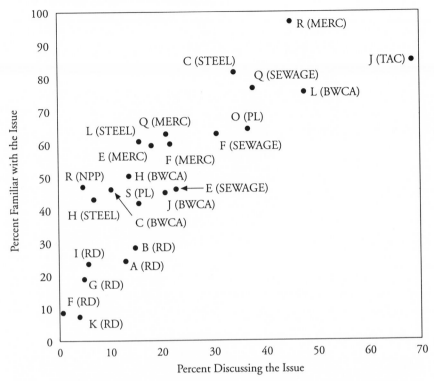

Figure 1.3. Percent Discussing the Issue and Percent Familiar with the Issue in Twenty-four Community Issue Comparisons. (Key to issues: BWCA = Boundary Waters Canoe Area; TAC = taconite; RD = regional development; NPP = nuclear power plant; MERC = mercury pollution; SEWAGE = sewage control; PL = power line; STEEL = steel plant)

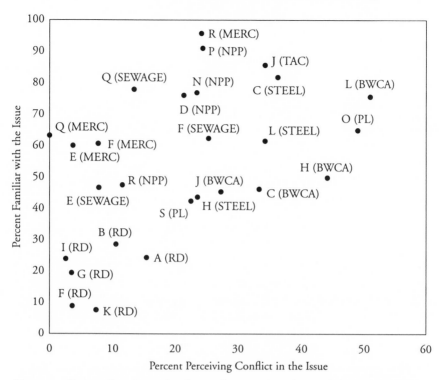

Figure 1.4. Percent Perceiving Conflict and Percent Familiar with the Issue in Twenty-seven Community Issue Comparisons. (Key to issues: BWCA = Boundary Waters Canoe Area; TAC = taconite; RD = regional development; NPP = nuclear power plant; MERC = mercury pollution; SEWAGE = sewage control; PL = power line; STEEL = steel plant)

Table 1.1. Rank Correlations among Communication Factors, Conflict, and Knowledge, across Community Issue Comparisons

	Newspaper Coverage Index	Perception of Conflict	Interpersonal Communication	Familiarity with Issues
Newspaper Coverage Index	X			
Perception of Conflict	.58	X		
Interpersonal Communication	.08	.50	X	
Familiarity Issue	.09	.51	.84	X

Conflict and Knowledge: A Pair of Case Studies

More detailed examination of the regionalization and power-line cases offered greater insight into the processes and relationships among conflict, dissemination of information, and citizen knowledge. These controversies provided an opportunity for studying these processes over time. Each case involves measures at different points in time during a period when increasing numbers of groups and agencies were being drawn into one controversy (the power line) while activity and attendant publicity was slackening in the other (regional planning).

Both communities in the regional planning study are in the same county of an eleven-county region. Community K, with population under 2,000, was once a farm service center, but is now partly a bedroom community for commuting workers. Nearby townships are dominated largely by farming, and the entire area is served by a weekly paper, the *Chronicle.* The other community, F, population near 30,000, is a transportation and small-scale manufacturing center with a number of ethnic groups, four-year colleges, and more than 1,000 places of business. The daily *Forum* serves the community, which, compared with many cities of its size, has a decidedly urban atmosphere.

The anticipated heavy publicity focusing on competing organizations and public controversy about regional planning did not develop in either the *Chronicle* or the *Forum* between the first and second interviews.

The power-line study also involved two areas. One is in a rural county near and including community O, population under 2,500, an agricultural trade and service center with relatively few residents commuting to other cities for work. The weekly *Observer* circulates locally and in surrounding farm areas. The community O area also includes several rural townships northwest of the town and other townships to the east. All rural townships are largely agricultural and relatively homogeneous in ethnic background.

Community S, the other study area in the power-line issue, includes two adjacent incorporated places. They are Metville, with a population of about 6,000 and Metfield, with 3,000 persons living mostly on farms and former farmsteads. Community S as a whole has more total population, a higher concentration of young people, more places of business, and a wider variety of professions and occupations than community O. Both Metville and Metfield are served by two jointly owned weekly papers that are different regional editions of the same basic newspaper. Since they carried identical coverage of the power-line topic, both are referred to as the *Sentinel*.

Among the different power-line study areas, the controversy varied in intensity even at the time of the first interviews. In the community O area, especially strong opposition arose in townships northwest of town, where power association representatives and landowners discussed easements before the power associations asked the state agency to designate a corridor. However, few talked seriously about the line going through the incorporated limits of community O itself or through the townships to the east.

In the community S area, concerns were quite different, focusing on residential areas and the hearing procedure itself, in part because end points of the line had been fixed before the corridor hearings began. At a major corridor hearing there in August 1975, statements emphasized that regardless of other corridor routes, the lines would go through both Metville and Metfield, near the end of the line.

In mid-September 1975, a citizens' advisory committee recommended to the state agency that the corridor be diverted from most of the agricultural area northwest of community O where the proposed line had been hotly disputed. On 3 October 1975, the state agency designated a corridor that accepted most of the area proposed by the hearing officer, including much of the area sharply opposed by farmers and suburban residents. As a result, the agency designation was not in agreement with several recommendations of the advisory committee.

The first interviews in the power-line study were conducted between 18 September and 2 October 1975, just before the corridor designation. A short time later, the power associations applied to another state agency for a certificate of need, emphasizing a projected increase in demand for electrical power by their rural consumer members. The certificate of need had not yet been issued when the second wave of interviews was conducted between 10 February and the end of February 1976. Hearings, however, had been held, both on the certificate of need and on specific routes for the line. In late January 1976, the state agency specified certain routes that the power line could take within the larger corridor areas, routes similar to those proposed by the power associations. Those routes went through the rural townships northwest of community O and crossed both sections of community S.

Media Coverage

Compared with regional planning, the power-line question received considerable publicity in weekly newspapers serving both study areas. Whereas regional planning publicity centered around routine reports, the power-line coverage included articles about the intense opposition to the line, to procedures, and to interpretations of scientific evidence about effects of the line. Before the first interviews, the community O *Observer* devoted large amounts of space to technical issues. After the first interviews, coverage particularly in the *Observer* shifted from technical arguments about the safety of the line to procedures for locating it, to specific line routing, and to opposition.

At the time of the interviews, regional development and the power-line issue represented sharp contrasts in social organization, events, and media coverage. Regional planning was largely at the initiating stage and received low-key treatment by newspapers. The power-line topic, however, already had dimensions of an intense issue within the respective regions. Opposition groups had formed, first to deal with technical issues and later with procedure and organized protest and legal counteraction.

What People Know about Public Issues

The varying levels of media attention to the issues are reflected in the differing levels of familiarity and understanding which respondents expressed on regional planning and the power-line issue. In the first and second interviews on regionalism, no more than 8% had any accurate knowledge about the purpose of the regional development commissions and no more than 5% knew how the commissions were funded (table 1.2). Though these levels are low, they tended to decline even more in the second interviews—not a single respondent in community K knew the commission's purpose. The highest specific knowledge on the topic was on the subregion organization, which had been part of the structure for a longer period of time; 12% in community K had some accurate knowledge about it in the first study. Familiarity dropped sharply (to 3%) in the second interview, after the subregion agency had been absorbed quietly into the larger one, in what might be considered an accommodation to avoid an increase in conflict.

Table 1.2. Specific Items of Knowledge about Regional Planning

Percentage Who:	Community K		Community F	
	First (N = 194)	Second (N = 183)	First (N = 187)	Second (N = 92)
Have any accurate knowledge about "RDC" purpose	8	0	7	2
Know how "RDC" is funded	4	2	5	3
Have any accurate information on "revenue sharing"	28	23	33	28
Have any accurate knowledge about "subregion organization" purpose	12	3	3	2
Rate issue as "very important"	22	29	20	20
Call topic a "touchy subject"	33	39	36	33

Between a fourth and a third of the respondents had some accurate information on "revenue sharing," which is a concept related to regional planning.

In spite of the lack of knowledge about specifics, at least a fifth of the citizens saw the regional planning issue as "very important" and a third or more said "yes" when asked if it was a "touchy subject."

The power-line issue was characterized by higher levels of general familiarity, higher-rated importance, and higher levels of perceived conflict in the rural and open country areas than the regional planning issue. The proportion of citizens having some accurate knowledge about the power line varied from a low of 25% in the suburban community to a high of 70% or more in the most directly affected northwest rural area (table 1.3).

However, even with the continuing heavy publicity, overall levels of measured knowledge on the power-line topic did not increase between the first and second interviews. On specific aspects, some changes occurred with slight increases in percentage hearing about effects on health in all except the suburban community (table 1.4). On other aspects, including effects on agriculture, underground installation, names of utilities, and names of organizations opposed, declines equaled increases in familiarity.

This last finding may suggest a modification of the conflict-knowledge hypothesis. While conflict increases awareness of a topic, it may not necessarily lead to increased understanding of the underlying issues in the population at large. Perhaps as the issue progresses, newspaper coverage shifts to some extent from concentration on the scientific and technical aspects to concentration on procedure and legal opposition. The conflict itself, as a conflict, becomes the story. Accordingly, the percentage calling the topic a "touchy subject" increased in four of the five study areas, particularly in the

Table 1.3. Knowledge and Opinions about the Power-Line Issue in Two Studies (September 1975 and February 1976)

	Percentage Who		
	Have Any Accurate Knowledge about the Power Line	Say Issue Is "Very Important"	Say Issue "Affects Me Directly"
Community S			
Metville			
First (*N* = 68)	33	18	31
Second (*N* = 48)	25	21	25
Metfield			
First (*N* = 39)	49	22	22
Second (*N* = 43)	49	46	44
Community O			
Town			
First (*N* = 71)	62	17	14
Second (*N* = 48)	46	13	10
Rural area, east			
First (*N* = 34)	65	32	18
Second (*N* = 33)	67	42	12
Rural area, northwest			
First (*N* = 31)	74	61	45
Second (*N* = 36)	70	64	43

Table 1.4. Technical Knowledge and Perception of Conflict in Power-Line Issue in Two Studies (September 1975 and February 1976)

	Percentage Who			
	Have Heard of Effects on Health	Have Heard of Effects on Agriculture	Have Heard of Underground Installation	Call Topic a "Touchy Subject"
Community S				
Metville				
First (*N* = 68)	16	21	28	21
Second (*N* = 48)	8	8	8	23
Metfield				
First (*N* = 39)	25	26	28	19
Second (*N* = 43)	26	23	30	51
Community O				
Town				
First (*N* = 71)	14	25	32	44
Second (*N* = 28)	29	42	29	33
Rural area, east				
First (*N* = 34)	35	44	41	29
Second (*N* = 33)	39	48	36	36
Rural area, northwest				
First (*N* = 31)	55	71	68	52
Second (*N* = 36)	67	70	73	83

rural townships most directly affected. In this situation, however, one might not expect appreciable changes of knowledge about specific technical aspects of the issue.

Conflict, Importance, and Collective Interest

Other data relevant to the conflict-knowledge hypothesis include differences among subareas in the power-line study. Importance of the power-line topic and perceived conflict as measured by the "touchy subject" question differ sharply across community areas (table 1.4). In both community O and community S areas, the highest importance ratings were in open country locations and the lowest, particularly in the second interviews, were in the communities with more concentrated populations. The percentage saying "very important" in the Metfield portion of community S jumped from 22% in the first interviews to 46% in the second; a key event between the first and second interview studies was a well-publicized meeting of opposition groups in the community.

Such visible organizational activity as the opposition group meeting in Metfield is a key event in public arousal. Not only did perceived importance increase but also the direct impact on individuals was redefined. In Metfield, 22% of the respondents in the first interview said the issue "affects me directly"; in the second interview, after the new burst of organized opposition activity, more than twice as many (44%) answered the question affirmatively. Thus, the increases in perceived importance and perceived personal impact were almost perfectly parallel. This finding is particularly dramatic because in Metfield, the planned corridor routing remained unchanged between the first and second interview periods, since the entire community S area was near the "end point" of the line established months earlier in the power association and state agency announcements. Therefore, little new had occurred as far as power-line location was concerned. In light of that fact, the increased perception of importance and "direct effect" seems to be a direct outgrowth of organized activity and the intensity of conflict which that organization and its publicity produced.

The differences in perceived importance of the issue in the Metfield and Metville sections of community S may reflect differences in social structure. In the open-country areas of Metfield, where there is a lower degree of diversity, a problem in one rural sector is more likely to be seen as a problem by all in the area. In Metville, however, the greater population size and diversity means that the power-line issue was more likely to be submerged amid a variety of concerns and less likely to dominate public attention.

A further consequence of social structure can be seen in table 1.3 by comparing the different parts of the community O area. In community O itself, the percentage rating of the power-line issue as "very important" dropped from 17% to 13% between the first and second interviews. This is especially noteworthy, since the *Observer,* read by more than 90% of the community O town respondents, had given heavy attention to the issue and editorially opposed the power cooperatives, as described earlier. This finding indicates that neither heavy media coverage of an issue nor circulation could individually insure that people will see an issue as important. Judgments of importance also depend on how the issue is related to community self-interest. In this case, it appears that rural residents increasingly viewed the issue as a *general* rural area problem of individual rights, while town residents saw it in a quite different light. The town citizen may be more likely to see the problem as primarily one of energy needs, as might the urban citizen. The fact that the large urban media entered the reporting later, and editorialized as they did, seems to reflect this difference in problem definition. Such a similarity between small-town residents and the urban perspective may suggest that nonmetropolitan versus metropolitan differences may have a parallel in local farm-town divisions. Just as rural people tend to see things differently than big-city residents, so may similar differences exist at the local level between town and rural citizens.

Where People Get Information about Issues

In both the regional planning and the power-line studies, respondents who had heard of the topic were asked, "Where have you seen or heard about this topic? Has it been from other persons, from television news, from radio news, from newspaper articles, or where?" Most of the sources mentioned were either newspapers or other persons, or a combination, a reflection of the dominance of newspaper publicity on both issues in the time period studied. The power line had not yet become a major television topic; television coverage started rather abruptly about four months after the second interviews, following heavy local coverage of the topic in the print media.

These data make it possible to test a hypothesis from the diffusion literature: Citizens tend to get their first information about a topic from mass media (in this case newspapers) rather than from personal contacts or sources. This hypothesis, frequently supported in studies of diffusion of information about farming practices and consumer goods, should also apply to knowledge about communitywide issues.[10]

Evidence strongly supports the diffusion hypothesis (fig. 1.5). On the regional planning topic, the proportion citing newspapers, although quite low, is nevertheless higher in both communities than the proportion mentioning hearing it from other persons. But the most striking support for the hypothesis is in the results from the power-line issue, for which total attention was much higher. In four of the five subareas of communities O and S, the responses in the first interviews indicate that the percentage seeing it in newspapers is higher than the percentage hearing about it from other persons by at least twenty-two points. The one important exception is in the directly affected area northwest of community O, where the issue was already the dominant topic of conversation in the first interview. In that area, organiza-

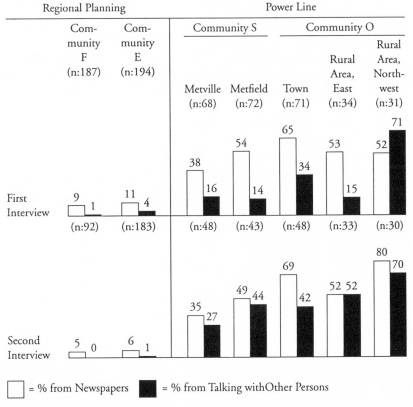

Figure 1.5. Percent Getting Information from Newspapers and from Talking with Other Persons

tional activity had been high with extensive individual contacts concerning the issue; the potential impact of the power line on local self-interest had already been discussed in a highly organized setting.

In the second interviews, the sources of information patterns as shown in figure 1.5 are different. This time, the percentage talking to others about the issue more nearly equaled the percentage reading about it in papers. In all areas except northwest of community O, the proportion citing newspapers as sources of information stays roughly the same as in the first interview and citing other persons increases. In Metfield, mention of "other persons" jumped from 14% in the first study to 44% in the second, even though the percentage naming newspapers dropped slightly, from 54% to 49%. In the area east of community O, the increase in citing "other persons" was from 15% to 52%, so that in the second interviews, proportions are identical for the two sources. Seeking information from newspapers increased sharply in only one area, northwest of community O where it went from 52% to 80%.

The pattern in the power-line case may typify information seeking and receiving for a variety of public affairs topics in communities. People often get first word of events through the media, unless an organization exists for transmitting the information through primary sources, as occurred in the northwest townships. Most rural residents east of community O, who may have been less likely to have friends or relatives directly involved with power-line negotiations in earlier months, apparently got their first information by reading about it. But as the issue developed and the accompanying conflict and implications for the rural area became more widely publicized, the matter became a topic for interpersonal communication. Newspaper reading, however, did not fall off; the results suggest that newspaper coverage may have reinforced, if not maintained, the levels of discussion. In some cases, conversation can stimulate increased reading, as may well have occurred in the northwest township. There, general involvement increased to a point where people may have sought still further information wherever they could find it.

Newspapers and Knowledge

Since newspapers tend to be the most frequently cited source of information in both of the power-line studies, level of knowledge of the issue should differ according to the amount of newspaper reading. That expectation is supported (table 1.5) when data for the second surveys in communities O and S are divided according to newspaper reading patterns. In both communities, the percentage having any accurate knowledge about the issue is lowest for

Table 1.5. Knowledge about the Power-Line Issue, according to Newspaper Reading in Two Communities

	Percentage Having Any Accurate Knowledge about the Issue
Community O area (rural)	
Reads weekly *Observer* but no metropolitan daily (*N* = 24)	46
Reads weekly *Observer* and metropolitan daily (*N* = 7)	14
Does not read weekly *Observer* (*N* = 60)	7
Community S area (metropolitan)	
Reads weekly *Sentinel* but no regional or metropolitan daily (*N* = 44)	39
Reads weekly *Sentinel* and regional or metropolitan daily (*N* = 51)	53
Does not read weekly *Sentinel* (*N* = 52)	21

those persons who do not read the local weekly paper. In community S, knowledge is highest among those who read both the weekly and a daily, whereas in community O, those who read the weekly but not a daily tend to be most knowledgeable about the issue. In the latter case, however, only seven respondents read both the weekly and a daily, so those results should be viewed with caution.

The findings do, however, indicate the importance of the weekly newspaper in these two communities and on this issue, since the lowest level of knowledge is among nonreaders in communities with weekly newspapers. These findings reflect again the fact that the weekly papers reported the issue as a community concern and from a community perspective.

Measures of Technical Knowledge

The power-line study provides for an extensive examination of familiarity with, and knowledge about, various technical aspects of an issue. Several questions related to the proposed high-voltage power line involved interpretation of a variety of technical arguments and scientific evidence. These questions fit largely into three categories: effects on health, effects on agriculture, and the question of underground installation.

The human health question was a prominent one and was linked to a basic characteristic of the proposed line, "corona loss." Corona is an electric discharge around a power line that can vary according to weather conditions; corona loss is greater during rain, fog, and snow. The greater the corona loss, the greater the production of ozone and oxides of nitrogen. One of the frequently debated aspects of the power-line issue was the extent to which corona loss, through producing ozone, would present a danger to the health of workers around the line or to farm animals. Under certain weather and wind conditions, could ozone concentrate in certain areas at levels dangerous or perhaps fatal to livestock? The position of the cooperative power associations, supported by data supplied by their professional consultants (but challenged by opposition groups), was that the predictable concentrations of ozone and nitrogen oxides would pose no danger to humans or to livestock.

There were other health questions, such as whether the electric field would be injurious in other ways to persons working near the line for long periods of time. In various hearings, for example, there was a disagreement over translation of a Russian journal article summarizing a study of long-term effects of a high-voltage power line on workers. This journal article was cited frequently; at the time, very few places internationally had operated power lines with such high voltage (±400 KV DC) for an appreciable period of time. The power association consultants at one hearing cited one translation of the Russian article, which reported "disorders" of the functional state of the nervous and cardiovascular system of workers. Opposition groups cited a different translation of the same Russian journal article, which stated that a "shattering" of the central nervous system and cardiovascular system had occurred. Sharp and sometimes acrimonious exchanges over the various translations had occurred in the hearings.

Questions of effects on agriculture concerned such matters as amount of land taken up by the towers, inconvenience to farmers in working around towers and under the sag of the line (130-foot towers, about 1,000 feet apart), potential difficulties for irrigation equipment and aerial crop spraying, and interference with activities in nearby farm buildings and yard areas.

The possibility of putting the high-voltage power line underground was raised frequently by individuals and farmer groups as an alternative solution to the controversy. Analyses published by the power associations claimed that problems in undergrounding a high-voltage transmission line are quite different from undergrounding lower-voltage lines used in urban and residential areas and, therefore, opposed the alternatives as technically and economically unfeasible. One report from the power association stated that with current technology, undergrounding would require more than seven times as much steel and ten times as much copper as overhead lines. Furthermore, the same report indicated that undergrounding would require high-pressure pipe-type systems, containing enormous amounts of oil. The power associations concluded that no undergrounding system, including the pipe-type, would be justifiable because of time, cost, and resource considerations. As a result, the power corridor hearings had proceeded on the assumption that the lines would be above ground, mounted on the large towers.

Other technical arguments arose, such as the potential effect on radio and television transmission. Health, agricultural, and underground installation concerns appeared to include the most frequently made statements, however, and these three points were utilized in the survey instruments. Respondents were asked: "Now we'd like to ask about three questions that have come up in connection with the power-line issue. One is the question of possible effects of high-voltage power lines on human health. Have you seen or heard of any scientific viewpoints or evidence about that?" If the respondent said yes, a probe was used to learn what the respondent had heard and where it had been heard. Similar questions were asked about possible effects on agriculture and about the possibility of underground installation. Other technical questions were also asked, such as the height of the poles, length of the line, and voltage.

Knowledge and Conflict

Underlying this analysis of the special cases is the same basic hypothesis considered earlier: The higher the level of conflict surrounding an issue, the higher the level of citizen familiarity and knowledge concerning that issue. The test of that hypothesis, in the power-line case study, requires examination of data on the "touchy subject" question along with knowledge of individual technical issues (table 1.4).

Findings about technical knowledge in the power-line issue are generally supportive of the conflict-knowledge hypothesis, that is, in areas where the subject is more likely to be viewed as touchy, knowledge on all counts tends to be highest (table 1.4). Across all of the subareas studied, respondents in Metville were among the least likely to term the issue "touchy"; that subarea also displayed the lowest level of knowledge on all aspects including health, agriculture, underground installation, and names of organizations and utilities. At the other extreme, levels of knowledge on all those aspects were highest in the rural area northwest of community O where 52% in the first wave and 83% in the second (highest both times) called the issue touchy.

The relationship between perceived conflict and knowledge can be illustrated graphically by plotting the percentages on the touchy subject question

against familiarity or knowledge. Figure 1.6 (based on data appearing in table 1.4) depicts the relationship for the percentage who have heard of underground installation. While the relationship is not perfectly linear, the clear
tendency in both waves is for knowledge to be higher in areas where the topic is seen as more controversial. Furthermore, the line becomes straighter, and
the differences in knowledge are more extreme, in the second wave of studies when the topic was seen as more touchy in all except one of the five areas.

One respect in which the data do not support the conflict-knowledge
hypothesis is seen in figure 1.6. The power-line issue was seen as more con-

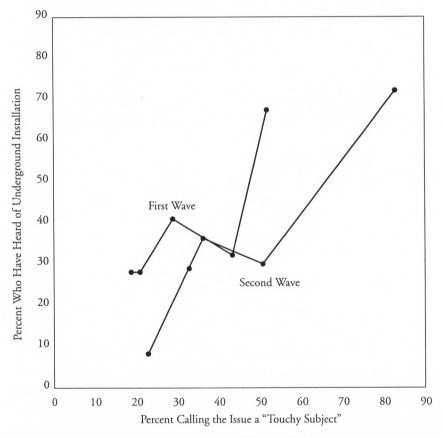

Figure 1.6. Percent Calling Power-Line Issue a "Touchy Subject" and Percent Familiar with Underground Installation in Five Sample Areas

troversial in the second wave of interviews; yet, level of familiarity with underground installation in each of the five subareas was actually lower. The changing pattern of media coverage with more newspaper attention to the technical aspects of the problem in the early phases than in following months may be operating here. The controversy had reached a point where conflict itself was the major news item, as suggested above.

Community Organization, Conflict, and Knowledge

The findings reported thus far in this chapter generally support the conflict-knowledge hypothesis but do not test directly the fundamental hypothesis: Conflict itself is generated as a result of organized social activity. A separate comparison of communities O and S, characterized by high degrees of organized opposition, with two additional communities (not part of the nineteen) where lower degrees of organization surrounded the issue facilitated a test of the relationship in the 1977 power-line issue. This comparison also allows for a more direct test of the hypothesis that the higher the degree of organization surrounding an issue, the higher the public knowledge of that issue.

The comparison of two pairs of communities was made in a separate telephone interview study, in late winter and early spring 1977, in communities O and S (high on organization) and the other two (low on organization), which we shall call T and U. The latter were selected for comparison for two reasons. First, community T, like S, is located within a metropolitan area, with a mixture of residential and open-country farm areas. Community U, like O, is a small town in a predominantly rural agricultural area. Second, as a result of participant observation, communities U and T were judged to have a lower degree of countervailing organization on the power-line dispute.

Communities T and U are geographically separated from O and S and are in what is called a southern region. They had their corridor hearings in 1976 and their route designation hearings in 1977, about a year later for each set of hearings than had occurred in O and S.

In neither community T nor U were there any organized demonstrations or confrontations associated with any of the hearings. No legal experts appeared at any of the hearings representing opposition groups, as had occurred in the central region where O and S are located. Also, community leaders and informants gave quite different impressions in the two regions. County extension agents, for example, in the central region regarded the opposition there as highly organized and intense. In the southern region, by contrast, the county agents regarded the issue as quiet and, as one put it, "quite unlike" the central region and without "very much organized opposition."

As a result, hearing testimony in the southern region took a different form. Whereas testimony in the central region was dominated by general and repeated questions of effects of the line, the southern region hearings particularly at the route hearings were characterized frequently by individuals speaking *as* individuals, seeking alterations of the route that would benefit them alone.

When the route designation hearings were completed in the central region in 1976 with a state agency decision in favor of the power associations, the utilities began land surveying in the route area. This resulted in open confrontations between farmers and survey crews that summer on a number of farms near community O and in other areas along the line. A temporary injunction against further surveying was issued in the county in which O is located, but potentially violent incidents continued to occur throughout the summer of 1976. These incidents led to several requests for law enforcement personnel and the Minnesota National Guard to protect surveyors. A group of suits against the line project, originating in the central region, were pending in the state supreme court when the telephone interviews were conducted in the late winter and early spring of 1977.

No demonstrations or major confrontations occurred in the southern region, and opposition groups issued few public statements about their positions on the issues, apart from some petitions at hearings. Although some organizations had members in both regions, public statements were made mostly by leaders in the central region. By comparison, the opposition in the southern region appeared much more quiescent.

Newspaper Content Differences

During the two years prior to the 1977 interviews, the papers in communities S and O combined quoted or cited statements from opposition groups more than five times as frequently as did the papers in T and U combined. However, the S and O papers also quoted the power associations more often, some six times as frequently as in the T and U communities. This finding indicates that existence of countervailing organizations led to increased coverage of their viewpoints. Indeed, if conflict is a state or condition of the system, this is to be expected. Intensity increased as a result of rising activity on the part of the power associations as well as among the opposing groups. In community O, where coverage was heaviest, the number of statements attributed to the power associations and to opposition groups was almost exactly the same.

In addition, the weekly papers in communities O and S had more total coverage of the issue. In the two-year study period, these papers printed 1,823 and 848 column inches, respectively, on the issue. This compares with about 634 in community T and 571 in community U.

The metropolitan daily newspapers gave the power-line issue heavy coverage from June 1976 through the following winter. The daily with the largest statewide circulation contained some 110 articles on the issue during the study period, and the topic was covered frequently as a major news item by television stations and radio stations around the state. At the end of 1976, one metropolitan television station termed the issue the "number two news story of the year," topped only by the taconite disposal issue of northeastern Minnesota, characterized also by organized groups with high levels of activity, including confrontation with government agencies and corporate groups.

Attention, Familiarity, and Knowledge

Data in table 1.6 are highly supportive of the hypothesis that the higher the degree of organization surrounding the issue, the greater the public knowledge. Citizens of the communities with higher levels of organization are more likely to have heard of the issue, to view it as controversial (that is, as a touchy subject), and to display more knowledge about the issue, both in response to an open-end item and in response to specific items about potential effects of the power line on health and agriculture and about underground installation.

The assumption about greater communicative activity in communities O and S is generally supported (table 1.7). Both of the communities with higher organizational levels show more respondents having heard about the topic from other persons, from television, and from reading newspapers. The one type of communicative activity not consistent with the assumption is hearing from radio, which occurred more frequently in community T (metropolitan area, lower level of organization) than in any other community, and lowest in community O (rural, higher level of organization). All communities are within range of metropolitan radio stations that gave the issue regular and frequent coverage during the previous year. Since local radio coverage was not monitored, no further explanation for the differences in radio listening is possible. However, it should also be pointed out that discussion of the issue was lowest in T, even though radio listening there was high.

Table 1.6. Perceptions of and Knowledge about the Power-Line Issue in Four Communities, 1977

	Communities with Higher Degrees of Organization among Opposition		Communities with Lower Degrees of Organization among Opposition	
	Community S (metropolitan) (*N* = 200)	Community O (rural) (*N* = 167)	Community T (metropolitan) (*N* = 131)	Community U (rural) (*N* = 149)
Percentage who:				
Have heard of issue	84	88	63	68***
Rate issue as "very important"	47	67	38	54***
Call issue a "touchy subject"	64	78	42	54***
Know name of opposition organization	14	26	4	13***
Make one or more accurate statements about power-line issue (open end)	66	52	31	48***
Percentage who have heard scientific evidence or viewpoints about:				
Questions of health	46	51	28	36***
Effects on agriculture	40	36	19	25***
Underground installation	55	44	32	38***

*** = difference across all groups, p<.001

Table 1.7. Sources of Information about the Power Line in Four Communities, 1977

	Communities with Higher Degrees of Organization among Opposition		Communities with Lower Degrees of Organization among Opposition	
	Community S (metropolitan) (*N* = 200)	Community O (rural) (*N* = 167)	Community T (metropolitan) (*N* = 131)	Community U (rural) (*N* = 149)
Percentage who heard from:				
Other persons	34	50	28	31***
Television	67	61	44	50***
Newspapers	66	78	53	64***
Radio	39	26	56	30***
Percentage who saw issue in:				
Local weekly newspaper	30	43	28	45**
Daily newspaper	57	30	34	45***

** = difference across all groups, p<.01
*** = difference across all groups, p<.001

Patterns of recall of the issue in weeklies and dailies vary from one community to another, although these differences are not extreme. As indicated in table 1.7, the percentage seeing the issue mentioned in a weekly is highest in the two most rural communities (O and U). Recall from a daily is highest in the metropolitan area community S and lowest in O. The daily most frequently mentioned in communities S, O, and T is the largest metropolitan newspaper in the state. In community U, the most frequently mentioned daily newspaper source is from a regional urban center about twenty-five miles away.

In general, then, the data offer considerable support for the hypothesis that degree of organization among countervailing groups is associated with higher community levels of awareness and knowledge about all aspects of the issue. The one finding that is not entirely in line with the hypothesis is the rating of importance of the issue; the rating (table 1.6) in community U (rural, lower level of organization) is higher than in community O (rural, higher organizational level). However, when comparisons are made between structurally similar communities, the importance ratings are, predictably, higher in O than in T and higher in S than in U.

Summary

Understanding the process of social conflict is basic to understanding the generation and spread of knowledge in a community. Conflict grows out of countervailing social groups seeking to reach their respective goals within the system. Conflict frequently gives rise to increased mass media publicity, which in turn tends to accelerate the intensity of the conflict.

As intensity rises, interpersonal communication about the issue increases among people in groups creating higher general levels of knowledge among the groups within the community. In this process, the impact of the newspapers is indirect, and the specific role of the newspapers may change as the issue develops. As expected from diffusion theory, citizens tend to get their first information about an issue from the mass media. The relative importance of interpersonal communication as a source increases with time and duration of the conflict. Even at high levels of intensity, however, newspapers and other mass media continue to receive high attention. At intense stages, reciprocal effects among media and discussion with other persons may occur. That is, reading may stimulate conversation, and conversation about a topic may stimulate the citizenry to pay more attention to future news about the topic.

Conflict is related not only to familiarity with an issue but also to technical knowledge about the issue. The more intense the conflict about the power line in different geographical areas, the more the respondents in those areas tended to know about technical aspects of the topic.

In general, the conflict-knowledge hypothesis receives considerable support from the data. At the same time, the data do not support the view that "nobody learns anything" in a conflict. It may well be that possession of technically incorrect information may also increase in a heavily publicized and intense situation. But what is often seen as misinformation in a conflict situation may be an aspect of conflict itself. By their nature, conflicts are characterized by differing interpretations of evidence and reality, and these differing interpretations may come from technical and scientific experts as well as from other observers. To be knowledgeable about the scope of a community conflict is to be aware of these differing perspectives, and the evidence supports the conclusion that such knowledge does increase as intensity increases.

Notes

This essay is reprinted with minor editorial changes from Phillip J. Tichenor, George A. Donohue, and Clarice N. Olien, *Community Conflict and the Press* (Beverly Hills, Calif.: Sage Publications, 1980), 139–73. © 1980 by Sage Publications, Inc. Reprinted by permission of Sage Publications, Inc.

1. W. Lippmann, *Public Opinion* (New York: Macmillan, 1922).

2. See G. A. Lundberg, *The Foundations of Sociology* (New York: Macmillan, 1939), and E. S. Bogardus, *Essentials of Social Psychology* (Los Angeles: University of California Press, 1920).

3. For example, J. R. Feagin, "Issues in Welfare Research: A Critical Overview," *Social Science Quarterly* 54 (1974), 321–28.

4. L. A. Coser, *Continuities in the Study of Social Conflict* (New York: Macmillan, 1967), and R. Dahrendorf, *Class and Class Conflict in Industrial Society* (Palo Alto: Stanford University Press, 1959).

5. Coser.

6. H. D. Graham, *Crisis in Print: Desegregation and the Press in Tennessee* (Nashville: Vanderbilt University Press, 1967).

7. I. Obeng-Quaidoo, "Hutterite Land Expansion and the Canadian Press" (Ph.D. diss., University of Minnesota, 1977).

8. See Phillip J. Tichenor, George A. Donohue, and Clarice N. Olien, *Community Conflict and the Press* (Beverly Hills, Calif.: Sage Publications, 1980), chap. 5.

9. North Central Regional Publication, *How Farm People Accept New Ideas (Report 1)* (Ames: Iowa State College Agricultural Extension Service, 1955); E. M. Rogers, *Diffusion of Innovations* (New York: Macmillan, 1962); E. Katz, *Personal Influence* (New York: Macmillan, 1955); and J. S. Coleman et al., *Medical Innovation: A Diffusion Study* (Indianapolis: Bobbs-Merrill, 1966).

10. North Central Regional.

2

The Black Press and the Black Community: The *Los Angeles Sentinel*'s Coverage of the Watts Riots

Susan M. Strohm

On 11 August 1965, a group of curious spectators in Watts watched as police arrested Marquette Frye, 21, for drunken driving. By 16 August, the smoke over Watts was clearing, cries of "Burn, Baby, Burn" were fading, and Gov. Edmund G. Brown Sr. was preparing to appoint a blue-ribbon panel, the McCone Commission, to examine the causes of rioting that resulted in death for 34 persons, injury for over 1,000, and arrest for nearly 4,000.[1] The actions of the previous days caused over $40 million in property damage, with more than 600 buildings damaged or destroyed by burning and looting.[2]

In the aftermath of the urban riots of the 1960s, the energies of social scientists, government officials, journalists, and laypersons focused upon the riots' causes and consequences. Questions were raised about the possible role of media in spreading and prolonging the rioting.[3] While the role of the dominant media received attention, questions about the nature of riot coverage in the black media were left largely unaddressed.

This is a study of the coverage of the Watts riots in the major black newspaper in the area, the *Los Angeles Sentinel*. The analysis included all riot stories that appeared in August through December 1965 and a second group of stories that appeared in the summers of 1970, 1975, and 1980. The newspaper's coverage of the riots is examined to determine the nature of social reality presented. Coverage patterns of this explosive event may provide some insight into broader issues about the functions of media in social conflicts.

This chapter begins with a brief discussion of the role of media in social conflicts, presents an overview of the community context in which the 1965 Watts riots occurred, reviews the interpretations given to these events by key social actors, examines the patterns of riot coverage in the *Sentinel,* and draws inferences about the newspaper's role from the coverage pattern.

Social Conflict and the Media

Lewis Coser defines social conflict as "a struggle over values and claims to scarce status, power and resources."[4] Theories of social conflict have addressed the types and causes of conflict; conflict group formation, resource mobilization, and confrontation; processes of conflict resolution, regulation, and institutionalization; and the functions of conflict for conflict groups and social systems.[5] Central to the study of social conflict is the role of media in the "development and control" of conflict.[6]

Communication channels long have been used as tools in the struggle to gain and maintain power. James Leith's discussion of the use of music, games, festivals, newspapers, and the theater by Jacobin leaders during the French Revolution,[7] Lawrence Goodwyn's study of the Populist movement and the National Reform Press Association,[8] Robert Morlan's analysis of the Nonpartisan League,[9] and Lauren Kessler's examination of ethnic and women's presses[10] provide examples of the uses of communication channels in social conflicts.

The role of media in social conflicts may vary with the nature of the conflict. Social conflict often stems from activities of organized conflict groups.[11] The role of media in this type of conflict is a critical area for inquiry, as media may play an integral role in the formation, mobilization, and maintenance of conflict groups. Leaders of conflict groups may seek to use media to gain attention,[12] create and reinforce an image of credibility,[13] and mobilize resources such as time, money, and commitment from group members and sympathetic others.[14]

Conflict groups, however, compete for sympathies and resources as they attempt to direct sentiment into structured group action. Established social movement organizations, such as the National Association for the Advancement of Colored People (NAACP), may have more success than informal conflict groups, such as the Black Panther party, in controlling media content, including success in using media channels to disseminate mobilizing messages.[15] To the extent these messages are effective tools for mobilization, resources may flow more readily through established, legitimized groups to legitimized social conflicts.

Although much sustained social conflict involves organized actors and socially sanctioned forms of collective action, riots and other short-term forms of collective action may occur outside organized channels under the minimum condition of a common target held responsible for collective grievances.[16] When riots and other unorganized conflicts burst upon the scene, government officials, organized conflict groups, and media are left with the task of "making sense" of the unexpected events.

As with organized conflicts, media coverage patterns—including language and images used to describe conflicts, sources used to interpret conflicts, and media editorializing about conflicts—may shape the "sense" made of the events. Selection of sources, for example, is a gatekeeping process that determines "who speaks" through the columns of the newspaper. In a case study of coverage of the 1967 Winston-Salem riots in the local mainstream media, David Paletz and Robert Dunn concluded that heavy reporter reliance upon local police and other government officials as sources led to reporting of the event from the point of view of local authorities.[17] As suggested by Edward Herman, the selection of "established" views for presentation as news may serve a social control function as divergent views become "confined to the fringes" of media coverage and the opposition becomes "marginalized."[18] Media may serve a social control function through the reinforcement of existing power arrangements within the social system.

Media, however, do not play an independent role in the manufacturing of meanings about social conflicts. As with the resource mobilization role, media coverage of issues, events, and conflict participants reflects the distribution of power in the social system. As media "mirror the conditions" of the social system, coverage of social conflicts reflects the concerns of "dominant power groupings" in the system.[19] As a result, media may function selectively to "accelerate, decelerate, clarify or redefine" social conflicts.[20]

As the dominant media reflect power arrangements in the broader social system, the black press may reflect the maintenance needs of the black power structure, both internally, in struggles to maintain its power position within the black community, and externally, in attempts to gain recognition from and access to the dominant power structure.

This implies that the long-recognized "protest" role of the black press may also be part of a broader internal and external social control function.[21] In his landmark study of race relations in the United States, Gunnar Myrdal characterized the black press as a "fighting press."[22] In his study of the black press during World War II, Lee Finkle concluded that even wartime pressures did not dissuade the black press from its Double V campaign, a campaign calling for victory abroad and victory against racism at home.[23] In her examination of the "dissident press," Lauren Kessler cited the black press for its "persistent struggle" against racism, a struggle carried on by men and women who "devoted their energies and sometimes risked their lives in hopes of bettering the conditions of their race."[24]

Within this "protest" pattern of coverage, the black press may reflect the power interests of the black community's established leadership. Coverage of the struggle for social justice may function to legitimize established black leaders, their organizations, and their methods for seeking change. The frustrations, energies, and resources of the black community may then be funneled through these channels. As a result, the internal and external power positions of established black leaders may be reinforced and conflict may take on a more predictable form.

Conflict regulation may occur through regularized contact between these leaders and representatives of the dominant power structure. Regularized contact may bring about the "binding" function of conflict, as contact gives rise to shared norms about the rules of conflict and new institutions for the resolution of conflict.[25] In addition, as black organizations formalize and black leaders gain a stake in the system, they may be more likely to choose social change strategies that serve organizational maintenance goals, as well as the goals of the broader movement. In short, they may engage in more "orderly" forms of protest.[26] The social control role of the black press, then, may be manifest as conflict becomes regulated and institutionalized.

The 1965 Watts riots provide an example of unorganized, short-term conflict within the broader civil rights struggle.[27] The riots caught both black and white leaders in Los Angeles by surprise. Governor Brown was shocked by the rioting and claimed, "Here in California, we have a wonderful working relationship between whites and Negroes. We got along fine until this happened."[28] Black leaders recognized the problems and frustrations in the ghetto, but they were "baffled and horrified" by the scope of the violence.[29]

In the months following the riots, many social actors struggled to make sense of what had happened. Government officials, the governor-appointed McCone Commission, black leaders, and the black press each interpreted the conflict in ways compatible with the power interests of those they represented.

The Watts Riots as a Challenge to the Local Black Power Structure

A shortage of adequate housing, employment, and educational opportunities, an inadequate transportation system, and a strained relationship with local police long had plagued residents of the Los Angeles black community.[30] Many black residents faced intense housing discrimination, and as a result, at the time of the 1965 riots, Los Angeles was more segregated than any of the cities in the South.[31]

A host of civil rights organizations, social, professional, and voting organizations, neighborhood clubs, and church-affiliated groups emerged in the black community of Los Angeles in response to community conditions.[32] Dominant among these groups were the local affiliates of the NAACP, formed in 1914, and the Urban League, established in 1921. These key organizations, along with local black politicians, the United Civil Rights Committee, and the Western Christian Leadership Conference, formed the basis of the local black power structure at the time of the 1965 riots.[33]

Despite efforts of black political leaders and these key organizations, living conditions remained difficult for many in the black community. At the time of the riots, the chairman of the California Fair Employment Practices Commission (FEPC) described ghetto areas as "literal islands of poverty and deprivation that have grown more depressed over the last five years."[34] Too often these civil rights efforts had little impact upon blacks in working-class sections of the Los Angeles area.[35] Protests against discrimination in housing often targeted expensive homes located outside ghetto areas, and efforts to combat job discrimination often resulted in the creation of positions for which few working-class blacks were qualified.[36] Calls for social justice by black leaders "produced only feeble echoes in the housing projects and parking lot social centers of Watts," where, "voiceless and isolated, the community observed the civil rights victories as news from a distant battlefield."[37]

By the middle of 1965, however, Watts was no longer voiceless. The explosion of the ghetto was seen by some as evidence of the failure of the established black leadership.[38] *Newsweek* called the Watts riots a "bruising setback for the Negro leadership and its cause" as it "represented a failure of the largely middle-class Negro leadership to reach the alienated ghetto masses and to mobilize them in community efforts to better their lot."[39]

Local black leaders also recognized the rioting as a sign that a leadership crisis had developed. Based upon testimony offered at the McCone Commission hearings, Robert Fogelson summarized the feelings of the local black leadership. These leaders

> realized that rioting would not only endanger the rioters, but, by alienating their friends and comforting their enemies, undermine the civil rights movement as well. . . . They understood that the rioters were challenging their leadership in the Negro community and subverting their positions vis-à-vis white

society. . . . Other than to join the rioting and assume its direction—which they were unwilling (and probably unable) to do—the Negro leaders had no alternative but to try to restrain the rioters.[40]

Despite several attempts, local black leaders had little success in their efforts to restrain the rioters. After they failed to quell the rioting, William Parker, the chief of the Los Angeles Police Department, called them "pseudo-leaders . . . who can't lead at all."[41] One N-VAC (Non-Violent Action Committee) leader conceded, "What's happening out there is out of the Negro leaders' hands."[42] Even Martin Luther King Jr. was jeered by the crowd as he attempted to talk with residents in the riot area. By some accounts, King "had to invoke the name of Elijah Muhammad to get a hearing" in the ghetto, leading some to conclude the local black Muslims were "powerful enough to challenge the established Negro 'leaders.'"[43]

Black activists emerging in the community also questioned the ability of established leaders to produce meaningful change.[44] One charged that the black leadership "couldn't lead a group of old ladies" and ignored the efforts of more aggressive leaders "out in the streets."[45] Many younger, lower-class blacks criticized established leaders for their mainstream orientation and lack of interest in ghetto problems.[46] Some concluded that these leaders and their moderate civil rights organizations were "of no more use to the Negro."[47]

The leadership void in the ghetto resulted in the formation of new black organizations in the months following the riots.[48] Some of these new groups rejected established black leaders as "Uncle Toms" and denounced their integrationist philosophies in favor of black power and/or black nationalist approaches.[49] Prominent among these groups were SLANT (Self-Leadership Among All Nationalities Today), a grass-roots black nationalist organization;[50] US, which emphasized cultural nationalism;[51] and the Sons of Watts Improvement Association, which emphasized black pride and self-determination.[52] These groups, along with the Black Panthers, the Nation of Islam, the Student Non-Violent Coordinating Committee (SNCC), Operation Bootstrap, and the Black Congress, were the most visible of the more militant black organizations in Los Angeles in the years after the riots.[53]

The leadership crisis faced by the black power structure stemmed from its "marginal" position in the social structure, a result of dual constituencies and its attempt to represent the interests of the black community while remaining dependent upon the dominant power structure for resources.[54] The Watts riots did not create the leader marginality problem; they served to make the problem more visible, as black leaders were "severely squeezed between the conservative white authority . . . and the revolt of ghetto Blacks."[55] The black leadership's stake in the system and its middle-class orientation, coupled with the need to maintain stability in the community, led to a disinclination to condone, much less engage in, the use of militant rhetoric or tactics.[56] Rather, established black leaders were "personally confident in orderly change and professionally committed to non-violent protest."[57]

The marginal position of the black leadership was reflected in the "bitter divisions" between black leaders and many in ghetto areas over strategy and tactics to be used in the fight for social justice.[58] These divisions reflected class-based differences in interests between ghetto residents and the middle-class leadership.[59] Black middle-class leaders often focused upon issues of discrimination and the attainment of "status" goals. Many ghetto residents, however, were more concerned with the improvement of daily living conditions and the attainment of "welfare" goals, such as adequate housing and increased employment opportunities.[60]

The conflict over goals extended to a dispute over tactics. Survey data collected shortly after the riots suggested two distinct groups were active in "the cause"—the traditional black leadership and an emerging militant group—and these groups had different ideas about how to create social change.[61] The militant segment, comprised of black nationalists, Muslims, ghetto youth, and black college students, focused upon welfare goals, questioned the slow pace of change, and approved of a wider range of tactics for the redress of grievances.[62] Violence was accepted as a legitimate tactical alternative by "a sizable and probably growing minority" in the black community.[63] The greater acceptance of rioting and violence as tactics led some to conclude that the "militants" were attempting to "accomplish through fear what has not been achieved through traditional processes of social change."[64]

Conflict over goals and tactics in the black community of Los Angeles reflected concerns expressed about the broader civil rights movement at the national level. As calls for "Black Power" began to ring across the nation in the summer of 1966, differences within the black community intensified over the direction of the civil rights movement.[65] These differences led to a shift away from accommodationist "Negro" leaders and toward a more aggressive "Black" leadership in the years that followed.[66] Established civil rights leaders, however, disapproved of black power activists and saw a strong black power movement as a threat to their integrationist goals.[67]

In this national and local milieu, competing views about the meaning, causes, and consequences of the 1965 Watts riots developed in the black and white communities. Black leaders and government officials deplored the rioting, the violence, and the destruction of property. Government officials, however, blamed outside agitators for stirring up local "riffraff" who then engaged in rioting, burning, and looting. Black leaders pointed to the deprivations of ghetto life as the underlying cause of the riots.[68]

Making Sense of the Riots

To riot participants and the crowds that cheered them on, the riots were most likely experienced as "a highly ambiguous, erratic alternation of insane noises, violent movements, fire and flashing lights, with long periods of eerie silence occasionally punctuated by gunfire, shouts, and sirens. In all likelihood, hardly anyone, black or white, could make much sense of the riot on the basis of his own fragmentary personal experience with it."[69]

To make sense of the riots, Chief of Police Parker, Governor Brown, Mayor Samuel Yorty, and the McCone Commission drew upon theories that attributed political violence to riffraff and outside agitators.[70] According to these explanations, community riffraff and/or outside agitators often linked to communist governments were responsible for riots and other forms of political violence. Governor Brown blamed a "hoodlum gang element" for the rioting.[71] Chief Parker concurred with his assessment and compared the rioters to "monkeys in a zoo."[72] In its December 1965 report, the McCone Commission called the rioters' actions "senseless" and placed blame for the riots upon local riffraff, members of the underclass, and southern newcomers unprepared for city life.[73]

Survey data collected shortly after the riots refute these positions. Riot participants were more representative of the community than many people had thought, as "every stratum of the ghetto contributed its share of rioters."[74] The data further refute official estimates that only one or two percent of area residents took part in the rioting. The data suggest that about 15% of area residents participated in the rioting and an additional 30% to 40% were "close spectators" who played a supportive role but were not actively engaged in the looting or burning.[75]

Despite contrary evidence, explanations blaming riffraff and outside agitators were widely used by government officials to account for the urban riots of the 1960s.[76] Reliance upon such interpretations served to shift the search for solutions to ghetto problems away from the improvement of ghetto conditions and toward a "riot control" perspective, which centered upon the need to control the unacceptable behavior of a small group of troublemakers.[77] In addition, to the extent this "riffraff" was seen as comprised mainly of recent arrivals from the rural South, local officials could argue that if change was needed, it should occur in the southern cities, not in Los Angeles.[78] According to Lewis Masotti, blaming riffraff and outside agitators made it possible to rationalize the violent events and relieve guilt about the society's failure to improve ghetto conditions.[79]

Unlike many government officials, black leaders and liberal whites rejected these explanations and drew upon relative deprivation interpretations of the riots.[80] Relative deprivation theories suggest that real or perceived inequalities in resources or status underlie political violence.[81] While black leaders condemned the rioting, they pointed to residents' anger and frustrations over the lack of housing, limited job opportunities, and police malpractice.[82] Councilman Gilbert Lindsay, a prominent black politician, called the rioting an outgrowth of an "economic situation" and argued that "the people reacted because they are frustrated and disgusted. They have come to the end and they don't know the proper end."[83]

Black leaders recognized the legitimate grievances underlying the riots, but they stood firm in rejecting rioting as a mechanism for change. One black minister called the actions of the rioters "misguided" and argued that "no amount of discrimination ought to cause a man to break into a liquor store. No amount of police brutality should cause a man to steal guns and beds."[84] Rev. H. H. Brookins, chairman of the United Civil Rights Committee, argued that "the surest road to ultimate defeat for all people, particularly minorities, is this sort of violence. Unjust means to achieve just ends will never work."[85] Reverend Brookins concurred with Chief Parker's estimate of the riot participation rate, saying, "In defense of the 550,000 Negroes of this city, less than 1 percent was involved, with the remaining 99 percent being just as opposed to this kind of violence as any white person in this nation."[86]

Black leaders urged local residents to channel their energies into orderly, constructive forms of political action.[87] Roy Wilkins of the NAACP called upon "the sober majority in the Negro community and in its leadership" to do the "unglamorous work" of helping ghetto residents take advantage of their opportunities.[88]

Although relative deprivation explanations have often been used to explain political violence, many political theorists argue that relative deprivation alone is not a sufficient condition for rioting to occur.[89] Rather, relative deprivation may serve as a predisposition that, coupled with the perception that traditional mechanisms for the redress of grievances are ineffective or blocked, may lead to an acceptance of political violence as an alternative form of political protest.[90] This interpretation of rioting gained some acceptance in the mid-to-late 1960s, as many black Americans saw the urban riots of the period as legitimate and effective forms of political protest.[91]

The perception that traditional redress mechanisms were ineffective was widespread among riot participants and many others in the black community of Los Angeles.[92] Many riot participants saw the civil rights movement, with its tactical emphasis upon sit-ins and marches, as a "hopeless cause."[93] Although many members of the black community disapproved of violence as a tactic, violence was seen by "a substantial majority" of ghetto residents as "either necessary, or if not, probable just the same,"[94] because violence was the only way to get white officials to listen.[95]

Use of rioting or violence as a tactic, however, does not suggest that the goals of riot participants were outside the political mainstream. Rather than seeking revolution, riot participants sought a "fuller participation in the social order and the material benefits enjoyed by the majority of American citizens."[96] Rioting, especially looting and burning, was intended as a protest against "the institutional fabric of the ghetto," most notably local merchants and police.[97] The message sent by the rioters was that "they would no longer quietly submit to the deprivations of slum life."[98]

Many riot participants hoped their actions would bring them visibility and respect.[99] As one explained, the riots had "put fear on them patties; they're scared. The only ones you give respect to are those you fear."[100] Many participants felt the riots had increased unity and pride in the ghetto, as "Everybody was sticking together" and "calling each other 'Brother'" in the days following the rioting.[101]

An interpretation of the rioting as an alternative form of political protest became widespread in the black community in the months following the riots.[102] The riots were often seen as a social reform action.[103] One prominent commentator concluded that the convergence of class and race had resulted in a "native uprising" reflecting the "mood and spirit of the low-income Negro community."[104]

This interpretation of the riots as an alternative political tactic included an expectation that the riots would produce beneficial outcomes for the community.[105] One study of post-riot attitudes in the black community found that more than half of those interviewed believed the riots were a political protest that would have a positive impact on their lives.[106] By contrast, 75% of whites interviewed expressed the view that the riots had hurt the blacks' cause.[107] Overall, many black residents viewed riot participants with sympathy and the riots with pride.[108]

These protest interpretations were even more pronounced in the "militant" segment of the black community. Militants were more likely to use terms from the "revolutionary lexicon," such as "revolt," when labeling the events, while more conservative and uncommitted members of the black community were more likely to choose labels that reflected a "violent public disorder" view of the events.[109] Militants expressed greater approval for the riots and were more optimistic about the riots' long-term impact on the community. Militants saw a greater likelihood of renewed rioting in the future and were more supportive of violence as a tactic for creating social change.[110]

In the aftermath of political violence, meanings are often developed in which the events "come to symbolize and glorify the rising up of an oppressed people."[111] These meanings may serve as "a rallying point for collective action" and function to "insure solidarity, act as a model for further violence, and justify similar future actions."[112]

As government officials, black leaders, and community residents developed meanings of the Watts riots, the community's black newspaper, the *Los Angeles Sentinel,* reflected and affected these processes. To what extent did the newspaper disseminate an ideology of political violence that glorified the "rising up" of oppressed ghetto residents? To what extent was rioting legitimized as an alternative mechanism for the redress of grievances? Whose view of reality was legitimized in the content of the *Los Angeles Sentinel?*

To address these questions, I conducted a content analysis of the *Sentinel's* riot coverage. Content analysis is a tool for creating understanding about media messages by reducing the messages' complexities through a search for the regularities and patterns in the messages. Berelson provided the classic definition of content analysis as "a research technique for the objective, systematic and quantitative description of the manifest content of communication."[113] In recent years, Berelson's approach has been the subject of some controversy, and concerns have been raised about the need to take into account the context in which messages are produced and received.[114] Regardless of approach, researchers using content analysis procedures determine how to sample content, the unit of analysis to be used, the construction of content categories, and processes for coding of content.[115]

The *Los Angeles Sentinel* Coverage

The *Los Angeles Sentinel,* a weekly newspaper, was founded in 1934 by Leon Washington Jr., who served as publisher until his death in 1974. In addition to the *Sentinel,* two local radio stations and several other weekly newspapers served the black community during the mid-1960s.[116] Founded in 1879, the *California Eagle* was the oldest black newspaper in the area. Changes in ownership and format in the midsixties did little to solve the *Eagle's* circulation problems and it subsequently ceased publication.[117] The *Herald-Dispatch,* founded in 1952, was a small-circulation paper with what Jack Lyle described as an "erratic" political position and a "thrown together" appearance.[118] Two lesser-known papers, the *News* and the *United Pictorial Review,* were also circulating during this period.[119]

It was the *Sentinel,* however, that was considered to be the dominant newspaper in the black community. Jack Lyle's 1963 examination of black newspaper readership found that seven in ten black residents read the *Sentinel,* one in ten read the *Eagle,* and one in seventeen read the *Herald-Dispatch.*[120] The *Sentinel* had the best-paid staff of these three papers, was the only audited circulation paper, and was a member of the black National Newspaper Publishers Association and the California Publishers Association.[121]

Over the years, the *Sentinel* enjoyed wide readership, broad community support, and financial success.[122] Results from Lyle's media users survey conducted close to the time of the riots suggested that 80% of the black community felt the *Sentinel* presented local issues accurately.

The *Los Angeles Sentinel* was closely tied to the economic and political power centers in the black community, which was reflected in its "healthy advertising linage."[123] Ties to sources of political power were reflected in the organizational affiliations of several of its regular columnists; officers of the local NAACP and Urban League and local black politicians were regular contributors to the newspaper.

Coverage of the Watts riots in the *Sentinel* began with the 19 August issue. I examined this issue and all subsequent issues through the end of the 1965 calendar year (*n* = 20) and I identified all stories containing mentions of the riots (*n* = 277). Included in this group were news stories, columns and features, editorials, letters to the editor, photographs, and political cartoons.

The number of riot stories that appeared in each month of the 1965 study period is shown in table 2.1. As indicated there, the early months of the period saw a large proportion of the total number of stories in this analysis. One-third of all stories appeared in the last half of August and more than 60% of all stories appeared in August and September.

I identified a second group of stories that appeared during the summer months of 1970, 1975, and 1980 to examine coverage in the post-riot years (*n* = 56). The summer months were selected for review because riot retrospec-

Table 2.1. Distribution of Stories over the 1965
Study Period

Month	Stories	
	Number	Percentage
August	92	33.2
September	78	28.2
October	33	11.9
November	30	10.8
December	44	15.9
	277	100.0

tives were more likely to occur near anniversaries of the initial events. These retrospectives tended to appear on the editorial pages of the newspaper, rather than in the news columns.

Using the 277 stories from 1965 and the 56 stories from the later period, I compiled a list of all connotative labels used to characterize the riots and riot participants; all mentions of causes and consequences of the rioting; all strategies for addressing the problems underlying the rioting; and all sources used in the stories.

These data suggest that the broad pattern of riot coverage in the *Los Angeles Sentinel* reflected relative deprivation explanations. The grievances underlying the rioting received extensive coverage, especially concerns about police malpractice and the lack of housing, employment, and educational opportunities.

Within this pattern of coverage, the rioting was condemned as an inappropriate action that would bring harm to the community. Traditional mechanisms for the redress of grievances were most often recommended as tactics to improve ghetto conditions. Socially sanctioned, orderly forms of change, such as voting, working with established black organizations, and building black businesses to create new jobs, were recommended. Established black leaders were heavily used as sources in the riot coverage.

Riot Coverage in August–December 1965

Labels Used to Describe the Riots

The terms used to refer to the riots were examined to determine the extent to which the events were identified as a political protest as opposed to a destructive outbreak of "senseless" violence as suggested in the McCone Commission report. All connotative labels applied to the events were identified and grouped into "protest," "destruction," and "other" categories. The heavily used, more neutral "riot" and "event" terms were excluded from these categories. All connotative labels identified in the coverage are listed in table 2.2. As all "other" labels had negative connotations, the "other" and "destruction" categories were combined for presentation in the table.

Over the five-month study period, "destruction" and other negative labels accounted for 72.8% (n = 169) of connotative labels identified and protest labels accounted for 27.2% (n = 63) of the labels. Initial riot coverage contained labels primarily from the "destruction" and "other" categories. The lead story in the 19 August issue of the *Sentinel* referred to the events as a "nightmarish week of rioting and pillaging" that resulted in "the most shameful and disgusting saga in the history of the Negro."[124] In the 2 September issue, the events were described as five days of "tragedy."[125]

The coverage included a higher proportion of protest labels by September 1965. One front-page headline in a 23 September story about the McCone Commission hearings read "Cure Revolt Causes."[126] The greater proportion of protest labels that appeared later in the period coincides with the spread of the political protest interpretation of the riots within the black community.[127] Despite the increased rate of appearance of protest labels, only limited conclusions can be drawn from these data because of the small number of connotative labels that appeared in later issues.

Table 2.2. Appearance of Protest, Destruction, and Other Negative Labels by Month of Issue, August–December 1965

Month	Protest[a] Labels	Destruction[b] and Other Negative[c] Labels
August	10.8% (n = 14)	89.2% (n = 116)
September	45.1% (n = 23)	54.9% (n = 28)
October	41.7% (n = 10)	58.3% (n = 14)
November	70.0% (n = 7)	30.0% (n = 3)
December	52.9% (n = 9)	47.1% (n = 8)
Category appearance	27.2% (n = 63)	72.8% (n = 169)

a. Protest labels = revolt, rebellion, insurrection, uprising, upheaval, unrest, strife, discontent.

b. Destruction labels = disorder, lawlessness, pillaging, burning, looting, bloodshed, crime-on-the-street, rampage, disturbance, wreckage, mess, mob rule, mob action, destruction (wanton, mass, self-, deplorable), riot-(torn, scarred, devastated, ravaged, burned).

c. Other negative labels = tragedy, disaster, outrageous, horrible, shameful, shameless, disgusting, senseless, disgrace, grim, turmoil, insanity, atrocity, catastrophe, holocaust, useless, maelstrom, chaos, conflagration, nightmare, violation, infamous, folly.

Labels Used to Describe Riot Participants

The terms used to refer to riot participants were examined to determine the extent to which sympathy for the rioters was reflected in the coverage and the extent to which they were characterized as political protesters. Few direct references to riot participants were found in the stories examined. In the 277 stories in the 1965 database, 20 connotative labels were identified as applied to riot participants. Thirteen of these labels related to destruction images. They included "destroying rioters," "looters," and "arsonists." Six of the labels reflected riffraff views, including "hoodlums," "gangs" or "gang members," "renegades," and "rabble-rousers." In the 19 August issue, for example, riot participants were described as "roving gangs"[128] of "young renegade Negroes"[129] who "ran amuck and destroyed all within their paths."[130] The remaining label applied was a protest label and appeared in an appeal by a *Sentinel* columnist to "the rioters or revolutionists to postpone the next disaster."[131]

Reasons for the Rioting

Mentions of the causes of the rioting were tabulated to determine the extent to which the riots were portrayed as resulting from legitimate grievances in the community. The data presented in table 2.3 report the causes of the rioting mentioned in the *Sentinel.* Police malpractice, lack of jobs and poor living conditions in the ghetto, and indifference to black community concerns on the part of the white community and government officials received the most attention.

The criticisms of Mayor Yorty's handling of Anti-Poverty Program funds that appeared in the *Sentinel* coverage provide examples of the broader concern about government indifference and reflect the anger of black leaders who felt they had been all but excluded from program participation.[132] Congressman Augustus Hawkins lambasted Mayor Yorty and argued that local civil rights organizations deserved a larger voice in Poverty Program decision making.[133] Father Samuel Morrison, vice-president of the local CORE affiliate, hoped that the rioting would "show Mayor Yorty and his friends that they just can't sit on that anti-poverty money and not let us have it."[134]

Sentinel columnist Stanley Robertson said that because government officials had not listened to "responsible members of the Negro Community," those officials were living in a "dream world" and had not noticed that Los Angeles had been "a racial tinderbox for at least the last five years."[135] An editorial appearing in the 19 August issue called the riots a "tragic disaster" born out of the "psychological fires of frustration . . . smoldering in the minds of thousands of deprived citizens in Watts."[136] A press release from the Los

Table 2.3. Mentions of Underlying Causes of the Riots, August–
December 1965 Issues

	Mentions	
Causes	Number	Percentage
Relations with police/government		
Police malpractice/Parker	41	24.6
Racism	13	7.8
White neglect	8	4.8
Anti-poverty program/Yorty	8	4.8
Don't listen to black leaders	7	4.2
	77	46.2
Ghetto conditions		
Unemployment	29	17.4
Poor housing	16	9.6
Poverty	13	7.8
Inadequate schools	10	6.0
Merchant exploitation	2	1.2
Lack of facilities/services	2	1.2
	72	43.2
Other		
Frustration/anger	12	7.2
Lack of black involvement	6	3.6
	18	10.8
Totals	167	100.2

Note: Percentages do not total 100.0 due to rounding.

Angeles Urban League that appeared in the same issue deplored "the wanton destruction of life and property" and called for more attention to the community grievances that "make such disturbances possible."[137]

Anticipated Effects of the Riots

Mentions of consequences of the riots were tabulated to determine the level of optimism about outcomes of the riots contained in the riot coverage. Specific consequences of the riots were discussed in about 6% of the stories examined ($n = 16$) and in these stories, harmful outcomes ($n = 13$) were mentioned more often than helpful outcomes ($n = 3$). Harmful outcomes of the riots included loss of jobs and businesses in the community ($n = 8$) and negative reactions by whites ($n = 5$). Included in the feared negative reactions was white anger and backlash, which might serve to "help the white man to live with his guilt, to justify what he has done."[138]

Helpful outcomes were mentioned less often and centered on the expectation that government officials and the society at large would pay more attention to black issues.[139] Dick Gregory, quoted in a *Sentinel* column, argued that "the Negro in the ghetto will not be able to list his needs any more than a sick man can diagnose his ills. . . . He makes his mark with a brick. And he knows that at least America cannot ignore his inarticulate brick the way it ignored the eloquence of his leaders."[140]

Tactics for Social Change

Recommendations of tactics for improving community conditions appearing in the *Sentinel* were tabulated to determine the extent to which traditional mechanisms for the redress of grievances were portrayed as blocked and the extent to which rioting was legitimized as an alternative form of protest. As the data in table 2.4 indicate, socially sanctioned forms of collective and individual action were the recommended tactics.

Building black businesses to create jobs in the community and working within established black organizations were mentioned most often as solutions to problems in the community. Community unity and increased middle-class and black leader involvement in ghetto issues were also mentioned as central to the improvement of community conditions. Congressman Hawkins encouraged greater participation in community affairs and suggested that "each of us get busy by volunteering our services."[141] Voting and participation in election campaigns, especially in voter registration campaigns in the black community, were also recommended tactics as "it is among the unregistered that troubles lie. These people harbor the frustrations."[142]

The *Sentinel* took a strong stand against rioting as a mechanism for the redress of grievances. One editorial stated that "all self-respecting Negro cit-

Table 2.4. Mentions of Tactics for Social Change, August–December 1965 Issues

Tactics	Mentions	
	Number	Percentage
Create new black businesses/jobs	10	33.3
Work with established black organizations	9	30.0
Increased middle-class involvement needed	5	16.7
Develop unity in the community	3	10.0
Vote/become politically active	2	6.7
Engage in peaceful protests	1	3.3
	30	100.0

izens here deplore the burning of buildings, the lootings and shootings and its staggering toll in human lives and property damage."[143] Sportswriter Brad Pye wrote, "This looting, burning and complete destruction of property isn't the answer . . . it isn't the way . . . it isn't the right way to get a redress of our grievances."[144]

Who Speaks?

The sources cited in the riot coverage were tallied to address the question of who speaks on the subject of the riots. The data presented in table 2.5 reveal that leaders of established black organizations, such as the NAACP and the Urban League, and black politicians, such as Congressman Hawkins, Assemblyman Mervyn Dymally, and Councilmen Lindsay and Thomas Bradley, accounted for more than 70% (n = 61) of the black community sources used in the riot coverage. The views of riot participants were cited less often. No militant spokespersons were cited as sources in any of the riot stories.

Riot participants were used as sources only a few times and tended to appear in the initial riot coverage issues. When riot participants were quoted, however, the quotes used tended to reflect the political protest interpretation of the events. One riot participant interviewed on the second morning of the five-day event told the *Sentinel* reporter, "What you see now ain't nothing. We're going to tear this —— town down. And if they mess with us, we'll set this whole —— world on fire."[145] Another, cited in the story as in the process of looting a liquor store when interviewed, was quoted as saying, "I'm a fanatic for riots: I just love them." But, he noted, "By the end of the week

Table 2.5. Black Community Sources Used in Riot Coverage, August–December 1965 Issues

Sources	Times Used	
	Number	Percentage
Leaders of established black organizations[a]	35	40.7
Black elected official	26	30.2
Black business leader	10	11.6
Black minister (non-Muslim)	6	7.0
Riot participant	5	5.8
Man-on-the-street (nonparticipant)	4	4.7
	86	100.0

a. Includes the NAACP, Urban League, United Civil Rights Committee, CORE, and Western Christian Leadership Conference. No "militant" spokespersons or Nation of Islam leaders were used as sources for the riot coverage during this period.

old liver-lipped Martin Luther King will come in here and everybody will be talking about how he came in and soothed the savaged beasts. He'll come in here with that old mess about 'Violence, whether black or white, is wrong.' Just wait, he'll be here."[146]

Summary of Coverage, August–December 1965

The terms applied to the riots and riot participants suggest the riots were portrayed as a protest within a broader emphasis upon the destruction they caused. Rioting was rejected in favor of socially sanctioned tactics and channels for creating social change.

Legitimate grievances were cited as the causes of the riots, although few beneficial outcomes were anticipated as a result of the rioting. The data in table 2.3 suggest that the explanations for the rioting found in the *Sentinel* coverage reflected grievances expressed by many in the black community. Survey data collected shortly after the riots found widespread frustration with the local police department, as many residents felt police officers lacked respect, used insulting language, stopped and searched black residents without cause, and used unnecessary force when making arrests.[147] Police raids on Nation of Islam headquarters in 1962 and again a few days after the riots compounded the tensions between the police department and the black community.[148]

Difficult living conditions and mistreatment by whites were also cited in various surveys as major grievances in the community. Reflecting the *Sentinel* coverage, 46% of respondents in one survey cited poor living conditions as a primary cause of the riots, and 14% cited mistreatment by whites.[149]

One key departure from community attitudes was the relatively few mentions of merchant exploitation as a cause for the rioting in the *Sentinel* coverage ($n = 2$, 1.2%). When asked to identify the main targets of the rioting, 38% of respondents in another survey named store merchants first,[150] and yet another survey found that one-third of ghetto residents felt they were frequently overcharged or sold inferior goods by local merchants.[151]

A pattern of pro-business coverage also emerged in other ways in the stories I examined. In addition to merchant exploitation's accounting for only 1.2% of all mentions of causes for the rioting, loss of businesses and jobs in the community accounted for 62% of all mentions of harmful outcomes of the riots, the building of new businesses accounted for one-third of all mentions of solutions to ghetto problems, and business leaders accounted for close to 12% of sources cited in the riot coverage.

Within this broad pattern of coverage, the established black leadership and black professionals did receive some criticism in the columns of the *Sentinel* for their lack of involvement in ghetto concerns. Commenting on this leadership vacuum, one columnist wrote that black leaders had not "really reached down and ever made contact with the people on the street."[152] The black leadership and the black middle-class were urged to get busy and help "pick up the pieces"[153] and "attack the problem where it exists."[154] Of the poorer black residents, another *Sentinel* columnist wrote, "These people are our people regardless to [*sic*] whether they are ignorant or educated. . . . We have all moved away and left them alone, trying to escape segregation and poverty. . . . We can't help them by being ashamed."[155]

The patterns of coverage identified in the 1965 stories reappeared in the retrospective riot coverage examined from the summers of 1970, 1975, and 1980. As in 1965, the *Sentinel* deplored the violence and feared the riots had hurt the community. Recommendations for facilitating change focused upon established black organizations and socially sanctioned tactics. Established black leaders were extensively used as sources in the coverage. One departure from 1965 patterns, however, was the appearance in editorials of pleas to community residents not to engage in renewed rioting.

Coverage in the Post-Riot Years

Similarities to 1965 Patterns

Although few connotative labels were identified in the post-riot years, the terms applied to the riots in 1970, 1975, and 1980 ($n = 29$) were similar to the terms found in the 1965 stories. Protest labels accounted for 51.7% ($n = 15$) of the connotative terms, a proportion similar to that in the later months of the 1965 coverage. By comparison, protest labels accounted for 48%, or 49 out of the 102 connotative labels applied to the riots in September through December 1965. No connotative labels were found for riot participants in the post-riot stories examined.

Reasons for the rioting again centered on the deprivations of ghetto life (54.1%, $n = 20$); government neglect of the community and its leaders (32.4%, $n = 12$); and anger and frustration born out of "deep and sincere wounds from oppression" (13.5%, $n = 5$).[156] Columnist Stanley Robertson charged that "years of unheeded warnings" had led to "the greatest tragedy that can befall a modern American city: riots, crime-on-the-street, insurrection, mass death."[157] Booker Griffin wrote that although he did not seek "to glorify or romanticize riots as acts that are sacred and redemptive," society must understand that riots are "symptoms of deep-seeded causes that society fails to cope with" and that rioting may serve as a means to "lash out against authority that is held to be unjust and unfair."[158] The *Sentinel* city editor concluded, "Urban riots are the ultimate reaction from the community as a whole to the frustrations of its daily experience."[159]

Consistent with 1965 patterns, the post-riot coverage did not associate riots with beneficial outcomes; the riots were seen as more harmful (77.3%, n = 17) than helpful (22.7%, n = 5). The problems underlying the riots were "still there and in greater numbers than before."[160] Fifteen years after the rioting, there were still "too many Blacks in Los Angeles without jobs, too many kids being turned out of schools with inferior educations, and too much frustration and hopelessness among the populace."[161] Fears expressed in 1965 about a white backlash were reiterated in the post-riot coverage. Writing about the "Ghetto Olympics of 1965," one *Sentinel* columnist concluded that the actions of "misinformed, misguided Blacks" only served to play into the hands of "The Man."[162]

As in the 1965 coverage, traditional forms of political action and work within established black organizations were most often mentioned as tactics for generating change (68.4%, n = 26). The other major approach mentioned was the creation of jobs through the building of new black businesses (28.9%, n = 11). "Peaceful demonstrations" were mentioned as a recommended tactic only once, and then for use only in "extreme cases" (2.6%, n = 1).[163]

Answers to the question of "who speaks?" suggested heavy reliance on established black leaders as sources, just as it had in 1965. Leaders of established black organizations (n = 10), black politicians (n = 6), and black ministers (n = 2) accounted for nearly 86% (n = 18) of the sources used in the post-riot coverage. No militant spokespersons were cited as sources in the stories examined.

Anti-Riot Messages

The key departure from 1965 coverage patterns was the appearance of editorials warning residents not to engage in rioting (16.1%, n = 9). One editorial writer argued the Watts riots were "holocaust enough to last a century."[164] Fears that tempers might flare and frustrations boil over in the summer heat were reflected in editorials warning residents not to let the hot weather make them lose their "cool."[165] In these editorials, the community was urged to "ignore those people who would stir up the emotions of the populace" as "their sole purpose is to create disruption."[166] The community was warned not to let "a few dissidents allow us to destroy all that we have worked for."[167] Residents were reminded, "Nothing can be proved by this kind of action, and, if we allow it to take place, then we are as guilty as if we were the actual perpetrators of the action."[168] Commenting on the 1980 urban riots in other cities, one *Sentinel* columnist argued, "When all is said and done, the communities will still be in shambles and the most damage Black people will have done will have been to themselves. . . . there is something nonsensical about fouling one's own nest."[169]

Along with the anti-riot messages were warnings to government officials that renewed rioting could occur unless change came quickly. In more than one-fifth of the stories (*n* = 12), *Sentinel* columnists called on government officials to pay greater attention to the black community and its leaders if they hoped to prevent renewed rioting.

Summary of Riot Coverage Patterns in 1965 and Later

The content analysis shows that some elements of the "political protest" interpretation of the riots were prominent in the *Sentinel*'s riot coverage. Excluding the initial coverage in August 1965, protest terms were applied to the riots at about the same rate as destruction or other negative terms. Although the events were often labeled as protest, the views of riot participants and militant leaders were not visible in the riot coverage. The views of established black leaders received greater attention.

Deprivations and legitimate grievances, including the lack of housing and employment opportunities and police malpractice, received attention as underlying causes of the rioting. To address these grievances, moderate tactics were endorsed. Rioting was not portrayed as a legitimate or effective means for seeking change.

Conclusion

This examination of coverage of the Watts riots in the *Los Angeles Sentinel* suggests that reporting of this event reflected the maintenance needs of the established black power structure at a time when it faced internal challenges and external criticisms.

The maintenance needs of an established black leadership in a "marginal" position, caught between an emerging militant segment of the community and the dominant power structure, may have been served by the newspaper's exclusion of the militant perspective on the riots, its emphasis upon established mechanisms for seeking social change, and its warnings that renewed rioting may occur if government officials refused to negotiate with established black leaders.

Although the desire to gain attention was cited by many riot participants as a primary reason for their actions, the resulting attention was drawn to ghetto conditions, not to riot participants or their perspectives. This lack of visibility, coupled with calls for unity and stability in the community, may have served to marginalize the militant perspective on the riots and bolster consensus in the community. Downplaying internal community conflicts may have served to reinforce the power position of the established black leadership.

The marginalization of the militant perspective may have served to reinforce the power position of the black leadership with its external constituencies as well. To the extent widespread participation in and support for the riots was denied, challenges to the legitimacy of established leaders' roles as spokespersons for the black community may have seemed less serious and potential threats to their negotiating positions may have been abated.

In addition, the rejection of rioting and other nonsanctioned tactics may have calmed representatives of the dominant power structure and moderate allies of the established black leadership. Black leaders were dependent upon the dominant structure and external allies such as trade unions and white liberals and could not afford to alienate these groups through the endorsement of militant tactics.[170]

As the rioting drew attention to ghetto conditions, established channels and sanctioned tactics were emphasized as appropriate mechanisms for addressing the legitimate grievances in the community. The emphasis in the riot coverage upon peaceful, integrationist modes of action reflected the established black leadership's commitment to and investment in orderly social change. Community grievances were used as a "rallying point for collective action" but rioting was not seen as an appropriate "model" for further action. Rather, the community was urged to rally around established leaders and their organizations. The *Sentinel* coverage may have functioned to funnel community frustrations and grievances through sanctioned outlets.

This is not to suggest that established black leaders escaped criticism in the *Sentinel*'s riot coverage. Neglect of ghetto residents and their grievances was noted by some *Sentinel* columnists as they urged black leaders to incorporate welfare goals into their integrationist and often status-oriented programs. Absorption of the militants' welfare goals, however, may have served to avert the internal threat to the established leadership's power position and expand its power base. Through absorption of welfare goals, established black leaders, not emerging militant leaders, may have been recognized as the legitimate spokespersons on welfare issues and the central agents of change in efforts to improve ghetto conditions.

To achieve social justice, no fundamental changes in existing institutions were required. Rather, the *Sentinel* called for greater inclusion in the dominant structure, a power realignment in which the established black leadership had a larger role in local decision making.

In the post-riot years, *Sentinel* columnists called on the dominant power structure to be more responsive to black leaders, lest renewed rioting occur. These warnings may have served to increase the leverage of the established black leadership in negotiations with the dominant power structure.[171] Peter Blau defined power as "asserting one's will against resistance owing to available sanctions."[172] With threats of renewed rioting, black leaders could argue that government officials would have to bargain now or pay later.

The use of militants by moderates in bargaining with the dominant structure is part of the cycle of change in protest leaderships.[173] Protest leaders emerge, gain legitimacy and recognition, develop a stake in the dominant power structure, and become more moderate. Their moderate stance often leads to an emergence of militant leaders who challenge the legitimacy and power position of the moderates. These challenges, however, may serve to increase the moderates' effectiveness, as representatives of the dominant structure become aware that real progress must be made on issues if they hope to stem the militants' influence.

The pattern of riot coverage in the *Sentinel* suggests that the media role in unorganized, unforeseen conflicts may parallel that in organized, sustained social conflicts. In both cases, the media may function to reinforce existing power arrangements within the social system.

Notes

1. For descriptions of these days' events, see Robert Conot, *Rivers of Blood, Years of Darkness* (New York: Bantam, 1967), and Jerry Cohen and William S. Murphy, *Burn, Baby, Burn!* (New York: Dutton, 1966).

2. Governor's Commission on the Los Angeles Riots, *Violence in the City—An End or a Beginning?* (Los Angeles: McCone Commission Report, 1965).

3. David L. Lange, Robert K. Baker, and Sandra J. Ball, *Mass Media and Violence,* A Staff Report to the National Commission on the Causes and Prevention of Violence (Washington, D.C.: U.S. Government Printing Office, 1969); National Advisory Commission on Civil Disorders, *Report of the National Advisory Commission on Civil Disorders* (New York: Bantam, 1968), also known as the Kerner Commission report.

4. Lewis Coser, *The Functions of Social Conflict* (Glencoe, Ill.: Free Press, 1956), 8.

5. Anthony Oberschall, *Social Conflict and Social Movements* (Englewood Cliffs, N.J.: Prentice-Hall, 1973).

6. Phillip J. Tichenor, George A. Donohue, and Clarice N. Olien, *Community Conflict and the Press* (Beverly Hills, Calif.: Sage, 1980), 18.

7. James A. Leith, *Media and Revolution* (Toronto: Canadian Broadcasting Company Publications, 1968).

8. Lawrence Goodwyn, *The Populist Movement* (New York: Oxford University Press, 1978).

9. Robert L. Morlan, *Political Prairie Fire* (St. Paul, Minn.: Minnesota Historical Society Press, 1985).

10. Lauren Kessler, *The Dissident Press* (Beverly Hills, Calif.: Sage, 1984).

11. Gary T. Marx and James L. Wood, "Strands of Theory and Research in Collective Behavior," *Annual Review of Sociology* 1 (1975), 363–428; Ralph H. Turner, "Collective Behavior and Resource Mobilization," *Research in Social Movements, Conflict and Change* 4 (1981), 1–24; Oberschall. Approaches in the study of social conflict have shifted away from social disorganization and alienation as explanations for social movements. Compare, for example, Gabriel Tarde's discussion of imitation (*Les Lois de l'imitation*, trans. Elsie Parsons as *The Laws of Imitation* [New York: Henry Holt, 1890, 1903]), Gustave LeBon's study of the crowd mind (*The Crowd* [New York: Viking Press, 1963], originally published as *Psychologie des foules*); Wilfred Trotter's discussion of herd instincts (*Instincts of the Herd in Peace and War* [London: T. Fisher Unwin, 1916]), and William Kornhauser's mass society approach (*The Politics of Mass Society* [Glencoe, Ill.: Free Press, 1959]) with discussions of the resource mobilization approach, as in Oberschall, and in John McCarthy and Mayer Zald ("Resource Mobilization and Social Movements: A Partial Theory," *American Journal of Sociology* 82 [1977], 1212–41).

12. Tichenor, Donohue, and Olien.

13. Charles Perrow, "Members as Resources in Voluntary Organizations," in *Organizations and Clients,* ed. W. R. Rosengren and M. Lefton (Columbus, Ohio: Merrill, 1970).

14. McCarthy and Zald.

15. Susan M. Strohm, "Black Community Organization and the Role of the Black Press in Resource Mobilization in Los Angeles from 1940 to 1980" (Ph.D. diss., University of Minnesota, 1989).

16. Oberschall.

17. David L. Paletz and Robert Dunn, "Press Coverage of Civil Disorders: A Case Study of Winston-Salem, 1967," *Public Opinion Quarterly* 33 (1969), 328–45.

18. Edward S. Herman, "Diversity of News: 'Marginalizing' the Opposition," *Journal of Communications* 35 (1985), 135.

19. Tichenor, Donohue, and Olien, 80, 219.

20. Ibid., 18.

21. These comments are not to be taken as a criticism of black press performance. Rather, one should be aware that, like the mainstream media, the black press reflects the distribution of power within the black community as well as the black community's power and status within the larger social structure.

22. Gunnar Myrdal, *An American Dilemma* (New York: Harper, 1944), 908.

23. Lee Finkle, *Forum for Protest* (Cranbury, N.J.: Associated University Presses, 1975).

24. Kessler, 21.

25. Coser.

26. Suzanne Staggenborg, "The Consequences of Professionalization and Formalization in the Pro-Choice Movement," *American Sociological Review* 53 (1988), 585–606; William A. Gamson, *The Strategy of Social Protest* (Belmont, Calif.: Wadsworth, 1990); Ralph H. Turner, "Determinants of Social Movement Strategies," in *Human Nature and Collective Behavior: Papers in Honor of Herbert Blumer,* ed. Tamotsu Shibutani (Englewood Cliffs, N.J.: Prentice-Hall, 1970).

27. Despite allegations by some government officials, no evidence was found to support the claim that the Watts riots were organized by black militant groups inside or outside the local black community. See, for example, David O. Sears and John McConahay, *The Politics of Violence* (Boston: Houghton Mifflin, 1973).

28. Roy Haynes, "Brown's Riot Area Tour Curtailed by Sniper Fire," *Los Angeles Times,* 16 August 1965, part 1, p. 1.

29. Sears and McConahay, *Politics of Violence,* 152.

30. Patricia Rae Adler, "Watts: From Suburb to Black Ghetto" (Ph.D. diss., Indiana University, 1977); James A. Fisher, "History of the Political and Social Development of the Black Community in California: 1850–1950" (Ph.D. diss., State University of New York at Stony Brook, 1971); Strohm.

31. Christopher Rand, *Los Angeles* (New York: Oxford University Press, 1967); Melvin Oliver and James Johnson Jr., "Inter-Ethnic Conflict in an Urban Ghetto," *Research in Social Movements, Conflict and Change* 6 (1984), 57–94.

32. Strohm.

33. Ibid.

34. "Minority Groups in California," *Monthly Labor Review* 89 (1966), 978–83, cited in George Frakes and Curtis Solberg, *Minorities in California History* (New York: Random House, 1971).

35. William Ellis, "Operation Bootstrap: A Case Study in Ideology and the Institutionalization of Protest" (Ph.D. diss., University of California, Los Angeles, 1969).

36. Ibid.

37. Adler, 330.

38. Robert M. Fogelson, "White on Black: A Critique of the McCone Commission Report on the Los Angeles Riots," in *Mass Violence in America,* ed. Fogelson (New York: Arno Press and the New York Times, 1969).

39. "After the Blood Bath," *Newsweek,* 30 August 1965, 13–17, 14 (quote).

40. Fogelson, 139.

41. "Parker Raps False Negro Leadership," *Los Angeles Times,* 15 August 1965, sec. A, p. C.

42. Jack Jones, "Area Appears Devoid of Community Leadership," *Los Angeles Times,* 14 August 1965, part 1, p. 1.

43. Charles E. Brown, "Say L.A. Muslims Challenge Negro Leadership in Ghetto," *Jet,* 16 September 1965, 50–51.

44. Paul Bullock, *Watts: The Aftermath* (New York: Grove Press, 1969); Douglas G. Glasgow, *The Black Underclass* (San Francisco: Jossey-Bass, 1980).

45. Tommy Jacquette, "Comments," in *The Black American and the Press,* ed. Jack Lyle (Los Angeles: Ward Ritchie Press, 1968), 75.

46. Glasgow.

47. "Watts Today: Brave Plans and a Sick Psyche," *Newsweek,* 13 December 1965, 29–32, 29 (quote).

48. Robert Blauner, "Whitewash over Watts: The Failure of the McCone Commission Report," in *Mass Violence in America,* ed. Fogelson; Celeste Durant, "The Watts Rebuilding Dream Is a Dream Deferred," *Los Angeles Times,* 23 March 1975, part 2, p. 3, in a special section entitled "Watts: 10 Years Later"; John Howard and William McCord, "Watts: The Revolt and After," in *Lifestyles in the Black Ghetto,* ed. William McCord et al. (New York: Norton, 1969); Bullock.

49. Glasgow; Cohen and Murphy.

50. Harry Scoble, "Effects of Riots on Negro Leadership," in *Riots and Rebellion,* ed. Louis H. Masotti and Don R. Bowen (Beverly Hills, Calif.: Sage, 1968); Bruce Tyler, "Black Radicalism in Southern California, 1950–1982" (Ph.D. diss., University of California at Los Angeles, 1983).

51. Imamu Amiri Baraka (LeRoi Jones), *Raise, Race, Rays, Raze* (New York: Vintage, 1972); Imamu Clyde Halisi, "Maulana Ron Karenga: Black Leader in Captivity," *Black Scholar* (1972), 27–34.

52. Glasgow.

53. Ellis; Strohm.

54. For a discussion of leader marginality, see Arthur Vidich and Joseph Bensman, *Small Town in Mass Society* (Princeton: Princeton University Press, 1968).

55. Tyler, 329.

56. Scoble.

57. Fogelson, 139.

58. Tyler, 281.

59. Tyler; Oberschall.

60. Nathan Cohen, "The Los Angeles Riot Study," in *The Los Angeles Riots,* ed. Cohen. For a discussion of welfare and status goals, see James Q. Wilson, *Negro Politics* (New York: Free Press, 1960).

61. T. M. Tomlinson, "Ideological Foundations for Negro Action: Militant and Non-Militant Views," in *The Los Angeles Riots,* ed. Cohen, 376; Raymond J. Mur-

phy and James M. Watson, "The Structure of Discontent: Relationship between Social Structure, Grievance, and Riot Support," in *The Los Angeles Riots,* ed. Cohen.

62. Cohen; Tomlinson.

63. T. M. Tomlinson and David O. Sears, "Negro Attitudes Toward the Riot," in *The Los Angeles Riots,* ed. Cohen, 312.

64. Cohen, 21; Tomlinson and Sears.

65. Robert C. Smith, *Black Leadership: A Survey of Theory and Research* (Washington, D.C.: Mental Health Research and Development Center, Institute for Urban Affairs and Research, Howard University, 1983).

66. Jerome H. Skolnick, *The Politics of Protest,* Report of the Task Force on Violent Aspects of Protest and Confrontation of the National Commission on the Causes and Prevention of Violence (New York: Simon and Schuster, 1969); Smith.

67. Smith.

68. H. L. Nieburg, *Political Violence* (New York: St. Martin's, 1969); Sears and McConahay, *Politics of Violence.*

69. Sears and McConahay, *Politics of Violence,* 147.

70. Blauner; Nieburg; Sears and McConahay, *Politics of Violence.*

71. Haynes.

72. Sears and McConahay, *Politics of Violence,* 151.

73. Governor's Commission.

74. Sears and McConahay, *Politics of Violence,* 25.

75. Ibid., 12; Cohen.

76. Nieburg; Cohen.

77. Sears and McConahay, *Politics of Violence;* Fogelson; Blauner.

78. James N. Upton, "The Politics of Urban Violence," *Journal of Black Studies* 15 (1985), 243–58; Fogelson.

79. Lewis Masotti, "Violent Protest in Urban Society," paper presented at the 1967 meeting of the American Academy for the Advancement of Science, cited in Nieburg, 20.

80. Sears and McConahay, *Politics of Violence.*

81. Nieburg.

82. Sears and McConahay, *Politics of Violence.*

83. "Reaction on Friction by Gil Lindsay," *Los Angeles Sentinel,* 19 August 1965, sec. A, p. 7.

84. David Felon, "Brave and Concerned Attend Watts Churches," *Los Angeles Times,* 16 August 1965, part 2, p. 1.

85. "7000 in New Rioting, Troops Alerted," *Los Angeles Times,* 13 August 1965, part 1, pp. 1, 3.

86. "Urge Parker Ouster; Police Attack Muslims," *Los Angeles Sentinel,* 19 August 1965, sec. A, p. 1.

87. "A Pertinent Answer," *Los Angeles Sentinel,* 16 September 1965, sec. A, p. 6; Gus Hawkins, "We Are All Guilty, Legislator Declares," *Los Angeles Sentinel,* 26 August 1965, sec. A, p. 2; Sears and McConahay, *Politics of Violence.*

86   Susan M. Strohm

88. Roy Wilkins, "Next Step in Rights Advance Is Negroes," *Los Angeles Times,* 16 August 1965, part 2, p. 5.

89. Nieburg; Sears and McConahay, *Politics of Violence;* Oberschall.

90. Oberschall.

91. Robert M. Fogelson and R. B. Hill, "Who Riots? A Study of Participation in the 1967 Riots," *Supplemental Studies for the National Advisory Commission on Civil Disorders,* 1968.

92. Glasgow; Howard and McCord.

93. Glasgow, 105.

94. McCone Commission data, cited in Fogelson, 136.

95. Bayard Rustin, "The Watts 'Manifesto' and the McCone Report," *Commentary,* March 1966; Cohen.

96. National Advisory Commission on Civil Disorders, 7; Oberschall; Cohen.

97. Glasgow, 115; Murphy and Watson; Fogelson.

98. Rustin, 30.

99. David O. Sears and John McConahay, "The Politics of Discontent," in *The Los Angeles Riots,* ed. Cohen; Sears and McConahay, 1973; Glasgow.

100. Glasgow, 118.

101. Ibid., 117.

102. Sears and McConahay, *Politics of Violence.*

103. Tomlinson and Sears, 305; Sears and McConahay, "Politics of Discontent"; idem, *Politics of Violence.*

104. Blauner, 183, 182.

105. Sears and McConahay, *Politics of Violence.*

106. Tomlinson and Sears.

107. Ibid.

108. Cohen.

109. Tomlinson.

110. Cohen.

111. Sears and McConahay, *Politics of Violence,* 170.

112. Ibid.

113. Bernard Berelson, *Content Analysis in Communication Research* (New York: Free Press, 1952), 18.

114. See, for example, Klaus Krippendorf, *Content Analysis: An Introduction to Its Methodology* (Beverly Hills, Calif.: Sage, 1980); Lynda Lee Kaid and Anne Johnston Wadsworth, "Content Analysis," in *Measurement of Communication Behavior,* ed. Philip Emmert and Larry L. Barker (New York: Longman, 1989).

115. For an introduction to content analysis methods, see Krippendorf.

116. Jack Lyle, *The News in Megalopolis* (San Francisco: Chandler, 1967); Roland E. Wolseley, *The Black Press, U.S.A.* (Ames: Iowa State University Press, 1971).

117. Lyle.

118. Ibid., 168.

119. Wolseley.

120. Lyle.

121. Ibid.; Wolseley.

122. Lyle.

123. Ibid., 168.

124. Betty Pleasant, "I Dodged Bullets While L.A. Burned," *Los Angeles Sentinel,* 19 August 1965, sec. A, p. 1.

125. Stanley Robertson, "LA Confidential," *Los Angeles Sentinel,* 2 September 1965, sec. A, p. 7.

126. "Cure Revolt Causes," *Los Angeles Sentinel,* 23 September 1965, sec. A, p. 1.

127. Sears and McConahay, *Politics of Violence.*

128. "Looting, Violence Cool Off with Weather," *Los Angeles Sentinel,* 19 August 1965, sec. A, p. 2.

129. "Flames," *Los Angeles Sentinel,* 19 August 1965, sec. A, p. 5.

130. "Salvation," *Los Angeles Sentinel,* 19 August 1965, sec. A, p. 5.

131. George Goodman, "Africa and the World," *Los Angeles Sentinel,* 7 October 1965, sec. A, p. 6.

132. Dale Marshall, *The Politics of Participation in Poverty: A Case Study of the Board of Economic and Youth Opportunities Agency of Greater Los Angeles* (Berkeley: University of California Press, 1971).

133. "Hawkins Blasts Poverty Control," *Los Angeles Sentinel,* 28 October 1965, sec. A, pp. 1, 3.

134. "The People Speak," *Los Angeles Sentinel,* 19 August 1965, sec. A, p. 10.

135. Stanley Robertson, "LA Confidential," *Los Angeles Sentinel,* 19 August 1965, sec. A, p. 7.

136. "Why the Rioting?" *Los Angeles Sentinel,* 19 August 1965, sec. A, p. 6.

137. "Urban League Deplores Racial Crisis," *Los Angeles Sentinel,* 19 August 1965, sec. C, p. 10.

138. Stanley Robertson, "LA Confidential," *Los Angeles Sentinel,* 28 October 1965, sec. B, p. 9.

139. Stanley Robertson, "LA Confidential," *Los Angeles Sentinel,* 30 December 1965, sec. A, p. 7.

140. Bill Lane, "The Inside Story," *Los Angeles Sentinel,* 9 December 1965, sec. D, p. 1.

141. Hawkins.

142. "Hawkins Blasts Poverty Control."

143. "Why the Rioting?"

144. Brad Pye, "Watts Has Rich Sports History," *Los Angeles Sentinel,* 19 August 1965, sec. B, p. 1.

145. "The People Speak."

146. Ibid.

147. Cohen; Sears and McConahay, *Politics of Violence.*

148. "Muslims Riot; Cultist Killed, Police Shot," *Los Angeles Times,* 28 April 1962, part 1, p. 1; Eric Malnic and Art Berman, "Most Troops Leave City, 3000 Remain," *Los Angeles Times,* 19 August 1965, part 1, p. 1.

149. Cohen.

150. Tomlinson and Sears.

151. Cohen.

152. Robertson, "LA Confidential," 19 August 1965.

153. Hawkins, 2.

154. "Assemblyman Urges Negotiation Session," *Los Angeles Sentinel,* 19 August 1965, sec. A, p. 9.

155. Maggie Hathaway, "A Woman's View," *Los Angeles Sentinel,* 19 August 1965, sec. B, p. 4.

156. Booker Griffin, "Ghetto Events Teach Nothing; Now Barrio Explodes," *Los Angeles Sentinel,* 3 September 1970, sec. A, p. 7.

157. Stanley Robertson, "LA Confidential," *Los Angeles Sentinel,* 6 August 1970, sec. A, p. 6.

158. Griffin.

159. Ed Davis, "15 Years Later, Watts Remains a Powder Keg!" *Los Angeles Sentinel,* 31 July 1980, sec. A, pp. 1, 17.

160. Jim Cleaver, "Ode to a Would-Be 1980 Revolutionary," *Los Angeles Sentinel,* 7 August 1980, sec. A, p. 7.

161. Stanley Robertson, "LA Confidential," *Los Angeles Sentinel,* 14 August 1980, sec. A, p. 6.

162. A. S. Doc Young, "Misinformed, Misguided Blacks," *Los Angeles Sentinel,* 28 May 1970, sec. A, p. 7.

163. "No Long, Hot Summer," *Los Angeles Sentinel,* 4 June 1970, sec. A, p. 6.

164. "Don't Get Hot and Blow Your Cool," *Los Angeles Sentinel,* 3 September 1970, sec. A, p. 6.

165. "Dog Days are Here Again," *Los Angeles Sentinel,* 9 July 1970, sec. A, p. 6.

166. "No Long, Hot Summer."

167. "No Margin for Error," *Los Angeles Sentinel,* 14 August 1980, sec. A, p. 6.

168. "The Need for Being Calm," *Los Angeles Sentinel,* 7 August 1980, sec. A, p. 6.

169. Cleaver.

170. Scoble.

171. Smith.

172. Peter Blau, *Inequality and Heterogeneity* (New York: Free Press, 1977), 222.

173. Everett C. Ladd, *Negro Political Leadership in the South* (Ithaca, N.Y.: Cornell University Press, 1966).

3

Perception of Mediated Social Conflict: Media Dependency and Involvement

Robert A. Baukus

Our perception of the world is based on direct experience and is cultivated through social relationships. The mass media provide a potential to expand this natural horizon. The limitations of temporal order and space have been, at the very least, altered if not removed. The mass media provide access to remote places and events. As Gitlin notes, "people are pressed to rely on mass media for bearing in an obscure and shifting world."[1]

The electronic media audience is able to see and hear distant events that are simultaneously occurring. This is most evident in television news programming. Media coverage of the 1991 Persian Gulf conflict illustrates how members of a vast audience can be simultaneously exposed to a series of "real-time" events. The conflict-related content drew enormous worldwide audiences. In the United States, as in many regions of the world, coverage related to the Gulf conflict dominated the news media. In fact, the news media provided the only access to information about the war. Individual differences in perception and social reality contributed to various interpretations of the war-related events and how they were reported. Nevertheless, all viewers were witnessing the same events, often without editing or interpretation by news personnel. For example, Cable News Network (CNN) provided direct feeds that were annotated by a field correspondent or a desk anchor in real time without preview or prior editing. Governments on both sides of the conflict relied on mediated reality for intelligence reports. The Allied Coalition forces possessed high-technology "intelligence assets" such as spy satellites and planes along with the various news media outlets. Iraq had only media and, as noted by Manheim, "Saddam had CNN and his very own correspondent Peter Arnett whose efforts he could monitor."[2] Government agencies also used on-line news services and satellite feeds to provide concurrent or timely coverage of war events.

Audiences can choose from a variety of media options, from the broad classifications of electronic or print to specific choices among television and radio stations or newspapers and magazines. New options, such as the Internet and the World Wide Web, are evolving, combining attributes of print and electronic media. All the media vie for our attention with conflict-related information.

Conflict is a frequent source of news programming content.[3] Conflict can be conceived as a component of society that exists in some underlying social context. Simmel defined conflict as a struggle over values or claims to status, power, and scarce resources.[4] Kriesberg characterizes struggle as a "relationship between two or more parties who believe they have incompatible goals."[5] The frequency, variety, and ubiquitous nature of social conflict provide ideal media content. The ambiguities and uncertain outcomes of conflict create interest and draw attention to information resources related to conflict. Events that emphasize conflict are the mainstays of televised news. According to Jamieson and Campbell, most "hard news is dramatic, conflict-filled and violent."[6] The context of the conflict is often presented in a format that emphasizes its dramatic elements and highlights or frames it in a manner that enhances its audience appeal. Appeal is important to media that must fulfill expectations of an audience that is selectively gathered with the intent of selling access based on its size and composition.

Conflict-related news items also can be considered as "knowledge-generating" messages in that they create or enhance information available to the audience.[7] Individuals may select the media option that has the greatest potential to satisfy their needs for conflict-related information. The form and content of news programs that successfully attract large audiences are frequently copied by competing media outlets in the hope of achieving larger audiences. While redundant program content increases the overlap among media audiences, each medium attracts specific audience profiles. It is assumed that the audiences are distributed among the available media options in a nonrandom manner that reflects intended behavior. In other words, people are motivated to select media that best meet their informational needs.

Differences among the news media may provide unique opportunities to learn about social conflict. Individuals may hold different beliefs regarding the media's ability to fulfill expectations and informational needs. People choose and subsequently depend on specific media when other information resources are restricted or cannot fulfill their information needs. The importance or personal relevance of the social conflict arena may also affect the development and maintenance of media dependencies.

The objectives of this study are to (1) identify audience beliefs related to social conflict presented in the mass media; (2) determine if the beliefs vary due to the type of media an individual depends upon and the degree of his or her involvement with the conflict event. An understanding of what people believe about mediated conflict may indicate how they come to depend on different media for the same information content. If perceptions and expectations influence media effects, then different belief structures that motivate media behavior should be associated with different patterns of media usage.

The following section provides a review of the literature and theoretical approaches relevant to the orientation, rationale, and design of the study of a person's orientation to mediated conflict.

Perspective and Theory Base

Media Dependency

"Dependency" theory suggests that reliance on the mass media develops when a person's informational needs concerning particular issues cannot be fulfilled by direct experience. What a person learns about the world beyond direct experience is influenced and shaped by the information offered by the media. Ball-Rokeach and DeFleur assert that media dependency increases to the degree that a medium adequately provides information consistent with a person's information goal.[8]

As noted by Miller and Reese, "dependency" implies that the satisfaction of needs and goals is contingent on resources external to the individual.[9] As dependency increases so does the potential of media to influence the audience. The audience is essentially reliant on the media and is consequently influenced by the restricted information available from the media options. Thus, dependency is related to the extent to which a person has information goals that require access to a particular medium. During major conflicts, such as war or social upheaval, the dependency model suggests that people will become more dependent on media and consequently subject to greater influence by the media. The media are often the only source of awareness and information about the conflict. Reliance is enhanced when the conflict takes place in a remote geographic region. During the Gulf war, news media exposure greatly increased. Pan et al. reported as much as a 4% increase in network television news viewing and an increased frequency of newspaper reading by half a day per week. Cable television networks, including CNN and C-SPAN, had the largest audience gains.[10]

Within the dependency framework, individuals can choose among media options that are limited by characteristics inherent in the social, political, and economic systems that produce and support them. In other words, the media outlets that have evolved are a product of the social environment in which they operate. Ball-Rokeach contends that a person's media dependency is often determined by "structural" relationships between the media and other social systems, such as economic and political systems, as well as by the personal and psychological characteristics of the individual.[11]

How a person thinks about social conflicts and his or her associated media selection behavior are constrained or limited by a reliance on media to acquire information about the conflict. The influence of the media on individuals is frequently categorized as cognitive, affective, and behavioral. The cognitive effects are important because they provide a key perspective on the mechanism underlying the development of a particular dependency. Cognitive effects include formation and modification of attitudes and beliefs concerning the relative potential for media to fulfill information goals. Affective effects are emotional reactions or associations with mediated content that can influence a person's orientation to conflict related events. Behavioral effects may be related to perceptions of media that lead to reliance on particular outlets for specific types of information.

Ajzen and Fishbein's theory of reasoned action provides a framework in which to examine the cognitive and behavioral effects related to media dependency.[12] This theory holds that behavior is directly linked to attitudes and beliefs, and that a predisposition is controlled by a set of beliefs that a person has learned to associate with the object of the predisposition. Thus, one way to understand media dependency is to determine the beliefs that people hold about mediated conflict. We may learn why individuals vary in their media dependency if we can determine the belief structures that are associated with particular media predispositions. This approach assumes that mediated reality may be perceived differently by the receivers rather than being embedded in media content. Potter reviewed a number of studies related to "perceived reality" from the perspective of the message itself and of the individual that receives the message.[13] He also presents a multidimensional construct of perceived reality that reflects (1) belief in the literal reality of mediated messages; (2) utility or the belief in the applicability of mediated information to one's own life; and (3) the closeness to or personalization of mediated characters.

In this study, perceived reality is operationally defined as mediated social conflict exemplified by the Gulf war. This is the object of the participants' information goal. One of the primary aims of this research is to determine if knowledge of a person's perceived reality of mediated social conflict, as revealed by the beliefs sets of individuals having different dependencies, is useful in understanding media dependency behavior.

The agenda-setting model provides another useful perspective on the impact of the media's informational content and its influence on audience awareness. In essence, the content of the information influences what the audience perceives to be important. By this process the media exerts social control. The agenda-setting effect can also be influenced by the importance of an issue to the audience. Agenda-setting theory posits that the public agenda, or the topics people most frequently consider and discuss, is influenced by what the news media choose to report. Frequently, the dependent variable[14] in an agenda-setting hypothesis is the level of importance attributed to a news-related topic.[15] Iyengar and Simon considered agenda setting during the Gulf war.[16] They found that increased coverage of the war led to increases in its importance; other major issues, except for the economy, were displaced from the public agenda to allow for greater war coverage.

Weaver suggested that agenda effects differ among individuals. Agenda effects were influenced by the relevance of the information and the degree of uncertainty concerning the subject.[17] This means that the agenda effect can vary according to the perceived importance of the presented topic and the amount of prior knowledge the audience has about the topic. This is applicable to the presentation of social conflict due to the dramatic personalization that is frequently a hallmark of its portrayal in the media. Zucker found that for inconspicuous issues of which the public may have less direct experience, frequent media coverage preceded increased awareness as reflected in public opinion polls.[18] However, a study by Demer, Craff, Choi, and Pessin found no support for the "obtrusive contingency" model. That model holds that as personal experience with an issue increases, the effects of agenda setting will decrease due to a decreased reliance on the media for guidance on determining an issue's importance.[19] In summary, as Manheim suggests, the public agenda is revealed by the familiarity, favorability, and personal salience of the topic.[20] The agenda-setting approach has been applied to a variety of topics with mixed results.[21]

From a functional perspective, one of the social roles of the mass media is to provide information. The relevance of the information presented by the media to the personal information goals of the individual may influence the agenda effect. This approach assumes that a lifelong exposure to and familiarity with media allows individuals to develop predispositions or expectations related to the manner in which the media depict social conflict issues and events. Also, through such experience one develops expectations that ultimately lead to preferences for specific media. Media preferences may vary according to the nature of the informational goals and the media options that are available.

Uses and Gratifications Studies

The agenda-setting theory concerns the media as a means of information distribution that influences the importance, legitimacy, and salience of issues or events. Dependency theory explains why people come to rely on mass media and the macro perspective of social influences as well as micro or individual cognitive effects of the media.[22] In contrast, the "uses and gratifications" perspective, illustrated by Katz et al., focuses on the extent to which a person's media-related needs are gratified by media consumption.[23] This perspective focuses on what the consumer does with the media. Audiences are more than passive receptors that soak up whatever the media have to offer. People have expectations that can influence media use. The assumption is that the user of the media is responsible for selecting content that meets psychological and social needs. Individuals seek gratification of needs based on expectations related to media content. When needs are met, those expectations are reinforced. A criticism of this model concerns the nature of a need and what a need actually represents. Rubin notes that uses and gratifications theory is primarily oriented toward the person's active participation in the mass communication process rather than the social context in which the consumption occurs.[24] A person's media behavior is motivated by the degree to which various media options can satisfy specific needs. People search for and select among the media options with the intent of receiving some specific gratification from the media experience.

However, the level of audience activity varies and not all audiences engage in the same type of activity. Media use may reflect the user's attitudes and expectations concerning the utility of the information to his or her goals. For example, Rubin describes media use as a "ritualized" or "instrumental" process. Ritualized orientation "is less active and less goal directed."[25] Instrumental use is characterized by selection of media content for specific informational goals. It implies greater involvement and is "more active and purposive."[26] Activity is influenced by the social context and attitudinal dispositions that "result from past experiences with a medium and produce future gratification-seeking behavior."[27] Levy and Windahl identified three types of media selection activity. Preactivity is the selection of specific media, such as a newscast, to gratify intellectual needs. Postactivity relates to selection based on perceptions of some personal or interpersonal value of the information. Attention to conflict-related news content with the intent of using the information for social interaction is an example of postactivity behavior. Duractivity is the degree of psychological attentiveness or involvement during the viewing experience. Duractivity is related to the person's interpretation of the mediated message.[28] Thus the audience actively selects media experiences related to pre-existing needs, values, and beliefs.

The audience's media selection behavior is, to various degrees, both active and constrained. A person's choice of media, or specific vehicles within a medium, is conditioned by previous experience with the media. Selection is also influenced by the current information needs of the person. Most of the considerations involved in the choice are intrinsic to the person. However, as dependency theory suggests, motives for particular selections may be influenced by overt or invasive social situations, such as military or political conflict, that generate a greater interest or need for information.

The set of media options available to the audience is constrained by what Ball-Rokeach refers to as structural dependency relationships.[29] In other words, the available media options are a function of social complexity. Economic, political, and other social systems are mutually dependent and interact to define the limits of the environment in which the media must function. Media systems often have goals and resources that are contingent upon one another. Cross ownership, shared technology, and competition for audiences limit the nature and diversity of the media outlets. Business and legal restraints delineate the boundaries of media access and content. Competition for audience produces pressure to model successful program types. For example, network evening news content is very similar among the major broadcast networks. The need of commercial media to attract advertisers also limits the scope of programming content. As a result, the audience is dependent on a limited number of media outlets that frequently offer redundant content. There is also a high degree of similarity in the program content among traditional and new media options. Emerging media such as the World Wide Web often compete for audiences by repackaging content and allowing greater audience interaction and control over access to information and program content. Consequently, the audience is free to choose, but only among a socially constrained set of media options.

Uses and Dependency

The variably active and constrained nature of the audience interaction with media is discussed by Rubin and Windahl. They posit a "uses and dependency" model that acknowledges audience selection within a socially constrained set of media options.[30] Social systems and media interact with audiences to create individual needs. An individual's information goals influence the selection of media and nonmedia sources of gratification, which subsequently leads to dependencies on the sources.[31] Consistent with the dependency model, the effects include cognitive, affective, and behavioral components. The audience impacts provide feedback to the systems that spawned them and ultimately reinforce the media options that best fulfill information needs and goals of the audience. The model suggests there are different media use patterns and dependencies as a result of ritualized versus instrumental use of media. In other words, a person's cognitive motivation and variations in involvement with content are manifest as variations in media activity. As Rubin explains, the model brings together personal goals, motivations, and information-seeking strategies that may produce dependencies on particular media options.[32]

The present study posits that knowledge of the dispositional beliefs shaped by previous experience with a media option will allow us to understand why a particular media option is chosen. This conforms with Rubin and Windahl's suggestion that people will focus their search for needed information on specific media and will therefore be susceptible to the influence of those media.[33] Within a given set of socially constrained media alternatives, it is up to the person to evaluate the potential of each medium to fulfill personal information requirements. It follows that a media option must be perceived as possessing some utility in order to be considered by the individual. For example, based on previous experience, a person may have expectations related to the potential for the Weather Channel to supply weather-related information. This enhances a person's tendency to seek out the Weather Channel, especially in urgent situations such as the threat of a storm. Subsequent satisfaction with the selection reinforces the person's dispositional beliefs and ultimately leads to a dependency on the Weather Channel for weather-related information.

This study is grounded in the uses and dependency theory and concerns the nature of the media selection process and the factors that influence the person's choice decision. Audience selectivity is considered to be contingent on inherent needs that the person brings to the media choice decision. As Rubin and Windahl observed, a person's existing salient information needs enhance his or her motivation to seek mediated information relevant to those needs.[34] Garramone notes that audience motivation affects attention to both channel and content aspects of a media presentation.[35] Prior experience may bias a person toward a particular media that is perceived to have the greatest potential to fulfill an information goal. In essence, an individually determined predisposition guides a selection from the socially determined media options.

Beliefs about Social Conflict

The perceived reality of a media-depicted conflict event is determined by personal interpretation of the mediated message. Perceived reality varies among people. It is not inherent in the media message itself. Exposure to informational alternatives related to specific informational goals may be affected by disposition as well as being situationally specific.[36] This information-seeking process is influenced by the individual's attitudes, beliefs, and existing perceptions that have been associated with various media during a lifetime of media exposure. People act to maximize the harmony and compatibility of attitudes and cognitions held toward an object.[37] These psychological states were further linked to behavior in Ajzen and Fishbein's theory of reasoned action.[38] Behavior is influenced by predispositions that are in turn influenced by sets of beliefs that a person has learned to associate with an object. Beliefs are knowledge or information associated with a particular issue or object. The information can be descriptive or evaluative. A belief structure is the total set of pieces of information that a person has concerning an object. A deficiency in the information needed to pursue an information goal can motivate one to search for information resources. Beliefs can also influence the search. Furthermore, the beliefs that a person holds toward a particular medium shape his or her disposition to respond to a particular media option. This means that experience with a medium that leads to favorable judgment concerning the medium's capacity to provide goal-related information will be associated with a dependency on the media option. If you believe that on a past occasion, television best provided the information you sought concerning a social conflict, you may turn to television to gain similar information in the future. You develop an expectation that you can depend on television to obtain the kind of information you desire.

Within this framework, media selection behavior by an audience is influenced by a person's dispositional beliefs. For example, unfavorable beliefs about a medium may reduce a person's motivation to develop a dependency on that option. Favorable evaluations of a medium that are consistent with an informational goal may enhance the probability that a person will become dependent on the medium, at least until a functionally equivalent or superior alternative that requires less effort becomes available.

In summary, this study assumes the perspective that knowledge of a person's beliefs concerning mediated social conflict can be useful in determining the nature of a person's media dependency.

Involvement

This study views involvement as a motivational property that can influence how a person processes message content. Involvement has been associated with an enhanced focus on the message content, an increased processing intensity related to the evaluation of message content, attitude change, and motives for media usage.[39] Consumer research acknowledges that the mechanisms of attention and comprehension are influenced by one's motivation to process goal-related information.[40] The motivation to process information is frequently related to a drive state conceptualized as involvement.[41]

An extensive review by Andrews et al. indicates that the "involvement" construct has been operationalized from a variety of perspectives.[42] Involvement is commonly related to the personal relevance of issues to an individual.[43] As suggested by Celsi and Olson, personally relevant information motivates overt behaviors such as "searching" and cognitive behaviors such as "attention." They further argue that involvement or degree of personal relevance "directs the focus of cognitive processing and thereby affects the interpreted meanings that are produced by attention and comprehension processes."[44] Low-involved users of media content are minimally interested and tend to respond to superficial cues and merely scan rather than carefully attend to message content.[45] Under low-involvement conditions, learning is a result of repeated exposure. Petty and Cacioppo's "elaboration likelihood model of persuasion" contends that influence occurs by either a "central" or a "peripheral" route depending on the person's involvement level.[46] A high-involved person will be strongly motivated to seek out carefully and review all information relevant to an information goal. In low-involvement conditions the person is not as highly motivated and focuses on peripheral cues associated with the message, such as source characteristics, rather than the message content.

Based on Zaichkowsky, involvement is defined as the perceived relevance of conflict-related media content based on a person's inherent needs, interests, and information goals.[47] This is similar to Houston and Rothschild's conceptualization of involvement as a function of a person's hierarchy of needs. The highly involved person uses a larger set of attributes to make decisions than does a minimally involved person.[48] Moreover, people develop an enduring structure of personally relevant knowledge derived from direct past experience and exposure to information.[49] This experiential knowledge base predisposes a person toward information resources in the environment that are instrumental to the fulfillment of information goals. Prior knowledge about mediated sources of information related to social conflict can affect a person's impression or belief structure concerning the usefulness of a medium to fulfill his or her information goals. In other words, people have a dispositional set of beliefs and needs that filters and interprets relevant information related to specific informational goals.

Lo, in a study of involvement and knowledge about the Gulf war, concluded that a person's involvement with an event increases motivation to seek more information about the event, which leads to even greater media use.[50] This seems consistent with the dependency model in that media use may lead to greater involvement with an event that, in turn, produces further motivated to seek more information about the event from available media resources.

In a study of comparative advertising, Muehling et al. noted that format is a cue that may initiate processing activity.[51] Different perceptions of the utility of the presented information are associated with prior experience with the content format. In the present context, the degree of relevance may be a consequence of prior experience with the media option concerning a specific information goal. Experience with the relative merits of the available media options, and the beliefs associated with each option, may be applied to future media comparisons. If the conflict-related message is consonant with the person's pre-existing knowledge of the topic, it may enhance the motivation to attend to the message. This is consistent with involvement as a mediating variable in the information search process.[52]

"High-involvement" persons should have a different interest in the acquisition of conflict-related information than that of "low-involvement" persons. Krugman's theory of involvement applied to advertising effectiveness argues that involvement influences communication effects.[53] Highly motivated people have a greater motivation to seek and process information in a careful manner to glean details related to their particular information goals. High involvement is associated with more immediate cognitive effects while low-involvement effects tend to be a result of repeated exposure. If the cost of a wrong decision is high, then a person will be motivated to make an extra effort to obtain knowledge related to an information goal. A low-involvement state is associated with reduced motivation to seek information. A medium may have less intrinsic relevance and consequence to the person's conflict-related information goals and therefore attract less attention.

In the context of this study, involvement is based on the perceived relevance of information to the fulfillment of personal informational goals related to mediated social conflict. High involvement leads to greater attention to media content consistent with information needs. For example, a person who is very interested in the Gulf war, perhaps due to business ties to the Middle East, would have a higher degree of involvement than a person who has no personal or business relationships that can be directly affected by the war.

This study will investigate whether beliefs associated with mediated social conflict differ across levels of involvement. Different levels of involvement should be associated with different levels of motivation, which should be manifest as different dispositional beliefs. Involvement is operationally measured on the basis of a scale derived by Zaichkowsky and is described below in the methods section.

The next section presents a series of research questions supported by rationales for their inclusion in this study.

Research Questions

The first two research questions are grounded in uses and dependency theory. The objective is to define the nature and composition of the dispositional belief structures used to evaluate social conflict.

Research Question 1   The first research question seeks to identify a set of audience beliefs that are related to mediated social conflict.

    A. How many dimensions are associated with the belief structures related to the perception of mediated social conflict?
    B. What belief attributes constitute each composite dimension?

Rationale: Audiences acquire a set of expectations of the various media's tendency to gratify their informational goals regarding social conflict. The selection of media is predisposed to the degree that the person's pre-existing beliefs and perceptions of a medium allow consideration of the vehicle as a viable source of social conflict-related information.

Research Question 2   The second research question examines the relationship between the belief structures associated with mediated social conflict across two different media dependencies and two levels of involvement.

    A. Do the belief structures related to social conflict held by television-dependents differ significantly from those of newspaper-dependents?

B. Do the composite beliefs significantly vary among persons classified by high and low levels of involvement and media dependency?

Rationale: Given the effect of disposition on media selection, what is the impact of holding specific belief structures concerning social conflict on the motivation to develop dependencies? If dispositional beliefs affect media consumption, then the composition of the conflict beliefs should differ significantly among people who depend on different media.

Media selection behavior is influenced by the degree of involvement during consumption. Wright found that the medium influenced the response given to the message.[54] Becker and Whitney propose that variations in media dependency lead to different audience effects due to the characteristics of the chosen medium. They found newspaper dependency was associated with greater knowledge of world news than was television dependency.[55] Research by Wicks suggested that information recall of messages with high degrees of personal relevance differed between television viewers and newspaper readers.[56] The recall differences attributed to personal relevance may be related to media dependencies developed by previous experience. Higher personal involvement increases motivation to seek media that provide information consistent with a person's information goals. The highly motivated viewer will become dependent on a medium that the person believes will best fulfill information goals related to the conflict event.

Research Question 3   Involvement, media dependency, and the variation in belief structures are explored in the third research question.

A. What is the relative importance of each of the composite beliefs in discriminating among the four participant groups?

Rationale: Each participant group should have a unique set of beliefs that reflects different motivation states related to fulfillment of information goals associated with mediated social conflict. Medium characteristics, together with content differences and timely dissemination of information, may predispose audience members who are highly involved with social conflict to develop media dependencies that differ from those of low-involved audiences. Past research has found differences between newspaper and television news. Television viewing has been associated with lower levels of knowledge than has newspaper usage. Differences have tended to be attributed to characteristics of the media. Because of time constraints that are inherent in the manner in which news is packaged, television tends to provide brief summaries of complex issues. Television, viewed in real time, lacks persistence in that once the news item is read or shown, the viewer cannot review the story and must rely on memory to analyze the content. Television's unique asset is its ability to provide live coverage of a breaking event and the dramatic impact that such coverage conveys to the audience. Even background or feature stories provide viewers with an audio-visual presence that can alter the perception of the event. On the other hand, newspapers are well suited to provide in-depth reflective analysis, supplemented by static pictures, which allows the reader to review and process the content at their own pace. Lo found that higher levels of cognitive-behavioral involvement led to greater knowledge about the Gulf war obtained from media use. He also found that when involvement was high, newspaper use was more strongly related to knowledge than was television usage. When involvement was low, the knowledge gain between newspaper and television usage was about the same.[57]

High-involved persons should have different dispositional belief structures related to conflict than those of low-involved persons. In a test of perceptions of several brands of the same product class, high-involved persons perceived greater differences among brands than did low-involved persons.[58] The explanation was based on Robertson's suggestion that high involvement implies that product beliefs are salient and strong.[59] High-involved persons seek more information to support an important choice decision. As a result, highly involved people use a larger set of attributes to make an evaluation than do low-involved people. Low-involved persons have less well defined belief structures.[60] Zaichkowsky further asserts that the strength of the belief system emphasizes the perceived differences among brands on the attributes that are strongly related to the most salient beliefs. High-involved persons seek information and make comparisons among information sources that lead to selections. Low-involved persons are less active information seekers and make fewer comparisons that lead to perceived differences among options.[61]

Differences in belief structures may also be related to the temporal sequence of cognitive and behavioral events. The traditional "hierarchy of effects" model assumes a cognitive ("thinking"), affective ("feeling"), and conative ("doing") sequence.[62] An extensive review by Barry and Howard reveals that at least six permutations of the three stages have been proposed.[63] Assael suggested that different sequences are associated with high and low involvement. In the high-involvement condition, beliefs may be formed through the active search for information prior to an anticipated selection. A different sequence may occur in low-involvement conditions, in which beliefs may result from passive learning that is a byproduct of viewing behavior. The search for information is less active, and media dependency may be in the form of what Assael terms a "spurious loyalty" based in viewing "inertia."[64]

The following section describes how the variables used in this study were operationally defined and measured. It begins with the methods used to identify the people who participated in this study and how they were classified on the basis of media dependency and level of involvement. The results section describes how each of the beliefs related to mediated social conflict were derived and the statistics used in the analysis. Technical points related to the test procedures are included in the appendix.

Method

Participants

A four-page questionnaire was distributed in university and shopping settings in three mid-Atlantic and New England states. Despite the accepted superiority of probability sampling methods, in which all elements have a known probability of inclusion in the sample frame, this exploratory study relied on a nonrandom convenience sample. A total of 385 people were surveyed based on availability and willingness to participate in the study. Quotas were set for equal proportions of males and females, and age ranges were set by decades. This procedure yielded 300 usable questionnaires; the rest had to be discarded due to incomplete or illegible responses. The respondents ranged in age from 19 to 30 years, with a median age of 23.5; 54% were female, 46% were male.

Participant Group Classification

One goal of this research is to identify belief structures that discriminate among types of media dependency and involvement levels. Television and newspapers were selected as media options because they use very different technology to convey information. Television and newspapers are frequently used in media research to avoid confusion or confounding effects due to similarity in form and structure.[65] Research summarized by Miyo emphasizes the differences between television and newspapers in format, content, social function, and audience effects.[66]

Four participant subgroups for the discriminant analysis procedure were defined by scores on the two classification variables. They were identified as: (1) High-Involved Television Dependents (HiTv); (2) Low-Involved Television Dependents (LoTv); (3) High-Involved Newspaper Dependents (HiNs); (4) and Low-Involved Newspaper Dependents (LoNs). Groups such as the low-involvement television dependents were over-represented among the 300 respondents. A proportional subsample was randomly selected to balance closely the number of people in each subgroup. The N of each group was 49, 48, 48, 48, respectively, for a total of 193.

Dependency Measure

The measurement of dependency has been approached in a variety of ways. Robinson discusses reliance on an outlet for information.[67] Wenner considers the degree to which media would be missed.[68] O'Keefe relates dependency to the use of media in voting decisions.[69] The dependency measure used in this study was derived from a series of indicators identified and discussed by Gaziano.[70]

The respondents were told that this study was related to their media use during major social conflicts such as the Gulf war. Respondents were asked to apply the following scale to the five questions below: 1 = Always newspapers; 2 = Mostly newspapers; 3 = Neither newspapers nor television; 4 = Mostly television; 5 = Always television.

1. What media source would you choose for information related to *social conflict?*
2. Which media do you pay most attention to for reports related to *social conflict?*
3. Which media provide you with the most important information concerning *social conflict?*
4. Which media do you prefer as a *source of conflict-related information?*
5. If you lost access to a *medium,* which would you feel most lost without?

These questions assume that the participants were sufficiently self-aware to describe their own media behavior. The score range is 5 to 25. A score of 10 or less operationally defined newspaper dependency, 20 and above represented television dependency.

Involvement Measure

The operational measure of the classification variable "Involvement" was derived from Zaichkowsky's Personal Involvement Inventory (PII).[71] The PII scale was originally developed to measure involvement related to products and consists of twenty bipolar scales. In this study the "product" rated on the PII scale is news, specifically news concerning social conflict. The twenty-item PII scale produces a score ranging from a low of 20 to a high of 140. The mean scale score for all participants was 85.4. This breakpoint was used to classify participants as low or high on the involvement construct represented by the scale. Cronbach's Alpha coefficient of reliability for the social conflict involvement scale was .89 indicating an acceptable level of reliability among the indicators.[72] Because the PII scale was initially designed to measure product involvement, a manipulation check procedure was used to determine that the scale could be applied to measure social conflict involvement. See appendix for the manipulation check.

Mediated Social Conflict Belief Inventory

An initial inventory of belief statements was based on a review of literature and an exploratory study. Belief statements reflected the information that a person has about mediated social conflict. Descriptive and evaluative items were included to reflect some of the core concepts of conflict theorists. Conflict has been considered as a positive force that increases social cohesion and as a safety valve to relieve social tensions.[73] Conflict is also perceived as a contributor to the maintenance of society.[74] The opposite of these contentions was also included as statements in the questionnaire; that is, conflict is bad for society, or conflict has destructive consequences for society. The belief statements are listed in table 3.1.

Table 3.1. Mediated Social Conflict Beliefs

Belief Items	Factor Loadings
Informative	
In1 Media give detailed explanations that provide information about the nature and type of the current conflict.	.79910
In2 Media give information that helps me understand the impact the conflict could have on the world.	.72716
In3 Media give information that helps me understand the effect the conflict could have on my own life.	.71866
In4 Media give background information that develops the context and reasons for the social conflict.	.69920
In5 Media help me learn about attempts at reconciliation among those involved in the conflict.	.59065
In6 Media report on peace efforts and activities by external influences to reduce or end conflict.	.53350
Functional	
Vi1 Social conflict contributes to the maintenance of groups in society.	.79664
Vi2 Social conflict functions as a social safety valve to relieve tensions in society.	.77370
Vi3 Social conflict is necessary for a healthy society.	.64823

Table 3.1. (cont.)

Belief Items	Factor Loadings
Vi4 Social conflict usually leads to socially constructive consequences.	.56545
Vi5 Social conflict compels opposing forces to resolve differences.	.49589
Influential	
Ma1 Media are now a force that shapes and influences rather than just observes social conflict.	.73464
Ma2 Media coverage can accelerate the events of a conflict.	.73023
Ma3 Coverage draws attention and legitimizes conflict.	.68745
Ma4 Extended coverage by media exploits conflict for their own self-interests.	.55105
Vigilant	
Vg1 Media warn of potential social problems before crisis.	.69460
Vg2 Media monitor the world for social conflicts.	.62102
Vg3 Media rally people against a common threat.	.59826
Vg4 Media influence the audience perceptions of the importance of the conflict.	.54764
Manipulated	
Mi1 Media are "used" by some groups that believe they will receive coverage if they do certain things.	.77620
Mi2 Media coverage can act to suppress the conflict itself.	.65036
Mi3 Media should establish guidelines to reduce the distorted coverage of issues related to conflict.	.61039
Dramatic	
En1 Major social conflicts seem more like "situation dramas" than news events because of the way they are "packaged."	.81027
En2 I feel more entertained than informed about conflict events.	.75621
En3 I enjoy getting information about social conflicts from the media.	.69778
Destructive	
Ne1 Social conflict is bad for society.	.60362
Ne2 Social conflict is a destructive force with negative impact.	.59468
Ne3 Social conflict is a violent way to resolve differences.	.54233

Additional beliefs related to the presentation of social conflict in the media were also solicited from a separate convenience sample of 55 people. All respondents reported exposure to television and newspaper news an average of at least five times per week. The respondents (average age 26, range 19–32) were asked to respond to the following open-ended request: "Please describe how you believe social conflict is presented in the mass media, specifically television and newspapers." Each sentence of their response was considered as a statement and separately analyzed by two trained coders. Eighty-three statements were selected as descriptive personal beliefs relevant to media coverage of social conflict. A second evaluation judged redundant belief statements that were eliminated. Scott's pi value of .82 indicated acceptable intercoder reliability or agreement between the judges during the final selection process.[75] This procedure produced the final version of the belief scales administered to the 300 respondents in the study. The belief inventory developed for this study consisted of 50 Likert-type statements designed to indicate beliefs related to the depiction of social conflict in television and newspapers. The statements concerned the impact of social conflict on individuals and society. Statements also addressed the form and content of media coverage of conflict. Each statement was scaled (1 = strongly agree, to 5 = strongly disagree). Participants were asked to indicate the degree to which they believed the statement to be true about mediated social conflict such as the Gulf war.

Results

First Research Question

The first part of research question 1 concerned the identification of the belief dimensions associated with the perception of mediated social conflict. Factor analysis was used to reduce the relatively large set of belief scales to a smaller set of composite belief factors.[76] The factors represent the underlying set of belief dimensions that are inherent in the larger set of 50 belief scales. The idea is to retain as much information as possible in the original scales yet reduce the number of beliefs to a manageable set of composite beliefs. These composite belief factors are used to investigate differences in belief structures across levels of involvement and media dependency. The process began with the responses of the 300 participants on the 50-item belief scale inventory. The belief items were factor-analyzed utilizing principal components with varimax rotation.[77] The initial factor procedure identified 9 factors with eigenvalues greater than one and accounted for 65.4% of the variance. Statements with multiple loadings greater than .35 were eliminated and the remaining 32 belief statements were re-factored. The Scree test was used to identify the number of common factors retained in the factor model.[78] A total of 7 factors qualified with eigenvalues greater than one. These factors account for 14.4%, 12.2%, 7.8%, 7.6%, 5.7%, 5.3%, 4.9%, respectively, for a total of 57.9% of the variance.

The second part of research question 1 addressed the beliefs associated with each of the derived dimensions. The subjective labels assigned to each of the seven composite dimensions reflect the overall nature of the highest loaded beliefs.[79] Five of the factors seem to reflect beliefs concerning the media's relationship to social conflict events. Two factors appear to relate directly to the nature of social conflict.

The Seven Mediated Social Conflict Beliefs

The first composite factor reflects the belief that the media are *informative* about social conflict. This composite includes the beliefs that the media: are a source of first awareness about the nature of social conflict; facilitate understanding of the impact on the world and on their personal lives; provide reasons for the conflict; allow them to learn about attempts at reconciliation and peace efforts by parties external to the conflict.

The second belief reflects the *functional* role of social conflict. Conflict is believed to be a social force that contributes to social stability. Conflict is a necessary process for a healthy society and is viewed as a social safety valve to relieve social tensions among clashing groups. Conflict is also seen as having generally constructive consequences.

The third belief factor, *influential,* represents the belief that the media influence the nature and duration of social conflict. Media coverage accelerates and legitimizes conflict. Media exploit conflict due to the attention generated by their coverage.

The fourth belief factor represents the *vigilant* coverage of social conflict by the media. Media warn of potential social problems and monitor the world for social conflict events. Media also provide a means to rally people against a perceived social threat.

The fifth belief factor, labeled *manipulated,* reflects the belief that the media are influenced and used by agents of social conflict to achieve their ends. It is also believed that media can act to suppress conflict. Participants believe that media should establish guidelines for coverage of conflict events.

The sixth belief factor, labeled *dramatic,* reflects mediated conflict as dramatized coverage of conflict events. Major social conflicts are packaged to resemble entertaining programming such as situation dramas.

The seventh factor identifies the belief that social conflict is a *destructive* force in society. Social conflict is a violent way to resolve differences and has a negative impact on society.

The seven composite measures derived from the factor procedure were operationalized as factor scores and used as the belief variables in all subsequent analyses.[80] Each factor was labeled to reflect the nature of the beliefs that had unique factor loadings above .49. The belief factors and the associated belief items are presented in table 3.1.

Second Research Question

For research question 2 the participants were classified in four distinct groups based on the contingencies of involvement and dependency. MANOVA was used to test for the effects of involvement and dependency on the belief structures.[81] The MANOVA procedure revealed significant interactions (Wilks' Lambda = .83, F[7,256] = 5.24, p ≤ .001). The significant MANOVA interaction suggests differences in the belief structures among the two levels of dependency and two levels of involvement.[82] The significant univariate F ratios for all seven composite beliefs are reported in the appendix. Next, discriminant analysis is used to determine which of the composite beliefs account for the differences in the score profiles of the four participant groups.

Third Research Question

Research question 3 addresses the relative effectiveness of each of the seven belief dimensions to distinguish among the four participant groups. The discriminant procedure produces a discriminant score for each person in each participant group.[83] The score is derived by multiplying each belief score by its corresponding discriminant weight and adding these products together. The discriminant weights are derived in a manner that maximizes the between-group variance relative to the within-group variance. The goal is to produce an equation that separates or discriminates between groups based on a set of variables, in this case, composite beliefs that were derived from the proceeding factor analysis procedure. The resulting composite belief score is averaged for all individuals in each group. This mean score, called a centroid, is plotted along the dimension of each factor being analyzed to determine the relative distance between the groups. See Hair et al. for greater details of the procedure.[84]

The Discriminant Functions

A stepwise discriminant procedure that maximized the Mahalanobis distance between the four groups was used.[85] All seven of the composite belief dimensions evaluated by MANOVA were retained by the stepwise discriminant analysis. The analysis produced two significant discriminant functions. The first function accounted for 75.9% of the variance (eigenvalue = 6.57, Wilks' Lambda = .32; χ^2 = 635.75, df = 24, p ≤ .001). The second function accounted for 16.0% of variance for a total of 91.9 for the model (eigenvalue 1.48, Wilks' Lambda = .24, χ^2 = 259.88, df = 14, p ≤ .001). The Lambdas indicate that ample discriminating power exists in the belief dimensions.

Classification Accuracy

A validity test was applied to the discriminant functions. The total sample of respondents was randomly divided into two groups. The functions were developed for one group of individuals and then applied to another group called a holdout sample. The classification matrices are detailed in the appendix. Results indicate that the percentage of correct classifications (82.4%) in the holdout sample is significantly larger than chance. Therefore, it is feasible to use the discriminant functions to develop group belief profiles that uniquely identify membership in each of the four participant groups.

Interpretation

The relationship of the composite beliefs to the discriminant functions is examined to identify conceptually meaningful combinations that could be useful in making distinctions among the participant groups. First, the discriminant functions will be reviewed to determine the relative importance of each of the composite beliefs in maximizing differences between the groups. Then the group means, or centroids, for each important composite belief will be reviewed to profile the groups.

Discriminant Loadings

The discriminant loadings, also known as structure coefficients, measure the product-moment correlation between each independent variable and the discriminant functions.[86] They can be interpreted like factor loadings to evaluate the relative contribution of each composite belief to the corresponding discriminant function. To facilitate interpretation, the composite beliefs are rank-ordered by their loadings as an indicator of relative discriminating power. The signs indicate a positive or negative relationship with the function and do not affect the rankings. The discriminant loadings are listed in table 3.2.

The loadings indicate that the first discriminant function had unique loading for beliefs that the media are informative about social conflicts that are packaged in a dramatic manner. Social conflicts are believed to be a destructive, negative force in society. The second function is composed of beliefs that: the media are vigilant in providing warning of impending social crisis; media coverage has an influential relationship with social conflict that can shape and accelerate events of a conflict; social conflict has a functional role that relieves tensions and contributes to a healthy society. These beliefs have a negative loading, while the belief that the media is manipulated or used by perpetrators of social conflict has a positive relationship.

Table 3.2.

Discriminant Loadings		
Composite Beliefs	Function 1	Function 2
Informative	−.44768	−.16156
Dramatic	.38006	−.11433
Destructive	.20551	.07472
Vigilant	.10021	−.49468
Influential	.09829	−.34325
Functional	−.12025	.31077
Manipulated	−.03475	.11526
Group Centroids		
Participant Groups	Function 1	Function 2
Television dependent		
high-involved	−2.917	−2.525
low-involved	−1.434	1.306
Newspaper dependent		
high-involved	1.865	−0.332
low-involved	2.523	1.582

Group Centroids

The centroids are the means of the discriminant function scores for each participant group.[87] Centroids show the typical location of a person from a participant group on a discriminant dimension. The distances or separations of the centroids of the groups are compared to see how far apart or distinct the groups are from one another. The centroids in table 3.2 indicate that the first function separates the television dependents from the newspaper dependents. The largest difference is between television-dependent group and newspaper-dependent group centroids. The second dimension also divides the groups, resulting in the four centroids' coordinates. The second function separates the high-involvement from the low-involvement groups. The greatest difference is between the high- and low-involved television dependents. The least-separated groups appear to be the low-involved and high-involved newspaper dependents. All four participant groups differed in their respective beliefs sets about mediated social conflict. Tests of equality of the group centroids, listed in table 3.2, were all significantly different at the .001 level.[88] See the appendix to this chapter.

Participant Group Belief Sets

To determine how the groups differ on the seven composite beliefs, Overall and Klett suggest a spatial relationship derived from vector plots for each composite belief; these plots are straight lines originating from the center of a graph to the coordinates of a specific belief.[89] The vectors are stretched by multiplying each rotated discriminant loading by its respective univariate F value. The vectors point toward the participant groups having the highest mean score on the respective composite belief and away from groups having the lowest mean scores.[90] In other words, the vector procedure isolates the composite beliefs with the greatest contribution to the separation of the four participant groups. A taxonomy of the beliefs associated with each participant group is provided in table 3.3.

Table 3.3. Mediated Social Conflict Beliefs by Participant Groups

Group	Beliefs	Stretched Coordinates	
		Function 1	Function 2
Television dependent			
high-involved	Informative	−18.72	−6.75
low-involved	Manipulated	−0.71	3.15
	Functional	−1.54	3.97
Newspaper dependent			
high-involved	Influential	16.71	−5.85
	Vigilant	4.96	−24.50
	Dramatic	3.44	−4.48
low-involved	Destructive	4.50	−6.75

Participants classified as High-Involved Television Dependents were most distinctive on the belief that media were *informative.* The High-Involved Newspaper Dependents were most associated with the *influential, vigilant,* and *dramatic* beliefs. Beliefs associated with the Low-Involved Television Dependents were *manipulated* and *functional.* The Low-Involved Newspaper Dependents were separated from the other three groups by the belief that conflict is a *destructive* force in society.

Discussion

The uses and dependency, involvement, and reasoned action models provide a framework to explain the nature of the media selection process and the cognitive and behavioral effects related to media dependency. While social systems constrain the nature and type of media available to the audience, media selection is affected by the information goals of the individual. Essentially, an individually determined predisposition guides a selection from a socially determined set of media. Knowledge of the dispositional beliefs influenced by previous experience with media will aid in the understanding of a person's tendency to develop specific media dependencies.

This study has sought to: (1) identify audience beliefs related to social conflict presented in the mass media, and (2) determine the set of beliefs that distinguish or separate individuals classified by the type of media they depend upon for information related to conflict events and by the level of personal involvement with the conflict event. Ajzen and Fishbein's theory of reasoned action was used to examine the cognitive and behavioral effects related to media dependency. Reasoned action links behavior to attitudes and beliefs. A behavioral predisposition is influenced by a set of beliefs that a person has learned to associate with the object of the predisposition. Therefore, one approach to understanding media dependency is to determine the set of beliefs people hold about an object, in this case, mediated conflict. One may learn why people vary in media dependency by determining the belief structures that are associated with the media they select for information related to mediated conflict. Consistent with the reasoned action model, this study found significant differences in the patterns of belief among participant groups. Results indicate that people classified on the basis of type of media dependency and level of involvement hold different beliefs related to mediated social conflict.

The first finding identified a set of beliefs that can be attributed to the presentation of social conflict by the television and newspaper media. Factor analysis was used to identify seven underlying dimensions inherent in fifty statements of beliefs that participants hold toward social conflict. Seven distinct dispositional belief structures were identified, as displayed in table 3.1. The belief dimensions termed informative, influential, vigilant, manipulated, and dramatic seem to concern the media's role in and interaction with social conflict. Within this group, mediated conflict events are believed to be affected or shaped by media attention and coverage. The belief dimensions termed functional and destructive reflect opposite orientations and appear to describe the perceptions of the intrinsic nature of social conflict. The functional dimension is similar to Simmel's view of conflict as a positive social force and is in opposition to the destructive dimension, which holds conflict as a negative force in society.

The result of the second research question found significant main and interaction effects for identifying beliefs that differ among groups based on type of media dependency and level of involvement. The interaction revealed differences in belief sets among both media dependencies and level of involvement. This result supports involvement as a mediating variable in an information search. The degree of relevance is a result of prior experience with a media option as a specific source of information. High-involved people have a greater motivation to seek knowledge salient to their information goals. Thus, different levels of involvement associated with different levels of motivation should reflect different dispositional belief sets. This is supported by the results indicated in table 3.2; the second discriminant function separated the high- and low-involved individuals. The greatest distinction in beliefs was the functional dimension for the low-involved groups and the vigilant dimension for the high-involved groups. (See table 3.3.)

Discriminant analysis was used to investigate the third research question. The belief sets differed significantly among people who were grouped according to their type of media dependency and their level of involvement with mediated social conflict. The discriminant procedure found that knowledge about beliefs related to mediated social conflict can be used to classify people based on media dependency behavior and involvement level. The belief dimensions that contributed most significantly to the distinctions between groups are revealed in table 3.3. While specific belief sets were identified, their importance may be more closely related to the finding that distinct cognitive differences exist, manifest by the unique belief sets among the groups, and that these may predispose motivations to select different media options. The beliefs listed in table 3.3 should not be considered to be static. According to the reasoned action model, the dispositional beliefs result from prior experience with the media relative to an informational goal. The media selection behavior is influenced by sets of beliefs that a person has learned to associate with an object. Beliefs are subject to modification as additional experience with the media refines a person's perceptions concerning how well a selected media fulfills a specific information goal.

This study provides additional evidence that an individual's perception of a medium is influenced by involvement, or the personal relevance of the goal-related information presented by a medium. One way of viewing dependency from an individual's perspective is to determine the relation of an individual's belief structures to mediated conflict. If beliefs predispose behavior, the knowledge of why people develop different media dependencies may be enhanced by determining their belief sets.

Media dependency is contingent on socially determined constraints and individual actions. The uses and dependency model acknowledges that the audience is proactive in media selection behavior. Dependency is not totally determined by a medium and the social environment in which it is used. People hold distinctive beliefs, probably acquired by past experience with the media, that can affect their choice of a specific information goal. Consistent with the dependency paradigm, a primary reliance on a particular medium is considered to occur when a functionally equivalent alternative is not available to meet a specific information goal. Usually there is no mandate or sanction tied to the choice between newspapers or television. A decision with a restricted set of alternatives allows personal predispositions to have a greater influence in the selection and subsequent dependence on a medium. Information concerning the relative effectiveness and efficiency of the available media options in providing information about social conflict also may be influenced by the nature of the conflict.

Limitations and Implications for Future Research

This study employed accepted standard factor analysis procedures, yet many opinions exist concerning the number of factors to extract, rotation methods, and the subjective process of naming the derived factors. Measurement errors associated with the various assumptions underlying any particular procedure may also occur. These can influence the results of any single analysis. The same type of criticism applies to discriminant procedures. It is important to note that plausibility of the results of a single analysis is no guarantee of validity or stability.

This exploratory study revealed that for this sample, with respect to mediated social conflict, it is possible to classify a person as television or newspaper dependent with high or low involvement on the basis of a set of beliefs. Generalization of these findings needs to be limited pending further study. Media consumption does not occur in a static environment. As consumers become aware of new media options, knowledge and comprehension may lead to a trial selection. The subsequent media exposure may lead to an enhanced impression and may reinforce exposure to the novel media option. This may generate a new set of beliefs and expectations concerning the medium's ability to meet information needs. The reinforced viewing behavior can result in a new dependency on the medium for selected information. Additional research is needed concerning the circumstances associated with changes in the perception of alternative and emerging media. The increased interactivity of new media options may be as important as the content in shaping receptions of the utility of the media to fulfill information goals. Identification of the attributes of new media and the corresponding consumer belief structures can be used to develop image and positioning strategies useful for marketing new information technologies.

Future research should investigate the stability of the social conflict belief structures among various demographic segments and other media such as radio and news magazines. The beliefs may be goal-specific, and their composition will probably vary across information goals. For example, one might expect that salient beliefs related to sports would differ from those related to politics. The stability of the belief structures throughout different social conflict situations may also differ. Beliefs may not influence dependencies after a threshold of uncertainty is passed. There is a variation in personal involvement in crises such as severe economic depression, the aftermath of natural and social disasters, and major military confrontations. Situational factors, such as a lack of access to goal-related information, may overwhelm conventional expectations and motives that would constrain selection in a less traumatic environment. The intensity and novelty of a disruption may induce a uniformly high level of involvement without previous experience or information on which to build expectations that a particular media option would fulfill a person's information needs. Situations in which no media options are available present unique opportunities to study the interaction of interpersonal and media resources. Catastrophic disruptions can severely restrict access to electronic media for large numbers of people. After hurricane Andrew struck south Florida in 1992, long-distance telephone networks were used to obtain information about the local damage reports and relief efforts as reported by the national electronic media. Northern media were describing the carnage and relief efforts to Floridians, sometimes in real time, as shown on television channels essentially dedicated to the event. People still depended on media for information although it was conveyed via interpersonal channels. Knowledge of belief structures, involvement, and situational influences may increase understanding of how and why dependencies develop, change, and break down.

Appendix

Manipulation Check

Since Zaichkowsky's Personal Involvement Inventory (PII) scale was originally applied to consumer products, a "manipulation check" was performed. A five-item involvement-check index was used to indicate the degree of attention to, notice of, concentration on, involvement with, and thought put into mediated social conflict.[91] The score on the involvement-check index for the PII high-involvement group was significantly greater than the score of the PII low-involvement group (t = 262, df = 191, p < .01).

Second Research Question MANOVA Summary Statistics

The main effect of media dependency was significant (Wilks' Lambda = .80, $F[1,268] = 6.43$, $p \leq .001$). Lambda is interpreted as a measure of the total variability not explained by the group differences. A canonical function was derived for the television and newspaper dependency groups (Wilks' Lambda = .20, $\chi^2 = 298.15$, df = 5, $p \leq .0001$). Wilks' Lambda indicates that 80% of the total observed variability in the beliefs is attributed to media dependency group differences.

Classification Accuracy

The classification accuracy of the dispositional belief set was tested by applying the discriminant functions to a holdout sample. The holdout sample is a group of respondents withheld from the total sample when the discriminant function is computed. The derived functions are applied to the holdout sample to validate the accuracy of the functions. The accuracy of the classification matrices for both the analysis and holdout samples must exceed levels expected by chance alone. The discriminant scores were converted to probabilities of group membership and compared to the actual membership in a classification matrix. Table 3.4 includes predictions based on the analysis sample used to derive the discriminant function and the predictions using the holdout sample.

Table 3.4. Classification Table

Actual Classification	Number	Predictor Classification			
		HiTv	HiNs	LoTv	LoNs
Analysis sample					
HiTv	41	40	1	0	0
HiNs	40	2	38	0	0
LoTv	40	0	1	35	4
LoNs	40	0	2	9	29
	161				
Correct classification = 88.1%					
Hold-out sample					
HiTv	33	30	3	0	0
HiNs	28	0	24	0	0
LoTv	26	0	0	18	2
LoNs	21	0	0	4	17
	108				
Correct classification = 82.4%					

A comparison of the analysis and holdout samples indicates an acceptable amount of upward bias in the discriminant function. Correct predictions for the holdout were 5.7% less than those of the analysis sample. The discrimination is weakest between the low-involvement groups. The maximum chance criterion is 30.5. Compared to the hit ratio of 82.4, the discriminant model's classification predictions are well above what could be expected by chance alone.

Centroids

The F ratios based on Mahalanobis D2 contrasts of the four group centroids were significant (p's < .001, df = 8,181.6).

Notes

1. Todd Gitlin, *The Whole World Is Watching: Mass Media in the Making and Unmaking of the New Left* (Berkeley: University of California Press, 1980), 1.

2. James B. Manheim, "A Model of Agenda Dynamics," in *Communication Yearbook,* vol. 10, ed. Margaret L. McMaughlin (Newbury Park, Calif.: Sage, 1987), 499.

3. Akiba A. Cohen, Hanna Adoni, and Charles R. Bantz, *Social Conflict and Television News* (Newbury Park, Calif.: Sage, 1990), 25.

4. Georg Simmel, *Conflict and the Web of Group-Affiliations,* trans. Kurt H. Wolff and Reinhard Bendix (New York: Free Press, 1955), 13.

5. Louis Kriesberg, *The Sociology of Social Conflicts* (Englewood Cliffs, N.J.: Prentice-Hall, 1973), 17.

6. Kathleen H. Jamieson and Karlyn Kohors Campbell, *The Interplay of Influence: News, Advertising, Politics and the Mass Media* (Belmont, Calif.: Wadsworth, 1992), 33.

7. "Knowledge generating" is a term attributed to James J. Bradac; see Bradac, ed. *Message Effects in Communications Science,* Sage Annual Reviews of Communication Research, vol. 17 (Newbury Park, Calif.: Sage, 1989), 8.

8. Sandra J. Ball-Rokeach and Melvin L. DeFleur, "A Dependency Model of Mass Media Effects," *Communication Research* 3 (1976), 3.

9. M. Mark Miller and Stephen D. Reese, "Media Dependency as Interaction: Effects of Exposure and Reliance on Political Activity and Efficacy," *Communication Research* 9 (1982), 227.

10. Zhongdang Pan, Ronald E. Ostman, Patricia Moy, and Paula Reynolds, "News Media Exposure and Its Learning Effects during the Persian Gulf War," *Journalism Quarterly* 71 (Spring 1994), 7.

11. Sandra J. Ball-Rokeach, "The Origins of Individual Media-System Dependency: A Sociological Framework," *Communication Research* 12 (1985), 488.

12. Isaac Ajzen and Martin Fishbein, *Belief, Attitude, Intention and Behavior: An Introduction to Theory and Research* (Reading, Mass.: Addison-Wesley, 1975), 5.

13. W. James Potter, "Perceived Reality in Television Effects Research," *Journal of Broadcasting and Electronic Media* 32, no. 1 (Winter 1988), 24.

14. The dependent variable is assumed to depend on or is caused by another variable. For example, for the discriminant procedure used in this study, media dependency was a dependent variable. It is a categorical dependent variable that has two values that merely identified or classified people as television or newspaper dependent. The discriminant procedure used the seven beliefs as a set of independent variables that were weighted and combined in a manner that would correctly classify a person solely on the basis of his or her beliefs related to mediated social conflict.

15. Shearon Lowery and Melvin L. DeFleur, *Milestones in Mass Communication Research: Media Effects* (New York: Longman, 1983).

16. Shanto Iyengar and Adam Simon, "News Coverage of the Gulf Crisis and Public Opinion," in *Taken by Storm: The Media, Public Opinion, and U.S. Foreign Policy in the Gulf War,* ed. W. Lance Bennett and David L. Paletz (Chicago: University of Chicago Press, 1994), 176.

17. David H. Weaver, "Political Issues and Voter Need for Orientation," in *The Emergence of American Political Issues: The Agenda Setting Function of the Press,* ed. David Shaw and Maxwell E. McCombs (St. Paul: West, 1977), 107.

18. Herbert G. Zucker, "The Variable Nature of the News Media Influence," in *Communication Yearbook,* vol. 2, ed. Brent D. Rubin (New Brunswick, N.J.: Transaction, 1978), 225.

19. David P. Demers, Dennis Craff, Yang-Ho Choi, and Beth M. Pessin, "Issue Obtrusiveness and the Agenda-Setting Effects of National Network News," *Communication Research* 16:6 (1989), 793.

20. Manheim, 499.

21. Maxwell McCombs and Donald L. Shaw, "The Evolution of Agenda-Setting Research: Twenty-five Years in the Marketplace of Ideas," *Journal of Communication* 43:2 (1993), 56.

22. Garth S. Jowett and Victoria O'Donnell, *Propaganda and Persuasion,* 2d ed. (Newbury Park, Calif.: Sage, 1992), 147.

23. Elihu Katz, Jay Blumler, and Michael Gurevitch, "Utilization of Mass Communication by the Individual," in *The Uses of Mass Communications: Current Perspectives on Gratifications Research,* ed. Jay Blumler and Elihu Katz (Beverly Hills, Calif.: Sage, 1974), 25.

24. Alan M. Rubin, "Uses and Gratifications: Quasi-Functional Analysis," in *Broadcasting Research Methods,* ed. Joseph R. Dominick and James E. Fletcher (Boston: Allyn and Bacon, 1985), 202.

25. Alan M. Rubin, "Media Uses and Effects: A Uses and Gratifications Perspective," in *Media Effects: Advances in Theory and Research,* ed. Jennings Bryant and Dolf Zillman (Hillsdale, N.J.: Lawrence Erlbaum, 1994), 417.

26. Ibid., 427.

27. Ibid., 426.

28. Michael Levy and Sven Windahl, "Audience Activity and Gratifications," *Communications Research* 11 (1984), 51.

29. Ball-Rokeach, 488.

30. Alan M. Rubin and Sven Windahl, "The Uses and Dependency Model of Mass Communication," *Critical Studies in Mass Communication* 3 (1986), 184.

31. Jowett and O'Donnell, 150.

32. Rubin, "Media Uses and Effects," 421.

33. Rubin and Windahl, 187.

34. Ibid., 189.

35. Gina M. Garramone, "Audience Motivation Effects: More Evidence," *Communication Research* 11:1 (1984), 80.

36. Dolf Zillman and Jennings Bryant, "Affect, Mood and Emotions as Determinants of Selective Exposure," in *Selective Exposure to Communication,* ed. Zillman and Bryant (Hillsdale, N.J.: Lawrence Erlbaum, 1985), 157.

37. Michael J. Rosenberg, "Cognitive Structure and Attitudinal Effects," *Journal of Abnormal and Social Psychology* 53 (1956), 367.

38. Ajzen and Fishbein, 6.

39. William J. McGuire, "An Information Processing Model of Advertising Effectiveness," in *Behavioral and Management Science in Marketing,* ed. Harry L. Davis and Alvin J. Silk (New York: Ronald Press, 1978), 156; Richard E. Petty, John T. Cacioppo, and David Schumann, "Central and Peripheral Routes to Advertising Effectiveness: The Moderating Role of Involvement," *Journal of Consumer Research* 10 (1983), 135; Alan M. Rubin and Elizabeth M. Perse, "Audience Activity and Soap Opera Involvement: A Uses and Effects Investigation," *Human Communication Research* 14 (Summer 1988), 246.

40. Rajeev Batra and Michael L. Ray, "Situational Effects of Advertising Repetition: The Moderating Influence of Motivation, Ability and Opportunity to Respond," *Journal of Consumer Research* 12 (1986), 432–45.

41. Joel B. Cohen, "Involvement and You: One Thousand Great Ideas," in *Advances in Consumer Research,* vol. 10, ed. Richard Bagozzi and Alice M. Tybout (Ann Arbor, Mich.: Association for Consumer Research, 1983), 325; Michael J. Houston and Michael L. Rothschild, "Conceptual and Methodological Perspectives in Involvement," in *Research Frontiers in Marketing: Dialogues and Directions,* ed. S. Jain (Chicago: American Marketing Association, 1978), 184; Andrew A. Mitchell and Jerry C. Olson, "Are Product Attribute Beliefs the Only Mediators of Advertising Effects on Brand Attitudes?" *Journal of Marketing Research* 18 (1981), 316; Richard E. Petty and John T. Cacioppo, "Issue Involvement as a Moderator of the Effects on Attitude of Advertising Content and Context," in *Advances in Consumer Research,* ed. Bagozzi and Tybout, 20.

42. Craig J. Andrews, Srinivas Durvasula, and Syed H. Akhter, "A Framework for Conceptualizing and Measuring the Involvement Construct in Advertising Research," *Journal of Advertising* 20:4 (1990), 27.

43. Robert Apsler and David O. Sears, "Warning, Personal Involvement and Attitude Change," *Journal of Personality and Social Change* 9:2 (1968), 162.

44. Richard L. Celsi and Jerry C. Olson, "The Role of Involvement in Attention and Comprehension Processes," *Journal of Consumer Research* 15 (1988), 210.

45. Ven-Hwei Lo, "Media Use, Involvement, and Knowledge of the Gulf War," *Journalism Quarterly* 71 (Spring 1994), 43.

46. Petty, Cacioppo, and Schumann, 138.

47. Judith L. Zaichkowsky, "Measuring the Involvement Construct," *Journal of Consumer Research* 12 (1985), 341.

48. Houston and Rothschild, 184.

49. Celsi and Olson, 215.

50. Lo, 50.

51. Darrel D. Muehling, Jeffery J. Stoltman, and Stanford Grossbart, "The Impact of Comparative Advertising on Levels of Message Involvement," *Journal of Advertising* 19:3 (1990), 41.

52. James R. Bettman, *An Information Processing Theory of Consumer Choice* (Reading, Mass.: Addison-Wesley, 1979), 97.

53. Herbert E. Krugman, "The Impact of Television Advertising: Learning without Involvement," *Public Opinion Quarterly* 29 (1965), 349.

54. Peter Wright, "Analyzing Media Effects on Advertising Responses," *Public Opinion Quarterly* 33:2 (1974), 192.

55. Lee B. Becker and D. Charles Whitney, "Effects of Media Dependencies: Audience Assessment of Government," *Communication Research* 7 (1980), 95.

56. Robert A. Wicks, "Schema Theory and Measurement in Mass Communication Research: Theoretical and Methodological Issues in News Information Processing," in *Communication Yearbook,* vol. 15, ed. Stanley A. Deetz (Newbury Park, Calif.: Sage, 1992), 115.

57. Lo, 52.

58. Zaichkowsky.

59. Thomas S. Robertson, "Low Commitment Consumer Behavior," *Journal of Advertising Research* 16:2 (1976), 19.

60. Michael L. Rothschild and Michael J. Houston, "The Consumer Involvement Matrix: Some Preliminary Findings," in *Proceedings: AMA Educator's Conference,* ed. Barnett A. Greenberg and Danny N. Bellinger (Chicago: American Marketing Association, 1977), 95.

61. Krugman, 354.

62. Charles U. Lavidge and Gary A. Steiner, "A Model for Predictive Measurements of Advertising Effectiveness," *Journal of Marketing* 25 (1961), 59.

63. Thomas E. Barry and Daniel J. Howard, "A Review and Critique of the Hierarchy of Effects in Advertising," *International Journal of Advertising* 9 (1990), 121.

64. Henry Assael, *Consumer Behavior and Marketing Action* (Boston: Kent, 1984), 87.

65. Jack M. McLeod and Daniel G. McDonald, "Beyond Simple Exposure: Orientations and Their Impact on Political Processes," *Communication Research* 10 (1983), 3.

66. Yuko Miyo, "The Knowledge-Gap Hypothesis and Media Dependency," in *Communication Yearbook,* vol. 7, ed. Robert N. Bostrom and Bruce H. Westley (Beverly Hills, Calif.: Sage, 1983), 626.

67. Marie J. Robinson, "Television and American Politics: 1956–1976," *Public Interest* 48 (1977), 3.

68. Lawrence A. Wenner, "Gratifications Sought and Obtained in Program Dependency: A Study of Network Evening News Programs and 60 Minutes," *Communication Research* 9 (1982), 539.

69. Garrett J. O'Keefe, "Political Malaise and Reliance on Media," *Journalism Quarterly* 57 (1980), 122.

70. Cecilie Gaziano, "Media Dependence for News: Some Neglected Groups," *Mass Communication Review* 17:3 (1990), 2.

71. Zaichkowsky, 345.

72. A good scale is one that yields stable and consistent results. A reliable measurement scale will produce the same data each time it is used to measure the same concept. Cronbach's Alpha is a measure of internal consistency of the items in an index. Alpha ranges from 0 to 1.0 and indicates how much the items in an index are measuring the same concept. Higher values indicate higher reliability among the scale items.

73. Simmel, 14.

74. Lewis A. Coser, *The Functions of Social Conflict* (Glencoe, Ill.: Free Press, 1956), 151.

75. Intercoder reliability indicates the consistency with which rules or measurement procedures are followed by human judges. Scott's Pi accounts for the percentage of coder agreement and chance agreement. A Pi of 80 or higher indicates acceptable reliability. Pi is equivalent to Alpha (see note 72) at the nominal level with two coders. The greater the specifications provided for each classification category, the less leeway a coder has to apply personal judgment. This yields greater consistency of classification provided the judges are adequately trained.

76. Factor analysis techniques are used to examine the underlying patterns in a large number of variables. The procedure condenses the information into a set of summary composite dimensions or factors that retain as much of the information inherent in the original data as possible. For example, consumer perceptions of a product can be portrayed as a linear combination of factors or dimensions that represent product attributes such as durability, value quality, and prestige. Factor analysis helps to reveal underlying patterns that may be present, although not readily observable, in a large set of data. See Jae-On Kim and Charles W. Mueller, *Introduction to Factor Analysis: What It Is and How to Do It,* Sage University Paper Series on Quantitative Applications in the Social Sciences, 07–013 (Beverly Hills, Calif.: Sage, 1978), 9.

77. Rotation of the factors often improves the interpretation by reducing some of the ambiguities inherent in the initial factor solution. Varimax factor rotation keeps

the axes at right angles and assumes that the derived factors are not correlated. This produces a structure that is essentially simple and therefore easier to interpret. The logic is that interpretation is easiest when the variable-factor correlations are close to either +1 or -1. See Joseph Hair, Rolph E. Anderson, Ronald L. Tatham, and William C. Black, *Multivariate Data Analysis with Readings,* 3d ed. (New York: Macmillan, 1992), 231.

78. The Scree tail test is used to identify the optimum number of factors that should be extracted and interpreted during the factoring procedure. The eigenvalues, which represent the amount of variance accounted for by a factor, are plotted against the number of factors and the shape of the resultant curve is examined to determine the cutoff. The point at which the curve flattens out is used to indicate the maximum number of factors to extract. Another possible criteria is to stop extracting factors when the associated eigenvalue drops below one. See Raymond B. Cattell, "The Scree Test for the Number of Factors," *Multivariate Behavioral Research* 1 (1966), 249, for additional detail.

79. Naming the factor dimensions is a subjective procedure that facilitates the presentation and understanding of the nature of the factor structure. Interpretation is based on the loadings of concepts associated with each dimension.

80. Factor analysis reduces an original set of variables (factors) to a smaller representative set of composite variables used to represent the larger original set of variables. The measure of a score is comprised of the scale items with the highest and most unique loadings on a individual dimension. The composite scale produces a measure referred to as a factor score. The factor score indicates the degree to which an individual possesses a particular belief represented by the factor. See Hair et al., 225.

81. MANOVA, or multivariate analysis of variance, is used to assess group differences throughout a set of dependent variables simultaneously. Each treatment group is measured on more than one dependent variable. The dependent variables are represented as a weighted linear combination rather than a single value. For example, several characteristics of individuals can be considered simultaneously in a manner that more realistically models a person's decision to purchase one brand over another.

82. Interaction effects refer to the joint synergistic effects of the treatment variables that cannot be explained by simply adding the contributions of individual treatment variables. The independent variables produce an effect on the dependent measures that is different from their individual contributions.

83. The purpose of discriminant analysis is to estimate the relationship between a categorical dependent variable and a set of metric independent variables. The objective is to understand and distinguish group differences based on several measurable characteristics. Discriminant analysis can be used to classify people by creating categories and assigning individuals probabilities for membership based on scores produced by the discriminant functions. An example would be classifying a person's mortgage credit risk based on variables such as age, income, marital status, and credit history.

84. Hair et al., 89.

85. The forward stepwise procedure used in this study begins by including the individual belief that provides the greatest univariate discrimination between the groups. The process continues to select belief variables until remaining variables do not contribute a sufficient unique increment to the separation of the groups. The selection criteria maximized the Mahalanobis squared distance between the pairs of group centroids. For a review of discriminant stepwise inclusion procedures, see William R. Klecka, *Discriminant Analysis,* Sage University Paper Series on Quantitative Applications in the Social Sciences, 07–019 (Beverly Hills, Calif.: Sage, 1980), 52.

86. Structure coefficients are useful for identifying the nature of the information associated with each of the functions which is useful for finding differences in the participant groups (see Klecka). The size of the coefficient indicates how closely a variable and the function are related.

87. In this study, there are four centroids, one for each participant group. Centroids are Z scores and can be interpreted as the number of standard deviations each group is from the average of all the groups.

88. Each of the participant group centroids are statistically different from the overall mean of the groups.

89. John E. Overall and C. James Klett, *Applied Multivariate Analysis* (New York: McGraw-Hill, 1972), 292.

90. Vectors originate from the grand centroid and point toward the groups with the highest mean level of the belief and away from the groups having the lowest mean scores. The longer the vector, the greater the influence the variable has on the group toward whose centroid it points.

91. Also see Darrel D. Muehling and Russell N. Laczniak, "Advertising's Immediate and Delayed Influence on Brand Attitudes: Considerations across Message-Involvement Levels," *Journal of Advertising* 17:4 (1988), 23; J. Craig Andrews, "Motivation, Ability and Opportunity to Process Information: Conceptual and Experimental Manipulation Issues," in *Advances in Consumer Research,* vol. 15, ed. Michael J. Houston (Provo, Utah: Association for Consumer Research, 1988), 213.

4

Who Owns Prime Time?
Industrial and Institutional Conflict over
Television Programming and Broadcast Rights

Ronald V. Bettig

This chapter provides a case study of the interindustry struggle between television program producers and the three major U.S. television networks (ABC, CBS, NBC) over who should be allowed to own and syndicate prime-time television programming.[1] In 1990, the sale of network rerun and first-run syndication programs to television broadcasters generated revenues of $3.4 billion in the United States and $2.3 billion globally; by 1995 the estimated total global value of this market topped $10 billion.[2] The economic significance of this market notwithstanding, this case study is more than an analysis of competition over revenue and profit shares between the television networks and Hollywood. Since the medium involved is network television, arguably the most pervasive and influential of present-day mass media, cultural, political, and social issues inevitably come into focus. Moreover, given that the commonsense perception of network television as a powerful mass medium is widely held, there has been continuous pressure on the U.S. government to intervene in this and related industries. The various branches and agencies of the U.S. government have responded accordingly, with a wide range of laws and regulations governing the institution of television, including the business of television program production and syndication.

Both the media and the state can be conceptualized as sites of class, race, and gender struggles.[3] Thus, when we examine the structure and regulation of the media, we find various sectors of industry and the public inserting themselves into relevant policy-making arenas and exerting pressure on the various departments of the state system in order to advance their particular interests. The interaction of these institutional forces, through the individuals, groups, and organizations that constitute them, helps to shape the general political-economic framework within which television production, distribution, and consumption take place.

Researchers who focus on media structures and practices seek to show how institutional and organizational forms and processes affect the context in which mass communicators work and thus the form and substance of media output (that is, their content). This case study sheds light on those institutional forces and processes that have shaped the current structure and operation of the prime-time television production, distribution, and exhibition industries. More precisely, it focuses on the conjunction of institutional and organizational forces involved in a contest over who should have financial interest in network prime-time programming and who should be able to sell reruns or first-run programs to television stations.

The contest concerns the Financial Interest and Syndication Rules (FISRs),[4] which Cantor and Cantor call the "most important" Federal Communications Commission (FCC) regulation relating to prime-time television.[5] The FCC promulgated the FISRs in 1970[6] and the Department of Justice (DOJ) subsequently incorporated them into a series of consent decrees to settle its antitrust action against the networks.[7] These efforts sought to break up the concentration of prime-time television program production, distribution, and exhibition and to curb the increasingly monopsonistic practices of the three television networks. The FCC and DOJ charged that the networks leveraged program producers to relinquish financial interests and syndication rights in exchange for access to prime time. By reducing network control over program production and distribution, the FCC and DOJ hoped to reduce barriers to entry to this market and thereby encourage more independent production. Venturing to capitalize on the deregulatory posture of the Reagan-appointed FCC, the three networks began a campaign in the early 1980s to gain repeal of the FISRs. The FCC and DOJ eventually allowed the rules to expire in the mid-1990s, effecting an immediate restructuring of the prime-time program production and distribution system.

The first section of this chapter introduces the theoretical framework that guides the investigation. The next section reviews the history and development of network broadcasting, with special attention to the regulatory efforts to control network–program supplier relationships that led up to the FCC's imposition of the FISRs. The third section briefly analyzes the events surrounding the FCC's move to repeal the FISRs in 1983. The final section looks at recent developments regarding the structure and performance of prime-time network television, summarizes the findings of the case study, and points out the contributions the study makes to the larger theoretical project of coming to a critical understanding of capitalism, the state, and the media.

Theoretical Approaches

The theoretical framework that guides this study is a combination of radical political economy and neo-Marxist and radical theories of the capitalist state. Political-economic media theory takes Marx's critique of capitalism as its starting point to demonstrate how this mode of production affects the form, substance, and range of media output. The constant drive for profit that is intrinsic to capitalism and defines the logic of capital, means that capitalists are forever enclosing the cultural and intellectual commons as they seek new markets.[8] In the domains of culture and information, it means commodifying whatever forms of this sort of human creativity that can be tangibly embodied and brought to the marketplace, from books to computer software. As Harvey puts it, "Precisely because capitalism is expansionary and imperialistic, cultural life in more and more areas gets brought within the grasp of the cash nexus and the logic of capital circulation."[9]

Two major areas of attention within political economy are, first, the structure of media ownership and control and, second, the effects of the logic of capital on the media marketplace. In the first area the focus is on who owns the media, the interlocking relationships between the media and the corporate sector as a whole, and the relationships between the media and the government. This research uncovers the institutional networks through which media owners promote their material and ideological interests and those of the class to which they belong. The second area of research—on the operation of the media marketplace—shows how the profit motive underlying the logic of capital produces an inevitable drive toward economic concentration. Thus, while capitalism is expanding ever further into new domains, the capital generated in this process becomes increasingly concentrated in a few hands. Consequently, in the media sector there are fewer and fewer families and individuals owning and controlling increasingly larger corporations operating in an increasingly oligopolistic marketplace.[10] For the capitalist class, the media sector is just one more site of investment where profits can be earned. The demand for profits results in "the reduction of independent media sources, concentration on the largest markets, avoidance of risk taking, [and] neglect of smaller and poorer sectors of the potential audience."[11] Thus the media marketplace is prone to failure, resulting in a restricted range of media output. Government intervention into the media marketplace is often required to counter these tendencies.

Political economists share an interest in media structures and performance with economists, but unlike the latter they do not relegate politics to the margins of their paradigm. Rather, political economy, as the term implies, makes politics a central focus of concern. Indeed, the approach takes state intervention into the economy as an essential feature of contemporary capitalism. Thus the need for political theory. Martin Carnoy divides the state theory of U.S. Marxists and radicals into three distinct areas: one focuses on the relation between the capitalist class and the state; the second stresses the relation between the logic of capital and state policies; and the third approaches the state as a site of class, race, and gender struggles.[12] This case study seeks to bridge these three areas of study in order to produce a holistic analysis of state intervention into the economic domain. Additionally, these three areas of theorizing about the state have their counterparts in political-economic media theory, making it possible to synthesize separate discourses carried on in different disciplines.

Accordingly, just as political-economic theory of the media is concerned with ownership and control, Marxists such as Miliband and power-structure analysts such as Domhoff are interested in the relationship between the capitalist class and the state.[13] The methodological objective here is to identify the organizational interlocks that constitute the social network of the dominant class or power elite and to demonstrate how the state is implicated in this system. The research, based on social network analysis, sampling of estate closings, and analysis of income-tax and census data, confirms that there is a ruling capitalist class in the United States, as well as in other capitalist societies, which is made up of the top 2 percent or so of the population. This class owns and controls most of the nation's productive capital that is held in such forms as stocks, bonds, franchises, real estate, and intellectual property rights.[14] This capitalist class is also a ruling class because it controls the state and has disproportionate influence in the policy-planning and implementation processes. In this case study, the questions Who owns the media? and Who rules the state? are posed in an effort to explain the outcome of conflict involving these and other institutions.

This brings us to the second area to which capitalist-state theory draws our attention: the relationship between the logic of capital and state policies. Again there is the parallel with political-economic theory, which examines how the logic of capital governs the mass culture industries. Logic of capital theory[15] holds that the contemporary capitalist state emerged as a response to the continuing economic crises produced by the contradictions inherent to the capitalist mode of production. Theorists of this school regularly point to the Great Depression of the 1930s as the moment when the interventionist state became essential to the continued existence of capitalism. Accordingly, this approach begins with an analysis of the capital accumulation process and its various crisis tendencies, from which it then derives the form and function of the capitalist state.

The tendency toward systemic crisis requires the state to intervene increasingly into the economy in an effort to produce countertendencies by reorganizing the processes of production, distribution, and consumption. For example, Keynesian economic policies served to counter tendencies of overproduction or lack of demand through government spending. Government antitrust action provides another example: in such cases the government seeks to counter the inherent tendencies within capitalism toward concentration by breaking up monopolies, oligopolies, or trusts. In this role of crisis manager, the state takes on the position of the "ideal collective capitalist," attempting to promote the long-term interests of capital as a whole through "discriminatory management of monopolistic competition."[16] State officials and workers constitute a "state managerial technocracy" that tends to operate in this manner due to its structural dependency upon the capital accumulation process from which the taxes for running the state are extracted. This makes state personnel especially sensitive to threats of a capital "investment strike" and limits their autonomy from the capitalist class. Also, because the state does not directly control capital, it can only indirectly intervene into the economy and this intervention is typically "reactive." This case study identifies the crises of accumulation and market failures in the television industry that prompt state regulation. The key question here is, What is the character of power and how is it exercised?[17]

Critics of capital logic theories of the state find them too functionalist and essentialist in their orientation, especially the idea "that the interests of capital are always realized in the final analysis."[18] A third area of capitalist-state theory highlights the dysfunctional, contradictory, and contingent nature of state intervention into the economy. The class struggle theory[19] also has its parallel with a third area of political-economic media research that highlights forms of resistance against industrialized culture. These theories stress the systemic nature of the state and the media as sites of class struggle in which interclass and intraclass conflicts are fought out. Accordingly, these approaches take the existence of both a unified ruling class and a law-like logic of capital as problematic. Moreover, state policies and actions and media forms and content are seen as specifically determined by the action of class forces struggling in and through the state and media systems. Thus, the state or media are not simply instruments that the capitalist class uses to advance its particular interests. Rather, the capitalist class, or a fraction thereof, must work in and through the state and media systems to maintain its ruling-class status and resist challenges arising from nondominant groups and classes.

However, as Jessop points out with regard to the state, there *is* a "bias inscribed on the terrain of the state as a site of strategic action," a bias that privileges the strategies of "some forces over others, some interests over others, some time horizons over others, [and] some coalition possibilities over others."[20] By underscoring the fact that the site of struggle is by no means a level playing field, Jessop avoids lapsing into pluralism. State structures are tilted in favor of the capitalist class. Thus the state becomes a "vehicle for building and maintaining class power, without appearing to do so."[21] Rather, the state appears as a mediator in a process of bargaining and compromise, while masking the underlying inequality of access to and influence within the state system.

The appearance of the state as mediator is also reinforced by the positioning of the state as a site of intraclass conflict. Various class fractions or industry coalitions seek to organize the individuals and organizations inside and outside of the state apparatus in order to promote their interests through state action. Jessop presents the concept of the "hegemonic project" to describe the process by which the hegemonic class (fraction) seeks to promote its long-term interests through mobilization of state officials and relevant forces in "civil society" in support of its favored policies.[22] It attempts to do so by casting these particular class interests as being in the general interest of the nation as a whole.[23]

A hegemonic project is more likely to be successful if it can be linked up with the prevailing "accumulation strategy" or "mode of regulation" operating in the economic domain. These concepts come from "regulation theorists" who argue that capitalists themselves are constantly forced to reorganize industrial structures and business practices in order to counter the inevitable tendency within capitalism of the rate of profit to fall. During the twentieth century, the capitalist class pursued an accumulation strategy based on the Fordist, mass-production model of production as a means of maximizing profit rates. This was based on huge, long-term investments in fixed plants and a well-paid yet generally acquiescent labor force. This accumulation strategy was only a temporary fix for a crisis-prone economic system and we are presently experiencing a shift to a new one commonly called "post-Fordism"; the basic strategy is to minimize risks through short-term investments and capital mobility and thereby to intensify the exploitation of the global labor force. Instead of the rigidity of Fordism, post-Fordism involves flexible accumulation with respect to labor processes, labor markets, products and services, and patterns of consumption.[24]

Following Jessop, this case study bridges the approaches of capital logic and class struggle with these concepts of "hegemonic project" and "accumulation strategy." The former concept is used to examine how the networks sought to use the state system to advance their interests and the various forms of resistance they met. The latter concept is used to explain why the efforts to gain repeal of the FISRs, even though thwarted in the early 1980s, came to fruition by the mid-1990s. It is argued that there is a particular logic of capital at work here, based on a particular accumulation strategy, that required the U.S. state to free the television network companies from a variety of regulatory constraints, including the FISRs, in its role as "ideal national capitalist."

History of Network Broadcasting and Regulation

A review of the political-economic history of the broadcasting industry in the United States is essential for understanding the nature of its contemporary structure. Indeed, it is a useful and important historical lesson for illustrating the way corporate capitalism works. Commercial radio broadcasting took shape in the period immediately after World War I. A handful of large corporations determined the formation of the radio industry, mainly General Electric (GE) and Westinghouse, which sought to extend their lucrative wartime production of radio and electrical equipment for the military to new markets, and American Telegraph and Telephone (AT&T), which needed to protect its monopoly over the telephone industry. The U.S. government, particularly the navy, also played a direct role in helping constitute the emerging broadcasting system by encouraging General Electric to establish the Radio Corporation of America (RCA) so it could take over the British-owned American Marconi Company. Soon after RCA was formed, its patents were pooled with AT&T, Westinghouse, General Electric, and United Fruit, permitting the continuation of the rapid development of radio that had begun under such an arrangement during World War I.[25]

Radio broadcasting emerged in the early 1920s, matured in the period 1926–34, and then passed on its form and many of its same functions to television in the 1940s.[26] A primary purpose of radio broadcasting at the outset was to sell radio receiver sets. Accordingly, the manufacturers of radio equipment and the retailers that sold it played a key role in developing the idea and system of broadcasting. However, it soon became apparent that the one-time sale of receiver sets simply would not provide the required income to cover program costs. Various models and mechanisms for organizing and financing radio broadcasting were proposed and discussed,[27] but given the economic forces and agents involved and the ideological mood of the times,[28] an advertiser-supported, network-based system eventually prevailed.

Economists of broadcasting claim that the development of advertiser-supported broadcasting and network systems is a logical outcome of a market engaged in the production and distribution of a "public good" such as a television program or film.[29] A pure public good is "one whose cost of production is independent of the number of people who consume it; more precisely, one person's consumption of such a good does not reduce the quantity available to other people."[30] Thus, once a television program is produced, the marginal cost of distributing the program to as broad an audience as possible is relatively small compared to the costs of production. Economists therefore see networks as inevitably determined by the logic of the market. A network can spend much more lavishly on programming than a single broadcast station can since the network can spread the costs over a much larger audience. Of course, these economists assume that the cost of producing a program is more or less related to its quality.

Another feature of public goods is the difficulty of excluding nonpayers from using them, that is, "free riders" who benefit from their existence and use without paying for them. Charging the members of a broadcast audience for receiving a program is inherently problematic since there is no way of determining exactly who is listening or watching. Various nations developed distinctive mechanisms for delivering radio programming to consumers and charging them for it. In the United States, corporate interests saw to the adoption of an advertiser-supported broadcasting system, which commodified audiences and concentrated on "excluding" advertisers. Rather than trying to charge audience members for the use of the programming, broadcasters found it easier, indeed quite profitable, to charge advertisers for access to the airwaves.

The economic analysis of the nature of broadcasting is useful for identifying some of its unique characteristics but does not entirely explain why and how any particular system comes into existence. Such explanations require an analysis of the key actors in both the private and public sectors involved in developing and promoting different systems; the relative power they are able to exercise in the marketplace and the state; and an understanding of the logic of capital that shapes and limits the range of possible outcomes. The key industry actors involved in originating broadcasting have been identified—AT&T, GE, RCA, and Westinghouse. They were joined in 1926, when the radio group—RCA, GE, and Westinghouse—set up the National Broadcasting Company to serve as its broadcasting arm, taking 30 percent, 50 percent, and 20 percent of the company's stock, respectively. The Columbia Broadcasting System, established in 1927 and taken over by cigar manufacturer William Paley in 1928, provided the basis for a national network oligopoly.

The key government actors involved in the development and regulation of radio included the military, the Department of Commerce, the Congress, the federal courts, and, after 1927, the Federal Radio Commission. Government action, or inaction, played into the hands of big corporations. Amateur radio operators, educators, union organizers, socialists, and other radicals did try to resist the commercialization of radio, proposing alternative visions and plans for a noncommercial broadcasting system, but they lacked consensus and were at a severe disadvantage in the face of the major broadcasters and the telephone monopoly.[31] Additionally, the structural bias of the state toward capital, the dominant ideological consensus around private enterprise, and the integral role of the capitalist class and its aligned agents inside and outside of the state greatly privileged the major private, commercial operations. Consequently, the number of nonprofit and noncommercial broadcasters rapidly diminished by 1933, to one-third their total in 1927, while the oligopolistic grip of NBC and CBS, in terms of hours and level of power, grew ever stronger.[32]

With regard to capitalism, we find that the nature of the emerging monopoly system was such that a handful of core firms had come to dominate a wide range of industry sectors, including the mass media, while large numbers of small firms languished at the periphery.[33] At about this time the theatrical film, music recording and publishing, and magazine, newspaper, and book publishing industries were taking on an increasingly oligopolistic form.[34] For example, by 1930 the theatrical film industry was a "mature oligopoly" and was vertically integrated from production through exhibition. Cross-media ownership and media conglomeration also expanded at this time. For example, RCA established the Radio-Keith-Orpheum Corporation, a motion picture production-distribution-exhibition subsidiary, to promote its sound projection system. RCA was also involved in music recording, transcription services, and artist management, as well as manufacturing electronics. Thus, RCA-Victor recording artists could broadcast over NBC and have their performances transcribed for further distribution. Artists managed by NBC could record for Victor, perform on the NBC radio network, or appear in an RKO movie.[35]

A large-scale, concentrated consumer-goods industry requires increasingly larger markets. The pursuit of national markets through national advertising began to grow in the late nineteenth century as capitalism became increasingly monopolistic.[36] The advertiser-supported national broadcasting network was perfectly suited to the needs of a capitalist system dominated by oligopolies. Advertising helped producers establish market power and "force distribution," meaning that distributors of consumer goods were increasingly forced to purchase at wholesale on the basis of brand name rather than price;[37] it helped the big firms establish barriers to entry through high advertising expenditures; and it led to further concentration in many sectors of the economy, including the media. This process was exacerbated with the emergence and development of network television broadcasting in the 1940s and 1950s.[38]

McChesney argues that the advertiser-supported, national-network radio broadcasting system became economically consolidated by 1932 or 1933; was politically consolidated with the Communications Act of 1934, which established the FCC; and became ideologically consolidated shortly thereafter. He shows how network owners and executives actively worked to convince the U.S. public and politicians that the economic structure of radio broadcasting as it stood was the best one and any recalcitrant elements who thought differently were fools.[39] From the late 1930s on, the U.S. government and most of the public accepted the basic structure and operation of broadcasting as natural and inevitable, a system that required, on the part of the government, only a minimal amount of fine-tuning to curb excesses by individual broadcasters or the abuse of network power by NBC and CBS. With regard to the latter issue, opposition forces did leave somewhat of an imprint on government legislation and officials. This influence provided the seed that grew into a system of federal regulation of the networks that includes the FISRs.

The Regulation of Network Radio

Federal government action against network power grew out of the debates in the 1920s over the structure and performance of the broadcasting industry. As network power continued to increase throughout the 1930s, the critics of this oligopoly forced the FCC to investigate the structure and operation of the radio industry. The resulting *Report on Chain Broadcasting* found that in 1938, the National Broadcasting Company, with its two networks, the

Red and the Blue; the Columbia Broadcasting System; and a fourth national network, Mutual Broadcasting, Inc. (established in 1934 and largely controlled by the Chicago Tribune Company and R. H. Macy and Company), accounted for nearly half of the total time sales made by the entire broadcast industry ($46 million out of $101 million total).[40] Much of this revenue-earning power was achieved by pushing contracts on affiliates, which kept them on a tight rein while requiring them to grant the networks unconstrained access to their air-time. The authors of the report recognized the efficiencies involved in networking but wrote that this fact did not mean that "the prevailing practices of the networks and their outlets [were] sound in all respects, or that they should not be altered."[41]

Accordingly, to curb network abuses vis-à-vis their affiliates, the FCC issued the Chain Broadcasting Rules saying it would refuse to grant or renew licenses of stations that contracted with networks in a number of specified ways. Additionally, the FCC struck at NBC's ownership of two networks, which it found being used in anticompetitive ways, by ruling that a station may not be licensed to a network if another station in the broadcast area is already owned by that network. Nor would a station be licensed if it planned to link up with a company that controlled two networks simultaneously in the same listening area.

The networks appealed all the way to the Supreme Court, which in May 1943 upheld the authority of the FCC to regulate broadcasting in this manner, in *National Broadcasting Co. v. United States*.[42] In the decision, the Court further ratified the spectrum-scarcity rationale upon which the FCC was building its regulatory framework for broadcasting. Shortly after the Court upheld the FCC's Chain Broadcasting Rules, NBC put the much weaker Blue Network up for sale. Among the forty-two bidders for the network were Paramount Pictures, the Mellon family, Marshall Field, Dillon Read and Company, and American Type Founders.[43] David Sarnoff, head of RCA, held out for his initial price of $8 million and eventually sold the network to Edward J. Noble, owner of radio station WMCA (New York) and founder of the Life Savers Candy Company. The Blue Network was renamed the American Broadcasting Company in 1945. Noble used the network to advertise his candy and gum products, which he found much cheaper than advertising on CBS and NBC. Kellner concludes that "on the eve of the introduction of television in the 1940s, the three networks—which ultimately would dominate television and serve as the oligopolistic kingpins of broadcasting—thus controlled the commercial system then in place."[44]

The Regulation of Network Television

Broadcast economists cite the FCC's allocation of the television spectrum in its 1952 *Sixth Report and Order* [45] as the key to understanding the basis of network power in the television industry. For example, Owen, Beebe, and Manning call this the most significant event in the history of television regulation for it created "an artificial scarcity of VHF-TV licenses" that ultimately resulted in "a system of powerful vested interests." [46] Noll, Peck, and McGowan agree that "most criticisms of the television industry are traceable to [this] single fact": the scarcity of VHF-TV stations. [47] Besen, Krattenmaker, Metzger, and Woodbury say that, in effect, the FCC's allocation plan "virtually guaranteed that no more than three full-scale, nation-wide commercial networks could arise to serve conventional, over-the-air, advertiser-supported stations." [48] These economists prefer to shift attention from corporate capital to government regulators as the cause of network television concentration. They thereby obscure the role of the former in determining who got what in the FCC's allocation of television broadcast licenses. They also tend to ignore or understate the industry roots and orientation of many FCC officials, the role of industry-bred engineers who developed the allocation plan, and the generally superior resources of the industry in terms of personnel, money, and political influence. [49] They are quick to lay the blame on the government since one of their normative assumptions is: the less government interference the more efficient the operation of "free market" forces.

Rather than seeing government regulation as determining the structure of the television industry, as the economists do, the FCC spectrum allocation plan for television should be seen first as a response to established corporate interests, mainly RCA and CBS, and the earliest television station operators—mainly radio broadcasters, publishers, electronics firms, and motion picture companies. [50] Instead of opening up television broadcasting to new competitors, the FCC ratified the dominance of existing firms. Thus, in preserving the 108 pioneer television stations operating in the VHF band, the FCC followed the policy preferred by RCA, which had the most advanced stake in the status quo in terms of receiver sales and broadcast operations. At the same time, responding to the interests of CBS, the FCC opened up the UHF band hoping that, with the adoption of a color broadcasting system (CBS being the most advanced here), all television broadcasters would eventually graduate up to UHF. However, the commission underestimated the intransigence of established VHF broadcasters and overestimated the viability of UHF.

The FCC's allocation plan did indeed mean that only two strong national networks had a chance of starting up right away, since the majority of the nation's communities were assigned only two VHF stations (the rest being UHF). NBC already controlled the VHF stations in the largest markets, and CBS, realizing that it was not going to win *this* "format war," moved quickly to expand its VHF holdings. ABC and the Dumont Television Network lagged far behind. The ABC television network remained a distant third until the 1970s, even after an infusion of $30 million as a result of a merger with United Paramount Theatres in 1952. The Dumont Network did not last past 1955. Resembling the dual economic structure of many other sectors of the economy, television broadcasting was divided into the "haves" (the networks, their owned and operated VHF stations, and their VHF affiliates) and the "have nots" (independent broadcasters operating mainly on UHF signals).

As if it were anticipating this extension of established network power into the new medium, the FCC made the Chain Broadcasting Rules applicable to television networks in 1943. The rules did little to check the growing power of the networks, especially NBC and CBS, and with ABC lagging behind, Dumont folding, and UHF floundering, Congress authorized a second inquiry into network structures and operations. The resulting "Barrow Report," issued in 1958, examined "the structure, operations, and practices of the networks in their relationships with other components of the industry."[51] However, the report did not address the issue of program production and procurement, thus the commission initiated another investigatory study in 1959, which generated reports in 1960, 1963, and 1965.[52] The reports ultimately led to the proposal[53] and promulgation of the FISRs in 1970.[54]

The studies of network program production and acquisition practices revealed that the three networks—usually as a *quid pro quo* for initial financing and eventual broadcasting of a program or series—would require program producers to give them a share of the profits (often 50%) earned by a program or series from its network runs; the right to distribute the program in domestic and foreign markets; the right to share in the profits from domestic and foreign syndication sales; the exploitation right and a share of profits from merchandising; and the right to share in other nonbroadcast interests (e.g., motion pictures, books, magazine stories and articles, phonograph records, and plays derived from the programs or series).[55] The studies also found that with financial control came stultifying creative control, with network insistence on regular series formats and program formulas. In the FCC's 1965 *Notice of Proposed Rulemaking,* in which the FISRs were first proposed, the commission found that the results of network program practices had been to concentrate ownership of program rights and creative control in the hands of the networks to the detriment of independent producers.[56]

To address this growing centralization of prime-time programming in the hands of the networks, the FCC proposed to restrict the networks' involvement in domestic and foreign syndication and to limit the amount of programming in which it had direct financial interest to 50% of prime time or a total of fourteen hours a week, whichever was greater.[57] The FCC hoped that the rules would strengthen independent program production and generate new sources of first-run syndicated programming, which might in turn strengthen UHF operations and facilitate the rise of a fourth network.[58]

For five years after the FCC proposed rules on network program practices, the networks, group broadcast operators, the Hollywood majors and independents, and others debated and argued over the form and content of the FISRs and Prime Time Access Rule (PTAR).[59] In the meantime, the FCC commissioned further research on levels of concentration in prime-time program production, which confirmed that the degree of network control of their evening schedules had been steadily increasing, substantially so since the 1965 proposal.[60] The record showed that networks were taking over more and more of their affiliates' prime time; that increased network control over prime time had provided increased leverage over program producers for obtaining ancillary rights; that there seemed to be a high correlation between giving up those rights and getting into a network prime-time schedule; and that the amount of independently produced and packaged prime-time network programming had declined sharply between 1957 and 1968 (from 32.8% to 3.3%).[61] The FCC was shown that programming commissioned by advertisers, the dominant form of production financing in radio broadcasting and early television, had virtually disappeared by the late 1960s.

After reviewing this record the FCC's majority concluded, "The public interest requires limitation on network control and an increase in the opportunity for development of truly independent sources of prime time programming."[62] With this goal in mind the FCC adopted the Financial Interest and Syndication Rules and the Prime Time Access Rule. The Financial Interest Rule prohibited the networks from acquiring any financial interest in programs, or in their distribution, that were independently produced, other than the network exhibition right itself. The Syndication Rule prohibited the networks from syndicating television programs to domestic television stations for off-network exhibition; distributing programs in foreign markets of which the network was not the sole producer; or participating in profit-sharing arrangements involving these activities. The Prime Time Access Rule limited the networks to scheduling no more than three hours of prime-time programming in the top fifty markets during the four hours of prime time each night.

FCC Chairman Dean Burch's dissent to the rules explained why he thought the FCC had moved ahead with their adoption: simply because they were there.[63] He figured that the rules at best would "shift some dollars from one pocket to another" or at worst could "very well harm the networks."[64] Burch's "nonexplanation" sounds very much like the one given by Besen et al., who can find "no satisfactory explanation, at least one based on public choice principles, of the preference for the interests of producers over those of the networks."[65]

While Burch was correct in predicting that the rules would shift some dollars from the pockets of the networks to those of producers and thereby shift television program production largely into the hands of the Hollywood majors and a few large independents, this obviously was not the intent of the FCC majority. The economists lack an explanation here because they lack political theory; their conclusions are based solely on their decontextualized economic modeling. By taking *politics* into account, the actions of the FCC majority *can* be explained. The class struggle perspective provides a strong explanation for why the rules were promulgated. They came in the midst of broad social and political activism that questioned and challenged the structure and operation of many major social institutions, including the mass media. It seems that the recent upholding of the Fairness Doctrine by the Supreme Court in *Red Lion v. Federal Communications Commission,* a decision that in many ways signals the peak moment of FCC reform of the broadcast media, clearly had emboldened the FCC majority, for they cite it a number of times.[66] For the FCC, the FISRs and the PTAR represented yet another means for shaking up the dominant vested interests in television, that is, the networks, and demonstrating some "autonomy" from such interests. Sterling argues that the FCC's efforts to limit network control of prime time can be traced back to the quiz show scandals and the building pressure on the FCC and the Congress to "clean up" television.[67]

A logic of capital explanation also serves to interpret the FCC's adoption of the FISRs. The FCC's majority cast the issue in terms of intraclass conflict: big capital, represented by the networks and their affiliates, versus small capital— the minor independent producers and the UHF operators. The FCC's majority cited the testimony of the latter throughout the 1970 *Report and Order,* as well as in a follow-up *Memorandum Opinion and Order* issued three months later, in which it reconsidered and then retained the rules.[68] Even the big capital represented by the Hollywood majors, who played an active role in promoting the FISRs, gets the big capital–small capital spin. This is found in a section of the *Report and Order* where the FCC majority cites evidence demonstrating that the majors were no more able to resist the leveraging of rights by the networks than were the small independents.[69] The inherent logic of capital toward concentration forced the government to step into this case of market failure and attempt to restore a greater degree of monopolistic competition.

Government action also served the larger interests of capital as a whole. The FISRs can be contextualized within the larger effort by big business, both large producers and users of information and information technology, to develop and promote a significant expansion and restructuring of the nation's communications industries.[70] Corporations inside and outside of the communications sector began challenging the established dominant powers in the telecommunications and electronic media areas—the three networks and AT&T—both in the marketplace and in the structure of state agencies and regulations. Serving as the "ideal collective capitalist," state officials involved with telecommunications policy began to impose constraints upon the market power of various oligopolistic or monopolistic sectors, such as network broadcasting and telephone communications. They also began to act to permit and facilitate the entry of new competitors developing new technologies, such as cable TV and satellites. This restructuring offered domestic and multinational corporations the opportunity to exploit new information and communications markets. It also hastened the development of an increasingly sophisticated global telecommunications infrastructure designed to serve transnational corporations in a post-Fordist international economic system.

The power-structure explanation underscores the interaction of industry and state officials within the policy-making and implementation processes, although only a brief outline of such an interpretation is possible here. The record of government hearings makes it clear that the Hollywood majors, independent program producers, and the broadcast groups played a significant role in the special-interest process as they lobbied Congress and the FCC for implementation of the FISRs and the PTAR. Donald M. McGannon, president and chair of the Westinghouse Broadcasting Company, led the campaign for broadcasters who sought greater autonomy from network control.[71] Indeed, Group W made the proposal to limit the amount of network broadcasting during prime time that later became the PTAR. As a program producer, Westinghouse had interests that also converged with those of other independents, and it later capitalized on the PTAR by producing first-run syndication shows for network affiliates seeking to program their new hour of prime time.

Lew Wasserman, head of MCA/Universal, led the major studios' campaign for the FISRs throughout the late 1960s.[72] Hollywood's clout extended beyond the special-interest process and into the candidate-selection process since Hollywood producers and stars have always been an important source of economic and cultural capital for politicians. Wasserman himself was very active in Democratic party politics and, during this period, recruited Jack Valenti, Lyndon Johnson's special assistant and confidant, to head the Motion Picture Association of America (MPAA).[73] Valenti has been successful in guaranteeing that Hollywood receives preferential treatment in Washington and has become one of the most powerful and well-paid lobbyists operating in the halls of the federal government.

The candidate-selection process also bears on this case as a result of the role of local broadcasters in U.S. election campaigns. Politicians facing election are wise to serve their local broadcasters well. Thus members of Congress involved in broadcast policy-making, through FCC oversight or law-making, would be inclined to favor the interests of this important constituency. The interests of elected Washington officials to serve local broadcasters converged with the Nixon administration's desire to punish the networks for what it perceived as negative news coverage and public affairs programming. Nixon's Justice Department filed the antitrust suit against the networks in 1972, which the government and the networks later settled by consent decree. The suit is seen by some as a blatantly political move especially since the consent decrees were basically redundant of the FCC's rules.[74]

If promulgation of the FISRs can be cast within the context of media-reform efforts, the attempts of the networks and the Reagan-appointed FCC to repeal the FISRs in the early 1980s can be seen as one more try by big business, as part of a broader deregulatory activity, to reverse the gains made in the 1960s and early 1970s by various activist forces within the state apparatus.

The Networks and the Effort to Repeal the FISRs

In his autobiography, Leonard Goldenson, chair of ABC, says that "from the moment it became clear that Reagan's FCC was intent on deregulation, all three networks began to push for rescission of the Financial Interest and Syndication Rules."[75] ABC's general counsel, Everett H. Erlick, among others, suggested to FCC chair Mark Fowler that the proceedings be reopened since competition from cable and independent stations had changed the marketplace. In Erlick's view, the networks remained "shackled with rules written for conditions, if they ever existed, that [were] twenty years old."[76] The networks claimed that they were at a competitive disadvantage against the new media, particularly pay-cable services such as Home Box Office (HBO) and Cinemax, because they could not syndicate or have financial interest in television programming, while their competitors could. The unfair-competitive-advantage argument was working for the networks with regard to other policy issues and they assumed it would work in helping to win repeal of the FISRs. The networks had gained, or were in the processing of gaining, loosened restrictions on ownership concentration (the number of stations a company could own and cross-ownership rules); relaxed ascertainment procedures; suspension of the Fairness Doctrine; reduced FCC supervision of children's programming; extended license terms; and eased renewal procedures, which aimed at limiting costly challenges to broadcast licenses. On all of these issues the networks were seeking to reverse the gains made through the earlier period of the "popular" struggles of the media reform movement.

The networks' efforts were part of a larger political attack led by big business against reformist legislation and regulation, an assault that had already begun in the early 1970s.[77] Rowland places the beginning of the communications deregulation trend at roughly this time also.[78] Horowitz argues that "more than any other factor, it was the growth of regulation which prompted the business political counterattack."[79] Much of the mass media deregulatory effort was targeted precisely at the policy reform movement, representing women, children, blacks, Latinos, and other "minority" interests, which had successfully increased media accessibility through legislation, regulation, and adjudication. But given the reassertion of corporate power in the form of a "hegemonic project" to reverse such access, and the simultaneous decline of political and social activism,[80] the policy gains made by the media reform movement were an easy target; they had been only an "illusion of fulfillment."[81] However, when it came to the FISRs the networks ran up against a more formidable foe, the Hollywood production community, which was able temporarily to derail the networks' deregulatory train.

Thus the networks' "hegemonic project" was to gain the revocation of a number of legislative and regulatory constraints, including the FISRs, that they claimed prevented them from competing with emerging cable and video media on equal terms. Network executives located a source among the policy-planning and discussion groups that could be used for advancing and justifying this deregulatory effort; that source was in the work of many of the economists previously cited in this text. Among the earliest inquiries into the economics of broadcast regulation are the Rand study of broadcast economics and regulation by Besen and Mitchell (1973) and the Brookings Institution publication by Noll et al. (1973), which began questioning the economic logic of the FCC's regulatory practices.[82] Besen, by 1983 the senior economist at Rand, was recruited by the FCC, along with Thomas K. Krattenmaker, a professor at the Georgetown Law Center, to codirect a $2 million study authorized by Congress in 1977, to examine whether the networks were engaging in anticompetitive behavior. Westinghouse Broadcasting prompted the study with its petition to the FCC in 1976 calling on it to investigate the production and programming practices of the three networks.

Although the networks initially opposed the study, its findings provided them with the ammunition they needed to launch an attack on the FISRs. Among the findings of the FCC's Network Inquiry Special Staff's (hereafter NISS) report, was that the FCC's FISRs were based on two "dubious" premises: that "regulation of networks imposes insignificant costs on the television system or viewers; and that the public interest is synonymous with the interests of affiliates or program suppliers."[83] The NISS sought to demonstrate in its report and several background studies[84] that the rules were harmful because they prevented the networks from engaging in "efficient risk-sharing" in program production. The rules denied the networks of the sometimes significant profits generated by a successful prime-time series in syndication and other ancillary markets. The result was that program producers had to take on a greater risk of failure in program production or were forced to go elsewhere to find someone with whom to share the risk. There was evidence, in the increased concentration of prime-time program production in the hands of the Hollywood majors, that the small independent producers had ended up doing the latter.

Another "inefficiency" was produced by diminished network investment in program production. The networks invested only as much in programming as could be profitably earned back from network exhibition. The result had been to force program producers into "deficit financing," wherein the cost of producing the program exceeded the price paid by the networks for the network runs. For example, MTM Productions claimed it paid $865,000 to produce each episode of "Hill Street Blues" for the 1982–83 season but received only $800,000 for two network runs, leaving it with a $65,000 deficit per episode.[85] The NISS said this deficit reflects inefficient risk-sharing; that if the networks could participate in ownership and ancillary rights they could pay more up front and producers would not have to engage in deficit financing.

Additionally, the NISS saw the FISRs as "doubtful solutions" to what were fundamentally structural problems rooted in the number of available outlets for prime-time television programming, that is, a consequence of the "scarcity" produced by the FCC's television spectrum allocation plan. The NISS recommended that instead of the FISRs and similar policies, the FCC should engage in accelerated elimination of barriers to entry for new television delivery systems that could serve as the foundation for new networks.[86] The findings of the NISS became the basis upon which the FCC, responding to the urging of the networks, built its *Notice of Proposed Rulemaking* released in June 1982, which announced the FCC's reconsideration of the FISRs and possible amendment or repeal thereof.[87]

This announcement triggered an intense amount of activity by industry officials and lobbyists; media workers, including journalists; media activists; and government officials. Most of the effort was aimed at opinion formation inside and outside of the state. The networks immediately took the case to their affiliates via closed-circuit television. The terms of their argument were set out in one such address by Robert E. Mulholland, president and CEO of NBC, which was reprinted for broader consumption in *Television/Radio Age* in October 1982.[88] Mulholland stressed the competitive disadvantage the networks faced vis-à-vis pay cable services; that these services had begun to be competitive bidders for prime-time programming; and that the concentration of program production in the hands of the Hollywood majors had increased. The affiliates, fearing that the networks might be inclined to begin cutting back on program expenditures in an increasingly competitive environment, fell in line with the networks.

The Committee for Prudent Deregulation, organized by and comprised of syndicators, producers, and independent stations, led the forces against rescission of the FISRs.[89] The committee's position, also presented early in the conflict in *Television/Radio Age,* was that repeal would harm independent television stations.[90] The opponents of repeal predicted that the networks would favor their owned-and-operated stations and their respective affiliates in the syndication market by making sure they got the best off-network programming, instead of competing independent stations. They also predicted that the networks would "warehouse" successful prime-time series by withholding them from the syndication market until they were long into their network run or until the network run was completed, instead of releasing them for syndication while they were at the peak of their popularity.

The independent stations had begun to make significant inroads into the network's share of prime-time. The total number of independent stations went from 73 in 38 markets in 1972 to 165 in 78 markets in 1982,[91] while their prime-time audience share went from an estimated 5% in 1972 to 16% by 1982.[92] Meanwhile, the networks' share of the prime-time audience had fallen from

90% in 1972 to 70% by 1982.[93] The members of the Association of Independent Television Stations, Inc. (INTV), "universally" agreed "that the unfettered availability of the most popular, most current off-network syndicated programs" had been the key to their success.[94] Such shows were scheduled during the "fringe day-part" (pre-primetime) hours—4 P.M. to 8 P.M.—and had become a popular alternative to the news and information programs run by the networks during this period.

The threat to independent stations brought advertisers into the debate on the side of the opponents of repeal. The Association of National Advertisers voted for retention of the FISRs based on in-house research demonstrating that advertising rates were 20% to 60% lower in markets with competitive independent broadcasters.[95] The American Association of Advertising Agencies (AAAA) supported holding off on repeal for a few more years until the new technologies, such as cable, videocassettes, low-power television, direct satellite broadcasting, and others were more developed.[96]

Finally, once again the issue was cast by opponents of repeal as a matter of "*life* or *death* for the small producer and/or distributor."[97] Norman Lear of Embassy Communications and Tandem Productions ("All in the Family," "Maude," "The Jeffersons"), Mel Blumenthal, executive vice-president of MTM Productions ("Mary Tyler Moore," "Hill Street Blues," "St. Elsewhere"), and Leonard Hill, partner in Hill/Madelker Films (producers of TV movies and mini-series), led the campaign by the independent producers. The large independent companies, such as Embassy/Tandem and MTM, were primarily concerned about losing the big payoffs that come with the sale of hit TV shows in the syndication market. They claimed that this income was essential for recovering the deficits accrued over the course of a network run and that the possibly big payoff in syndication served as a major incentive to enter and remain in the business.[98] The independents also argued that the rules preserved a certain amount of creative autonomy from the networks. The independents, knowing they had a chance of recovering any deficits in the syndication market, often would spend more in production than the networks were willing to pay.[99] At the very least, separating control of distribution from production was a good idea per se, since the networks were interested only in the largest possible audience with the right demographics, while the producer had interests beyond network exhibition and therefore tended to be more experimental than the networks.[100]

Media-reform and other activist groups generally came down on the side of retention. Many of them joined the Committee Against Network Monopoly, made up of thirty-seven organizations including representatives from consumer, religious, labor, minority, elderly, and other significant public interest groups. Repeating pretty much the same arguments as the production community and independent broadcasters, the committee argued that "network dominance persists in the video marketplace" and that the rules, while only a "palliative" and not a "cure" for this domination, had served the public interests "by allowing greater creative and financial independence to the creative community by reducing the three major networks' control over what [U.S.] Americans may view."[101] The networks were charged with failing to "serve special audiences," consequently the rules, which provided some space for competitors, were the best bet for "opportunities for greater diversity."[102]

Taking a compromise position, the Storer Broadcasting Company and Capital Cities Communications urged repeal of the financial interest rule but retention of some type of restrictions on network syndication to guard against "warehousing."[103] This compromise position recognized the long-term interests of the networks in deregulation but sought to keep some restrictions on them until the new media were established. This position could be seen as the one favored by the hegemonic fraction of capital as a whole. It is close to the stand taken by advertisers, particularly the AAAA, who were primarily interested in television as a marketing medium and thus the national networks' well-being in the long term. In fact, the final outcome of the repeal effort in 1983 was precisely what the AAAA had recommended. How this occurred is quite fascinating and reveals much about the day-to-day workings of the U.S. government, but it is too much to recount in any detail here. However, the highlights include the development of a split at the FCC between Fowler and other commissioners as the latter stepped back from total repeal to the compromise position put forward by Storer and Capital Cities. The Department of Justice, which would have had to revisit the consent decrees that had incorporated the FISRs, also initially took this position until instructed to withdraw it by President Reagan late in the year.

Congress joined the fray at the behest of the Motion Picture Association of America. A group of Congress members from California, along with Timothy Wirth (D–Colo.), the influential chair of the House's Subcommittee on Telecommunications, introduced and heard testimony on bills that would have deprived the FCC of authorization to repeal the rules for five years. The FCC and the Congress were headed on a collision course in the late summer and early fall of 1983, after the former had issued its tentative compromise decision in August[104] and moved toward adopting it and the latter moved toward imposing a moratorium on this action.

In October, it became apparent that Reagan was following the conflict with strong interest, having discussed it with Fowler and his cabinet on at least two occasions. In early November Reagan intervened on behalf of his old friends in Hollywood, mainly Lew Wasserman, who had helped launch Reagan's political career, and called for a legislated two-year moratorium on FCC action in this matter.[105] Shortly thereafter, Fowler took the initiative out of the hands of Congress and imposed a six-month moratorium on the proceedings. The FCC, knowing Reagan's views on the matter, left it on the shelf through the remainder of his presidency.

Reagan's intervention makes the power-structure analysis seem like the strongest explanation for the retention of the rules in the early 1980s. This outcome also seems to defy the logic of capital guiding the deregulatory movement. However, the class struggle and logic of capital explanations can be harmonized with the apparently contingent outcome precipitated by the Reagan-Wasserman connection. While the larger interest of capital lay in the deregulation of the economy, in this particular instance continued regulation was required since network hegemony over the prime-time television market remained largely intact even after the rules had been in place for over a decade. For this reason advertisers and major group broadcasters sought continuation of some version of the rules until emerging video services and technologies were more firmly established and competitive with the networks. These efforts converged with those of the media reform movement and permitted opponents of repeal to cast the issue in terms of media diversity and the national interest, something the networks were unable to do in promoting repeal.

The Repeal of the FISRs

Four key developments required the FCC to reconsider and revise the rules in 1991. First came the rise of a new television network, the Fox Broadcasting Company, and its petition in January 1990 to be exempted from the rules. Then, in November, came the expiration of certain restrictions on the networks imposed by the consent decrees, particularly the limits on the number of hours of prime-time programming that could be produced by the networks in-house. Third, by the end of 1990, four of the major Hollywood filmed-entertainment companies—Twentieth Century–Fox, Columbia, MCA/Universal and MGM/United Artists—had passed into the hands of transnational corporations based outside of the United States (News Corporation,

Sony, Matsushita, and Pathé, respectively). The extent to which the rules were shifting money "from one pocket to another" now became an issue of protecting the interests of national capital versus international capital. Additionally, the rules basically prohibited the merger of the remaining U.S.-based filmed-entertainment producers with any of the three networks, thereby blocking the emergence of a potentially more powerful, vertically integrated entertainment conglomerate that could compete in the international marketplace.

Finally, by 1990 the three networks' share of the prime-time audience had dipped to 65%, down from 95% when the rules were first promulgated in 1970, while the independent share rose to 19%.[106] In 1991, the FCC found that the networks monopsonistic power had pretty much dissipated; each network purchased only 16% of prime-time entertainment programming and garnered only 22% of the audiences viewing such programming.[107] At the same time the trend toward concentration in the program supply and program syndication markets had markedly increased with the large studios providing the networks with over 70% of their programming in 1990, as opposed to just 39% in 1970.[108] At the same time, Fox, Paramount, MCA, and Disney had moved significantly into broadcasting themselves, by buying up independent television stations.

The claims by the networks that the FISRs jeopardized their continuing investment in high-priced programming, and thus the future quality of "free broadcast television," was a clear threat to state officials of a possible "investment strike." The networks were also better able this time around to cast their particular interest in repeal of the FISRs as being in the national interest. Along these lines, NBC submitted a statement to the FCC in November 1990 arguing that the "declining competitive position" of the networks threatened "their continued ability to provide the levels of news, sports, and entertainment programs that the public now takes for granted."[109] Once again the various agencies and cabinet departments of the federal government dealing with communications came down on the side of significant revision (Department of Commerce and National Telecommunications and Information Agency) or repeal (Department of Justice and the staff of the Federal Trade Commission) of the rules. When President Bush's Council of Economic Advisors recommended repeal, it became clear in which direction that administration was leaning.[110]

A FCC majority, once again voting against its chair, rejected outright repeal of the rules and proposed a compromise that significantly relaxed the rules.[111] The June 1991 compromise was widely treated in the press as a disappointment for the networks.[112] However, a close reading of the compromise position reveals that the FCC permitted the networks to enter into several new lines of business from which they had previously been barred. Of vital importance is their nearly total freedom in the international program production and distribution marketplace. This provision was a response to the request of House Energy and Commerce Committee Chairman John Dingell, who repeatedly raised the issue of U.S. competitiveness and had threatened to intervene in the FCC proceedings unless this were taken into account.[113]

Although the FCC's April 1991 decision did relax the FISRs, it still contradicted the deeper logic of capital that necessitated a total deregulation of the prime-time program marketplace in order for the networks to be competitive within a post-Fordist regime of accumulation. The U.S. Court of Appeals for the Seventh Circuit, in Chicago, ratified this logic in November 1992, when it found the FCC's revisions of the FISRs "arbitrary and capricious," in *Schurz Communications v. FCC.*[114] The court demanded that the FCC provide better justification for the revised rules or come up with a new set of rules that would meet its approval. The court expressed concern that the FCC had not shown how the rules had enhanced the diversity of the television program marketplace nor had it refuted the networks' argument that they were in fact having the opposite effect. Writing on behalf of the three-judge panel, Judge Richard Posner, who in 1977 had testified as an expert witness on behalf of CBS in the DOJ's antitrust suit against the networks, argued that the FCC's treatment of the Fox network in revised rules was contradictory with their intent to enhance competition with the three major networks. In the revision, a network became subject to the rules once it reached fifteen hours a week of prime-time programming, which the Fox network was soon to reach. Once it did, the company would be forced to either spin off its production arm or severely curtail its output. Judge Posner also believed that the FCC had not successfully refuted the networks' argument, built on the NISS study, that the rules inhibited efficient risk sharing between themselves and program producers, and therefore limited market entry by independents. The court gave the FCC 120 days to return with a better case or new rules.

In April 1993, in a decision seen as favoring the networks, the FCC voted to lift most of the restrictions imposed by the FISRs.[115] The FCC permitted the networks to once again take a stake in programs they broadcast that are produced out-of-house; to take a share of the rerun sales when the programs are syndicated; and to produce and own as much of their prime-time schedule as they wish. The FCC continued to bar the networks from the domestic syndication market for two years. This requires the networks to use an outside company to syndicate programming produced both in-house and by outsiders and also prevents them from entering the first-run syndication business. The Fox network was exempted from the rules but not from the reporting requirements imposed on all networks to monitor their program production and distribution practices. The FCC declared it would revisit the remaining rules two years after the scheduled expiration of the consent decrees in November 1993. Hence, if no compelling case could be made for their retention, the FCC regulations would be allowed to expire in November 1995.

The networks took immediate advantage of the relaxed rules to reorganize their prime-time program production and distribution practices, particularly ABC. First, the company agreed with Wind Dancer Productions to continue the run of its prime-time series "Home Improvement" for three years in exchange for co-ownership of the producer's next two series.[116] Then it made last-minute changes in its fall 1993 prime-time schedule to add two programs from ABC Productions, the network's in-house production unit.[117] All three networks increased their output of prime-time television news magazine programming produced in house.[118] In November 1994, ABC announced a joint venture with Dreamworks SKG, the production studio formed by Steven Spielberg, David Geffen, and Jeffrey Katzenberg, to coproduce prime-time programming and share income from advertising, foreign sales, and domestic syndication.[119] Ironically, the alliance disclosed that its first joint production would be made for CBS.[120] CBS Entertainment Productions, in turn, sold network rights to its in-house production "Caroline in the City" to NBC, sacrificing potential losses in ratings in anticipation of profits from syndication.[121]

The major Hollywood studios responded to this changing market structure. Fox continued to expand its prime-time schedule and began to wage war on the big-three networks by signing away their affiliates. Paramount joined forces with Chris Craft Industries in late 1993 to launch a fifth broadcast network called United Paramount Network (UPN), with the four independent stations owned by Paramount and the six independents owned by Chris Craft serving as the network's core. Paramount's "Star Trek" spinoff, "Voyager," served as the bait to lure independent broadcasters into affiliation. A week after the UPN announcement, Time Warner and the Tribune Company launched yet another network, the WB Network (WBN), to be built around the Tribune Company's seven independent stations. Paramount and Time Warner formed these networks based on the assumption that network identity will be essential for attracting viewers in the emerging multimedia marketplace. The costs of launching these networks are high; in 1995 UPN and WBN lost $129 million and $66 million, respectively.[122]

After hearing arguments for and against the rules in the summer of 1995, the FCC decided to let them expire.[123] Repeal of the FISRs cleared the way for further consolidation of the media industry. On 31 July 1995, Disney announced that it would acquire Capital Cities/ABC for $19 billion in cash and stock. The deal was the first to link a major studio to one of the major networks and resulted directly from repeal of the FISRs. A day later, Westinghouse agreed to acquire CBS for $5.4 billion in cash. This deal brought together two long-time foes in the struggle over prime-time network regulations. The merger made Westinghouse the largest broadcaster in the United States with fifteen television stations reaching 33 percent of U.S. households. Disney/Capital Cities status as the world's largest entertainment conglomerate lasted only a month when, in late August 1995, Time Warner offered to acquire the 82% of Turner Broadcasting that it did not already own in a stock swap. Though this deal was not directly prompted by expiration of the FISRs, it produced further concentration of control over the media industry. More merger activity in the communications sector can be expected as a result of the Telecommunications Act of 1996, which lifted many of the barriers preventing the convergence of the media, computer, and telephone industries. The act can be seen as the capstone to the communications sector's hegemonic project to scale back state intervention into their markets.

Conclusion

The theoretical framework developed at the outset of this chapter will now be used to explain how the networks gained repeal of the FISRs. Turning to the first area of theoretical concern—who owns? and who rules?—the case study demonstrates the central role of the capitalist class, rather than the public or government officials, in shaping and controlling the mass media and the use of the state by this class to promote its general as well as particular interests. For example, Reagan's intervention on behalf of the his friends in Hollywood in 1983 can be seen as the workings of an interlocking network of the power elite. The intervention of the Bush administration on behalf of the networks can also be seen in this light. Schechter suggests that the networks stood strongly behind Bush during the Gulf war, and Kellner argues that the networks were soft on Bush even before that, by refusing to air a series of controversial and revealing stories about Bush the candidate, because they were seeking rescission of the FISRs and needed his help.[124] Such findings lead us to recognize the individual subjective positions and backgrounds of those who govern, for this *can* be determining in policy outcomes, though in both cases the intervention conformed to the long-term interests of capital as a whole.

The determination of media and state structures and processes by the logic of capital, the second area of theoretical concern, is also revealed in this case study. For example, the networks' effort to gain repeal of the FISRs, beginning in the early 1980s, can be seen as part of a larger hegemonic project of the dominant fraction of capital, in the guise of "deregulation," to move from the rigidity of Fordism and Keynesianism, which no longer could contain the inherent contradictions of capitalism, to a system of "flexible accumulation." This new accumulation strategy is based on small-batch production, "just-in-time" delivery of producer goods, and the general mobility of productive capital on a global scale. The significant decrease in the number of episodes of a series ordered by the networks each season, from over thirty to as few as five or six, is an example of "just-in-time" and small-batch production strategies. Repeal of the rules in 1995 gave the networks greater flexibility in procuring, financing, and producing prime-time programming at the same time the industry become more concentrated.

Additionally, after many continuous years of super profits, the networks began to see their profits level off somewhat.[125] Unable to count on guaranteed audiences, and facing rising labor costs, stagnating profits, and increasing competition from new media, the networks sought to restructure their business practices and enter new markets. They were particularly interested in international syndication and coproduction, however, the FISRs restricted them from entering these markets. Thus the networks were regarded by foreign broadcasters and producers "as the most *rigid* potential partners to work with."[126] In this case, the networks' hegemonic project to gain repeal of the FISRs and other regulations that restricted their business activities converged with the emergent accumulation strategy of the hegemonic fraction of capital based on flexibility and internationalization. Acting as "ideal collective capitalist," the state permitted the networks to enter into the international marketplace unfettered under the new FISRs adopted by the FCC in 1991.

The case study also bears on the third area of theoretical focus, that which takes the media and the state as a site of class, race, and gender struggles. For example, we saw that the FISRs were adopted in an era of broad social activism, including the media reform movement, and that the beginning of repeal efforts came in the midst of big business's move toward deregulation. The case of the FISRs is bound up with intraclass conflict as well. Here the state responded to the interests of one fraction of monopoly capital, the major Hollywood producers and their small-capital allies, independent producers, as network monopsony began to threaten the monopoly profits of the former and the very existence of the latter. The formal requirements on the state, particularly the FCC, to promote a diversity of program sources and broadcast media outlets, gave Hollywood and its allies the ability to promote their particular interests as the general interests of the nation as a whole. But given the domination of the state by capital, a viable public television program production system never emerged as an alternative, notwithstanding the establishment of the Corporation for Public Broadcasting at this time. The networks, in turn, were able to reverse the state's position, through articulation of a hegemonic project that stressed the viability of "free" broadcast television.[127] In this regard, they argued that restrictions on their business activities would lead them to abandon many areas and types of programming that the U.S. public had come to expect. That the networks were concerned with more than just their national audience share is clear from the arguments they made based on global competitiveness. These became especially potent as the Hollywood majors increasingly came under the control of foreign capital. We see here the state as a site of class struggle but also the workings of the bias of state structures toward the interests of fragments of national capital as well as capital as a whole.

Accordingly, this case study demonstrates that political-economic media theory and neo-Marxist and radical theories of the capitalist state can be useful tools for guiding investigations into institutional and industrial conflict, as well as providing explanations for what is discovered. These tools and the knowledge they generate give us the understanding we need to critique current media and state structures and practices, so that we may begin to move toward ones that are more democratic and participatory.

Notes

1. M. Cantor and J. Cantor define *prime-time television* as including: "programs produced in Hollywood and elsewhere for distribution to both U.S. and international audiences. These programs consist of series, serials, specials, movies made for television, and mini-series." *Prime-time Television* (Newbury Park, Calif.: Sage, 1992), 2.

2. D. Kneale and M. L. Carnevale, "In TV Rerun Ruling, Hollywood Interests Prove Special Indeed," *Wall Street Journal*, 10 April 1991, A1.

3. Douglas Kellner, *Television and the Crisis of Democracy* (Boulder: Westview, 1990), 7–8.

4. *Financial Interest and Syndication Rules,* 47 C.F.R. Ch. 1, Section 73.658(j)(1)(i) and Section 73.658(j)(1)(ii) (1990).

5. Cantor and Cantor, 45.

6. Federal Communications Commission, *Competition and Responsibility in Network Television Broadcasting: Report and Order,* 23 FCC 2d 384 (1970).

7. *United States v. National Broadcasting Co.,* 449 F. Supp. 1127 (C.D. Cal.), *aff'd mem.,* No. 79-3381 (9th Cir. 12 Apr. 1978) *cert. denied, sub nom.; CBS v. U.S. District Court,* 48 U.S.L.W. 3186 (1979); *United States v. CBS, Inc.,* Civ. No. 74-3599-RJK (C.D. Cal. 31 July 1980), *reprinted in* 45 Fed. Reg. 34,463 (1980); *United States v. ABC, Inc.,* Civ. No. 74-3600-RJK (C.D. Cal. 15 November 1980), *reprinted in* 45 Fed. Reg. 58,441 (1980).

8. See Ronald V. Bettig, "Critical Perspectives on the History and Philosophy of Copyright," *Critical Studies in Mass Communication* 9, no. 2 (1992), 131–55, and "The Enclosure of Cyberspace," ibid. 14, no. 2 (1997), 138–57.

9. David Harvey, *The Condition of Postmodernity* (Oxford: Basil Blackwell, 1989), 344.

10. Notable works include Herbert Schiller, *Culture Inc.* (New York: Oxford University Press, 1990); Janet Wasko, *Hollywood in the Information Age* (Austin: University of Texas Press, 1994); and Ben Bagdikian, *The Media Monopoly,* 5th ed. (Boston: Beacon, 1997).

11. Denis McQuail, *Mass Communication Theory,* 3d ed. (Thousand Oaks, Calif.: Sage, 1994), 82.

12. Martin Carnoy, *The State and Political Theory* (Princeton: Princeton University Press, 1984), 210.

13. Ralph Miliband, *The State in Capitalist Society* (New York: Basic Books, 1969); G. William Domhoff, *Who Rules America Now?* (Englewood Cliffs, N.J.: Prentice-Hall, 1983), and *The Power Elite and the State* (New York: Aldine de Gruyter, 1990).

14. For an excellent study of the distribution of wealth in the United States, see U.S. Congress, Joint Economic Committee, *The Concentration of Wealth in the United States* (Washington, D.C.: U.S. Government Printing Office, 1986).

15. Bob Jessop uses the term "state derivationist theory" to describe this set of approaches to the study of the state in *The Capitalist State* (New York: New York University Press, 1982).

16. Goran Therborn, *What Does the Ruling Class Do When It Rules?* (London: Verso, 1980), 89.

17. Ibid., 131.

18. Jessop, *State Theory,* 37, and idem, *State Theory: Putting the Capitalist State in Its Place* (University Park, Pa.: Pennsylvania State University Press, 1990).

19. Jessop terms this set of approaches the "class theoretical position."

20. Jessop, *State Theory,* 10.

21. Vincent Mosco, *The Pay-per Society: Computers and Communication in the Information Age* (Norwood, N.J.: Ablex, 1989), 102.

22. Jessop, *State Theory,* 207–9.

23. For further theoretical treatment of this essential point see Nicos Poulantzas, *Political Power and Social Classes* (London: New Left Books, 1975).

24. Harvey, 147.

25. The case is an interesting one for illustrating how the socialization of intellectual property facilitates innovation, the opposite of what is assumed in the philosophy of intellectual property rights, i.e., that privatization of intellectual creativity is the key to innovation.

26. Erik Barnouw, *A History of Broadcasting in the United States to 1933: A Tower in Babel* (New York: Oxford University Press, 1966); Sydney Head and Christopher Sterling, *Broadcasting in America: A Survey of Electronic Media,* 5th ed. (Boston: Houghton Mifflin, 1987); C. Sterling and J. Kittross, *A Concise History of American Broadcasting,* 2d ed. (Belmont, Calif.: Wadsworth, 1990); Robert McChesney, "The Battle for the U.S. Airwaves, 1928–1935," *Journal of Communication* 40, no. 4 (1990), 29–57.

27. See Mary S. Mander, "The Public Debate about Broadcasting in the Twenties: An Interpretive History," *Journal of Broadcasting* 28, no. 2 (1984), 167–85.

28. See F. Allen, *Only Yesterday: An Informal History of the Nineteen-Twenties* (New York: Harper, 1957), and Arthur Schlesinger, *The Age of Roosevelt. Vol. 1: The Crisis of the Old Order (1919–1933)* (Boston: Houghton Mifflin, 1957), 61–76.

29. S. Besen and B. Mitchell, *Economic Analysis and Television Regulation: A Review* (Santa Monica: Rand, 1973); R. Noll, M. Peck, and J. McGowan, *Economic Aspects of Television Regulations* (Washington, D.C.: Brookings Institution, 1973); B. Owen, J. Beebe, and W. Manning, *Television Economics* (Lexington, Mass.: Lexington Books, 1974).

30. Owen, Beebe, and Manning, 15.

31. See Barnouw; McChesney, "Battle for the U.S. Airwaves."

32. Robert McChesney, "An Almost Incredible Absurdity for a Democracy," *Journal of Communication Inquiry* 15, no. 1 (1991) 89–114.

33. See Samuel Bowles and Richard Edwards, *Understanding Capitalism: Competition, Command, and Change in the U.S. Economy* (New York: Harper and Row, 1985).

34. See Tino Balio, ed., *The American Film Industry* (Madison: University of Wisconsin Press, 1985); Douglas Gomery, *The Hollywood Studio System* (New York: St. Martin's, 1986); and Thomas Guback, "Theatrical Film," in *Who Owns the Media? Concentration of Ownership in the Mass Communications Industry,* ed. B. Compaine, C. Sterling, T. Guback, and J. Noble (White Plains, N.Y.: Knowledge Industries, 1979), 179–249, on the theatrical film industry. See Simon Frith, "The Industrialization of Popular Music," in *Popular Music and Communication,* 2d ed., ed. J. Lull (Newbury Park, Calif.: Sage, 1992), 49–74, on music recording and publishing. See Benjamin Compaine, "Magazines," 127–78, and "Newspapers," 11–53, both in *Who Owns the Media?* and Bagdikian, *Media Monopoly,* on magazine and newspaper industry concentration. See also J. Noble, "Books," in *Who Owns the Media?* 251–91,

and Janice Radway, *Reading the Romance: Women, Patriarchy and Popular Literature* (Chapel Hill: University of North Carolina Press, 1984), 19–45, on book publishing.

35. Federal Communications Commission, Network Inquiry Special Staff, *New Television Networks: Entry, Jurisdiction, Ownership and Regulation. Vol. 2: Background Reports* (Washington, D.C.: U.S. Government Printing Office, 1980), 39 (cited hereafter as Federal Communications Commission, *Background Reports*).

36. See Raymond Williams's chapter on the origins of advertising, "Advertising: The Magic System," in *Problems in Materialism and Culture: Selected Essays,* ed. Williams (London: New Left Books, 1980), 170–95.

37. Vincent Norris, "Advertising History—According to the Textbooks," *Journal of Advertising* 9, no. 3 (1980), 3–11.

38. See Head and Sterling, and Harry Skornia, *Television and Society: An Inquest and Agenda for Improvement* (New York: McGraw-Hill, 1965).

39. McChesney, "An Almost Incredible Absurdity," 109.

40. Federal Communications Commission, *Report on Chain Broadcasting,* Order No. 37, Docket No. 5060 (Washington, D.C.: U.S. Government Printing Office, 1941), 3–4.

41. Ibid., 4.

42. *National Broadcasting Co. v. United States,* 319 U.S. 190 (1943).

43. Leonard Goldenson, *Beating the Odds: The Untold Story Behind the Rise of ABC: The Stars, Struggles, and Egos that Transformed Network Television and the Man Who Made It Happen* (New York: Scribner, 1991), 97.

44. Kellner, 40.

45. Federal Communications Commission, *Sixth Report and Order,* 41 FCC 148 (1952).

46. Owen, Beebe, and Manning, 12.

47. Noll et al., vii.

48. S. Besen, T. Krattenmaker, A. Metzger, and J. Woodbury, *Misregulating Television: Network Dominance and the FCC* (Chicago: University of Chicago Press, 1984), 14.

49. Robert Horowitz, *The Irony of Regulatory Reform: The Deregulation of American Telecommunications* (New York: Oxford University Press, 1989), 28.

50. Federal Communications Commission, *Background Reports,* 72.

51. Federal Communications Commission, *Network Broadcasting* (Washington, D.C.: U.S. Government Printing Office, 1958), 3.

52. Federal Communications Commission, *Study of Radio and Television Network Broadcasting: Order for Investigatory Proceeding,* 24 Fed. Reg. 1605 (1959). The 1960 and 1963 reports were reproduced in U.S. House, Committee on Interstate and Foreign Commerce, *Television Network Procurement,* H.R. 281, 88th Cong., 1st Sess. (Washington, D.C.: U.S. Government Printing Office, 1963). The 1965 report is in Federal Communications Commission, *Second Interim Report by the Office of Network Study: Television Network Program Procurement. Part 2* (Washington, D.C.: U.S. Government Printing Office, 1965).

53. Federal Communications Commission, *Competition and Responsibility in Network Television Broadcasting: Notice of Proposed Rulemaking,* 45 FCC 2146 (1965).

54. Federal Communications Commission, *Competition and Responsibility . . . Report and Order.*

55. Federal Communications Commission, *Competition and Responsibility . . . Notice of Proposed Rulemaking,* 2151.

56. Ibid., 2154.

57. Ibid., 2160.

58. Ibid., 2158.

59. *Prime Time Access Rule,* 47 C.F.R. Ch. 1, Section 73.658(k) (1990).

60. Federal Communications Commission, *Competition and Responsibility . . . Report and Order,* 402.

61. Ibid., 389.

62. Ibid., 394.

63. Ibid., 416.

64. Ibid.

65. Besen et al., 178.

66. *Red Lion v. Federal Communications Commission,* 395 US 367 (1969).

67. C. Sterling, "Television and Radio Broadcasting," in Compaine et al., 104.

68. Federal Communications Commission, *Competition and Responsibility in Network Television Broadcasting: Memorandum Opinion and Order,* 25 FCC 2d 318 (1970).

69. Federal Communications Commission, *Competition and Responsibility . . . Report and Order,* 392.

70. See Vincent Mosco, *Pushbutton Fantasies: Critical Perspectives on Videotex and Information Technology* (Norwood, N.J.: Ablex, 1982), and Dan Schiller, *Telematics and Government* (Norwood, N.J.: Ablex, 1982).

71. See testimony in U.S. House, Select Committee on Small Business, Subcommittee 6, *Activities of Regulatory and Enforcement Agencies Relating to Small Business* (Washington, D.C.: U.S. Government Printing Office, 1966).

72. Goldenson, 454.

73. H. Williams, *Beyond Control: ABC and the Fate of the Networks* (New York: Atheneum, 1989), 176.

74. Sterling, 105.

75. Goldenson, 452.

76. Ibid., 453.

77. The airline, natural gas, and financial services industries were deregulated during the years of the Carter presidency.

78. Willard Rowland, "The Further Process of Reification: Continuing Trends in Communication Legislation and Policymaking," *Journal of Communication* 34, no. 2 (1982), 114–36.

79. Horowitz, 82.

80. Domhoff, *The Power Elite and the State*, 282.

81. Willard Rowland, "The Illusion of Fulfillment: The Broadcast Reform Movement," *Journalism Monograph* 79 (1982).

82. Besen and Mitchell, and Noll et al.

83. Federal Communications Commission, Network Inquiry Special Staff, *New Television Networks: Entry, Jurisdiction, Ownership and Regulation. Vol. 1: Final Report* (Washington, D.C.: U.S. Government Printing Office, 1980), 20 (cited hereafter as Federal Communications Commission, *Final Report*).

84. Federal Communications Commission, *Background Reports.*

85. See testimony in U.S. House, Committee on Energy and Commerce, Subcommittee on Telecommunications, Consumer Protection, and Finance, *Financial Interest and Syndication Rules: Hearings on H.R. 2250* (Washington, D.C.: U.S. Government Printing Office, 1983), 446.

86. Federal Communications Commission, *Final Report,* 519–23.

87. Federal Communications Commission, *Amendment of 47 CFR Section 73.658(j)(l)(i) and (ii), the Syndication and Financial Interest Rules: Notice of Proposed Rulemaking,* 47 Fed. Reg. 32959 (1982).

88. Robert Mulholland, "Viewpoints," *Television/Radio Age,* 18 October 1982, 65.

89. In a revealing example of the "revolving door" between government and industry, Dean Burch, who initially opposed the FISRs, now served as co-counsel for the Committee for Prudent Deregulation.

90. Don Taffner, "Viewpoints," *Television/Radio Age,* 1 November 1982, 37.

91. U.S. House, Committee on Energy and Commerce, *Financial Interest and Syndication Rules,* 236.

92. T. Ryan, "Viewpoints," *Television/Radio Age,* 31 January 1983, 49.

93. U.S. House, Committee on Energy and Commerce, *Financial Interest and Syndication Rules,* 236.

94. Ibid., 198.

95. Ryan, 49.

96. "Who's Saying What on Repeal of the Financial Interest/Syndication Rule," *Media & Marketing Decisions,* March 1983, 66–67, 66 (quote).

97. Taffner, 37.

98. U.S. Senate, Committee on Commerce, Science, and Transportation, Subcommittee on Communications, *Competition in Television Production Act: Hearings on S. 1707* (Washington, D.C.: U.S. Government Printing Office, 1984), 80.

99. Mel Blumenthal, "Reruns Pay Producers' Bills," *New York Times,* 28 August 1983, sec. 3, p. 2.

100. Ibid.

101. U.S. House, Committee on Energy and Commerce, *Financial Interest and Syndication Rules,* 467, 466.

102. Ibid., 468.

103. R. Sobel, "TV Affiliate Views on Financial Interest, Syndication Rules Re-

peal Vary Widely as Debate Intensifies," *Television/Radio Age,* 29 November 1982, 38–39, 64.

104. Federal Communications Commission, *Amendment of 47 CFR Section 73.658(j)(l)(i) and (ii), the Syndication and Financial Interest Rules: Tentative Decision and Request for Further Comments,* 94 FCC 2d 1019 (1983).

105. H. Williams, 175, and Goldenson, 454.

106. E. Andrews, "TV Rerun Ownership in Review," *New York Times,* 1 October 1990, D1.

107. Federal Communications Commission, *Evaluation of the Television Syndication and Financial Interest Rules,* 56(54) Fed. Reg. 11720 (20 March 1991), 11720.

108. Federal Communications Commission, *Evaluation,* 11720 and, "The Stale Rules that Stifle TV," *New York Times,* 30 November 1990, A32.

109. Cited in J. McManus, "MCA Deal Could Aid Fin-Syn Fight," *Advertising Age,* 3 December 1990, 10.

110. J. Aversa, "Economic Advisors Reiterate Bush Cable Policy," *Multichannel News,* 18 February 1991, 11.

111. Federal Communications Commission, *Broadcast Services; Financial Interest and Syndication Rules,* 56(109) Fed. Reg. 26242 (6 June 1991).

112. Kneale and Carnevale, A1; "The FCC Cages the Networks," *New York Times,* 11 April 1991, A24; J. Aversa, "Nets Win Little Fin-Syn Relief," *Multichannel News,* 15 April 1991, 37.

113. D. Wharton, "Finsyn Peace Treaty Kinder to Networks," *Variety,* 8 April 1991, 1.

114. *Schurz Communications, Inc. v. F.C.C.,* 982 F.2d 1043 (7th Cir., 1992).

115. Federal Communications Commission, *Broadcast Service; Syndication and Financial Interest Rules,* MM Docket No. 90-162, FCC 93-179 (1 April 1993).

116. Bill Carter, "Hollywood Isn't Smiling at an ABC Comedy Tactic," *New York Times,* 4 April 1994, D1, D6.

117. E. Jensen, "ABC Announces Primetime Lineup; All Nights Changed," *Wall Street Journal,* 11 May 1993, B9.

118. L. Wayne, "Networks Gain Riches from News Magazines," *New York Times,* 25 October 1993, D6.

119. Geraldine Fabrikant, "ABC and New Studio in TV Venture," *New York Times,* 29 November 1994, D1, D19.

120. Bill Carter, "In a Bid for Hits, Networks Buy Pieces of Rivals' Shows," *New York Times,* 16 January 1995, D1, D6.

121. Bill Carter, "A Castoff Show May Come Back to Haunt CBS from Its Lofty New Perch on NBC's Schedule," *New York Times,* 15 May 1995, D8.

122. Eben Shapiro, "Chris-Craft's 4th-Period Net Fell 67% on Losses at UPN, Weak TV Ad Revenue," *Wall Street Journal,* 15 February 1996, B6.

123. Federal Communications Commission, *In re Review of the Syndication and Financial Interest Rules,* MM Docket No. 95-39, 10 FCC Rcd 12165 (29 August 1995).

124. Danny Schecter, "Inside the Box: Gulf War Coverage," *Z Magazine,* December 1991, 22–25; Kellner, 164.

125. "CBS Sees Dip in First-Quarter Earnings,"*Broadcasting,* 21 March 1983, 162; "The Phoenix Ariseth," *Broadcasting,* 4 April 1983, 121–26.

126. E. Guider, "Nets Eye Global Finsyn Harvest," *Variety,* 11 March 1991, 21, 27; 27 (quote), (emphasis added).

127. Of course, broadcast television is not "free." Bagdikian (147) estimates that advertisers spend about $300 a year on each television household, money they recover by marking up the prices on the advertised product.

5

Conflict and Containment in Television News: A Case Study

Peter D. Moss

A television news program is no longer regarded as a statement or a presentation of an objective set of "realities." Rather, it is a sequence of messages created by codes of production, be they economic, technological, or ideological. The discursive critic or analyst has had to face the charge that regardless of the sensitivity of any explication of a television text, the meanings claimed are little more than mere opinion.

It has been the frustration and irritation at the gnomic quality of some interpretive critics that released the admirable intellectual and investigative effort involved in audience research, some results of which seriously undermine the more speculative claims of textual critics.[1]

These broad and contrasting approaches have produced dichotomies that, in the final analysis, still locate the observer in the iron cage of the "scientific" sociologist's endgame—How can you know that the general audience, however configured, understands messages in your way (individual analyst) or their way (audience researchers)?

While this search for the Real or the True (message) is a worthy endeavor, it is futile to allow the different research methods to lock in dispute, in rivalry for the key to meaning. It is especially pointless when sets of interpretive styles adopt controlling ideas such as *ideology* and *culture* to organize their critical claims. Such terms, particularly *ideology,* have lost much of their force in the postmodern world. The modern nation state, organized by its relationship to space, has disappeared and the postmodern state is organized by *time.* Television news, probably, will be a potent carrier of temporal signals for future audiences, signals that will structure and gloss general understandings of the world's events far more than in the past. In the new temporal world, where time is accelerated, the cultural significance of technological media cannot be overstated.

In his work on television news and ideology, Lewis concludes his review and analyses with the following: "Television news, with its fragmented narrative form . . . does not offer the viewer a coherent vision based on historical connections, it deals in a series of disparate associations. As long as these associations appear to float above the ebb and flow of historical reality, they are immune from the contradictions it may expose."[2]

He makes reference to attitudinal data that suggest that the more television people watch, the more likely they are to hold contradictory ideas simultaneously. Lewis concludes, "It is, perhaps, too much to hold the structure of television news entirely accountable for creating such confusion. What a qualitative study of the news tells us, nonetheless, is that the meaning of television is contingent upon its form—a form that alienates us, as a society, from our own history."[3]

This is another way of saying that television news, in its specific determinations, is an enemy of modern rationalism. This is a fair assessment, I suspect, but it is an unreflective judgment that fails to understand television's ability to move between two worlds—the modern spatial one and our postmodern temporal one.

Until very recently the world's powers, the big nation states, operated within psychic and physical boundaries. Modern history has been about containment—the Iron Curtain, the Berlin Wall. In communications, air space, wave lengths/bands, and radio jamming inscribed the limits of the potential for the exchange of views by the world's populations. Governments and their co-opted surrogates, broadcasting authorities and television networks, developed an ideological control by stealth, which has been demonstrated by media and news critics for two decades.

This essay attempts to show, albeit arguing from a small text base, that television news in form and content is an interesting and instructive example of our current condition of culture, straddling the modern and the postmodern, space and time. It traces the ideological containment structure within the cultural restraints of the modern world while indicating, in places, how the form of the news spills over into postmodern interpretive nuances.

Terrorism, conflict, cultural mayhem, and social disturbance seem to be endemic in contemporary global experience. Their generation and regeneration on the nightly television news programs, on the hourly radio news breaks, and in the daily press supply a rich source of general metaphors with which audiences and readers can take part in a mass mediated ritual. It is a primary ritual experience that news produces and, in our case, the small domestic screen is the arena for its expression. Conflict is both subject and style in the perennial ritual progressions. My argument is that both production and code coalesce in an elaborate spectacle that both wounds (in the selection of varieties of threat stories) and heals (by the encompassing of all stories within a predictable, and therefore reassuring, repetitive structure).

This study indicates that the presentation of a generalized cultural threat lurking in multiform aspect in world events is not a signal for social and political closure in order to maintain some gross social consensus, as Davis and Walton have argued.[4] My material suggests also that symbolic interactionist scholars may have overstated their case. According to their perspective, repetitive "ritualistic" productions, frames, and codes are designed to ensure an audience's assimilation of the dominant social structures and values. But no "dominant class" in a democracy would be so unsophisticated as to rely on representations of fear and danger as a structure for consensual power arrangements. Even the most pliant, naïve, or just plain dumb populations would sooner or later demand that the system of valuing and power be changed.[5]

My work indicates that, while the methods of news presentations and the details of narrative structure may be relatively complex, the "cultural design" is clear and that, fortuitously, many events in political and social history are conjunctural with the imperatives of this medium's entertainment principles.

The text analyzed in this chapter is a complete television news transcription, presented with visual reference and verbal quotation, on a main evening news program ("Eyewitness News") transmitted (7 March 1995) to viewers in Adelaide, South Australia.[6] In that Southern Hemisphere autumn, Channel Ten was the top-rated news provider in the city. It could claim, therefore, to be an important cultural broker between extant world knowledge and received new(s) knowledge. While television productions have no certain control over the way in which the differing segments of their audience interpret programs, analysis may reveal, with less of a problematic, the ways in which they structure and shape their narratives created from the "given" of selected world events.

For mass commercial television news productions the cultural judgments that must lie behind the selections pose cultural and social dilemmas. In Channel Ten's case, the tacit cultural and metaphorical structure of news is that of a world of isolated, settled communities (which might be large nation states or metropolitan cities or suburban towns) continually threatened by the active possibility of disruption, be it military, political, industrial, criminal, or, worse still, merely through the vagaries of chance. These nightly presentations of breaks in the routines of consensual social life cannot be allowed to develop a taken-for-grantedness, an aura of inevitability. Audiences would soon disappear if nightly news was always bad, however glossily packaged. Yet these anarchic conditions are the conditions of international relations in the world. Stability and security exist only within the boundaries of the nation state. That security is represented in a technological medium of communication by the way it represents culture, itself framed through ideological constraints of its narratives. Television networks overcome this in a gross way by paying careful attention to the nightly program schedules and by the placement of contrasting or diverting offerings over each evening's viewing. Within these, commercial breaks often play significant structuring roles in their attempts to inhibit possible unsympathetic audience reaction at the onset of an evening's viewing. These production principles are overlying ones. Of greater interest are the narrative creations within single items of news reportage, on the one hand, and the nature of the overall discourse methods across a complete news program, on the other. This kind of detailed micro-analysis is the real subject of this paper and my discussion will show how complex and interlocked are the different narratives across the complete program. More to the point, I will show how the emphasized themes of danger and disharmony, themselves underpinned by the style of production, are systematically and rhythmically contained by a parallel thematic and stylistic counterpoint.

Focusing on the Gaze

One of the unhelpful conventions of recent media critical practice has been the abolition of language. Critics have been absorbed with the purely visual; indeed, virtual lexicons of telecine semiotic systems have been produced. However, the verbal language used to encode news messages has been ignored for the most part. Such a partial "gaze" is inadequate for a consideration of Channel Ten news, partly for the obvious reason that most of the program is encoded verbally, mostly because this news transmission uses printed words to introduce every news item. Each item is framed by a "verbal box," a caption that in one or two words "headlines" the subsequent item-report. These verbal boxes are placed behind and either northeast or northwest of the anchorperson's three-quarter-frame screen presence. The words are crude agenda-setting devices for each news item, but they represent also an important framing device in the program's narrative of violence and disruption. Table 5.1 shows diagrammatically the messages of each box over the total news output,

Table 5.1. Verbal Boxes, in Sequence

1 PERRY CASE		
2 BOMB BID		A
3 OPERA ROW		
4 THANK YOU	COMMERCIAL BREAKS	
5 Nonverbal box		
6 RAID		
7 WALKER		B
8 WARNING		
9 SUBCONTRACT	COMMERCIAL BREAKS	
10 JAIL		
11 PLANE HORROR		
12 WORLD NEWS		
13 HEART IMPLANT		C
14 LEBANON BOMB		
15 EL SALVADOR MURDER		
16 NICARAGUAN FIRE		
17 WORLD WAR II BRIDGE	COMMERCIAL BREAKS	
18 NOAH		
19 CORDEAUX COMMENTS		D
20 BODY SEARCH		
21 HIGH LOAD		
22 NO DOPE		
23 KIDS' CRISIS	COMMERCIAL BREAKS	
24 PICKET		E
25 NEW BUY	COMMERCIAL BREAKS	

Note: Nos. 14–15 are world stories that are not verbally framed. The box titles are the author's.

interspered with the blocks of commercial narratives. Out of twenty-four verbal boxes (one of the twenty-five items listed is a nonverbal box), nineteen concern some element of disruption, violence or threat, confusion or mishap.

In each of the five sequences (A to E) there is a regular rhythmic "beat" of tension followed quickly by release. This is adopted in sequences A, B, C, and E, where final items in sequence are optimistic (B), entertaining (E), humanly connective (A), or conciliatory (C). All of these positive items are followed by advertisement sequences that also contain or suppress the dominant disruptive themes on the news reports by upbeat domesticity and by images of social construction and consumer plenty. Sequence (D), however, is disjunctive in that the rhythm is more complex and more extended. There is still the threat-release motif but it is followed by a final extreme item of unexplained, perpetual urban terror, with the report of missing children. This unexpected inclusion in the context of the rhythm of this program's news narratives is explained by reference to some local culture-knowledge.

Over the previous twenty years, South Australia had a number of unsolved cases of missing children. The popular media periodically have reminded the public of the events, usually under the guise of new, speculative guesswork (one such involved the possibility of extraterrestrial kidnapping). Coincidentally, only a number of weeks before this particular Channel Ten news broadcast, a "murder" case concluded that had involved the abduction of a ten-year-old girl and a bizarre sequence of clues, but no body. Despite this, a man was tried, convicted, and sentenced, but on appeal he was released owing to admitted perjury by prosecution witnesses. The report about missing American children (Kids' Crisis) would thus be irresistible for a major featured item and its placement an effective contrast with the trivial stories of a relocated giraffe (High Load) and a dope-sniffing pig (No Dope).

Although the above is a credible explanation for the inclusion of the missing children item, the local resonances it would produce require a carefully structured cultural suppression. This is begun immediately after the United States report ends. The Adelaide studio anchorman steps out of the institutional role and connects with the audience when he makes his remark, "What a frightening problem!" It is both an exclamation of outrage and a sympathetic affirmation ("Both I and the station know your fear and anger at the terror in our midst"). Such is the power of television's projected knowledge that this type of recognition takes on the potential for exorcism. But recognition and sympathy are not nearly enough; they are simply "reality" bridges to the advertisements (table 5.2), the commercial break that at this juncture in the news is the necessary "reality," one that soothes and distracts.

And "reality" is the theme of the first commercial, a zippy catalog of the contents of the only Sunday newspaper published in the state. The catalog of subjects and their regular reporters is a familiar and constant list. The normality extends beyond the ordinariness of the items. Ten of fifteen deal with sport, a mythic emblem in media versions of the Australian psyche. The journalists' names give further solidity and audience recognition. Apart from the one central European name, all others are reassuringly Anglo or, at worst, British in origin.

This advertisement dissipates the diffused anxiety by briefly focusing the audience on the natural world of the Australian environment. From demonstrable, institutional sympathy (the anchorman) to the locally known, familiar, and reliable (the Sunday journalists) to the commonly known and permanent (the nation's *natural* environment), the deflection of cruel reality is probably now complete.

Table 5.2. Commercials

Verbal		Visual
A.		
Voice-over (female)	1 Look what's happening in the *Sunday Mail!*	Facsimile of paper's page
	2 Geoff Roach, Australia's top sports writer	
	3 William Reschke on our heritage	
	4 Jim Dean, the man who knows football	
	5 Barbara Page speaks her mind	
	6 Randall Ashbourne, state politics	
	7 Ann Fulwood on sports	
	8 David Capel, fishing	
	9 Margaret Brenton, flair	
	10 Kevin Settle, racing	
	11 Ashley Porter, football	
	12 Helen Menzies, sport	
	13 Tom McKain, soccer	
	14 Ian Fewlings, trotting	
	15 Peter Brock, motor racing	
	16 Paul Kelly, from Canberra	Head shots of writers mentioned

And every Sunday a giant TV and entertainment liftout. There's always more in the *Sunday Mail.*

In a major publishing event the *Sunday Mail* this week introduces you to a spectacular new series of books, *Living Australia.* — Stills of animal and evironment photos contained in the book series

Volume 1 of *Living Australia,* worth $1.95, is free inside the *Sunday Mail* this weekend.

B.

Voice-over (male) — Chardhary's, Adelaide's finest Persian rug store, is closing down. Owing to financial difficulties they are sacrificing over $2 million worth of fine rugs. Two hundred Princess Bokiene rugs, an incredible $1; tribal wedding rugs, $17.50; *Tree of Life* rugs slashed to $179; classical rugs only $589 and elegant, 9' x 12' carpets were $4,000, now an unbelievable $895. All stock must go. See Saturday's *Advertiser* for details. — Various shots showing the rugs on sale in warehouse settings

C.

Voice-over (chuckling female) — Aren't you just a little late, Santa? — Santa Claus empties his sack—of jeans —each item illustrated by local models.

Voice-over (male) — Um. But this is worth waiting for.

Table 5.2. (cont.)

	Verbal	Visual
Female	Girls' jeans, two pairs for $20; and women's, two pairs for $25.	
Male	Boys' California jeans in school colors, $17.50. Student and men's also.	
Female	Plenty of stretch and baggies in denim and canvas. That's factory-direct; that's *Smile Jeans.*	
D.		
Voice-over	Kingston Biscuits, the delicious taste sensation from Arnott's. Arnott's takes two dainty home-style biscuits and in between puts a creamy filling that tastes like milk chocolate. You've never enjoyed anything quite like this. Kingston Biscuits. Try stopping at one.	An Edwardian scene, with demure uniformed maid preparing afternoon tea. She can't resist eating the biscuits despite the repeated ringing of the servant bell.

Unlike the standard TV ad, this commercial is more a reminder of what is strong and unproblematic, and it is nicely placed to confirm normality. The subsequent items in the sequence extend this to include good fortune for viewers—the bankruptcy sale of Persian rugs and the more regular sale of a staple item of clothing. Reality, newly reconstituted in selected areas, is extended into consumer opportunity on advantageous terms.

Finally, should the urge for possession not be normal enough, the final advertisement in the sequence closes the circle by stressing appetite through a quaint, if stilted, dramatic emblem for nourishment, domesticity, and reliability, sure bulwarks against the fearful narrative from far-off lands.

There is further confirmation of this conscious normalizing of the narrative in subsequent commercial sequences. In these advertising breaks the narrative themes consistently stress the domestic, the useful, the appetizing, the secure, and the hopeful. All the advertising sequences offer this reassurance of the locally familiar, as with the opening of the sequence just discussed. They also erect boundaries, and beyond the boundaries are silences. These are official (or news directors' or TV stations') containments that force the audience to be partner in the discourse. This is achieved by the sequencing of the verbal boxes.

Apart from box 5 (see table 5.1), which has no verbal headlining,[7] all the verbal boxes represent kinds of message making. Most of them offer the opportunity for members of the audience to make inchoate attempts at rapid-creation story making, small spaces in which to privately "exchange" stories and/or interpretations with the official discourse. Below, the box tags are grouped according to their potential for different kinds of narrative construction.

Adventure or Thrill or a Crime Narrative
PERRY CASE
BOMB BID
RAID
KIDS' CRISIS

Industrial Turmoil
OPERA ROW
PICKET

Military Adventure
BOMB BID

Personal Nightmare or Drama
JAIL
BODY SEARCH

Normality or Domesticity
THANK YOU
NEW BUY

The other verbal headliners as such are difficult to read off as narrative capsules. However, with one exception, they make story sense because they are accompanied by still pictures or by moving visuals. In the WORLD NEWS sequence the audience is plunged into the narrative, without preamble, as the headliners are presented as conventional action-news reporting. The still pictures, encased with the verbal tags, also suggest themes that audiences might begin to structure privately. Even the unpromising WALKER is rich with dramatic possibility for an Australian audience because the picture-still is a head shot of an aborigine.

These brief verbal codings offer a number of possible readings at the spontaneous level. For example, PLANE HORROR, a story involving a light plane crash in America, could be interpreted initially as generalized story string along the lines, COMMERCIAL JET FLIGHT—HIGH ALTITUDE ACCIDENT—

CRASH—MULTIPLE DEATHS. Such a story string is an ever-present sub-text of aviation mythology.

The news item's verbal text makes it clear that the plane incident refers to a single light aircraft, hardly of great moment in itself. However, this relatively minor piece of world knowledge is given heavy import by linkage to a similar accident in Melbourne, a week earlier, where four people were killed when a plane crashed into houses near the international airport.

The extensive coverage of the American crash, which has no intrinsic interest beyond the dramatic visual spectacle of a night-time urban blaze, is focused for the audience through the local referent, still fresh in the general recollection. The underlying text is "Accidents happen *all the time. Anywhere. It could happen to *any* one.*" It is another example of the program's loading of anxiety onto the domestic screen.

The only disjunctive occurrence in these narrative capsules is the segment CORDEAUX COMMENTS, an interesting and significant item because of its link with local media culture conventions and because it is placed in a position that helps contain the potential for social confusion present in the immediately preceding item, one concerned with the local fight against drugs.

NOAH (Narcotics, Opiates, Amphetamines, Hashish) is a code name for an initiative of the state police department to gain information that might aid in eliciting facts leading to the arrest of leaders in local drug dealings. Essentially, it is a community phone-in facility, in which anyone (even anonymously) can furnish the police with drug information. Clearly, such information might range from links to criminal intelligence to local gossip about backyard marijuana cultivation. The state police department made the inauguration of the scheme a media event. That Channel Ten is willingly complicit in this is clear in the discourse of the coverage (table 5.3).

On the surface, the coverage appears to be balanced, both verbally and visually, in that spokespeople with opposing attitudes toward NOAH are given public space. On two occasions the telephone number of the opposition's legal service is prominently highlighted. At this denotative level the discourse of this news item follows a familiar binary opposition principle, namely: Police–Public; Authority–Unknown Criminals; Mystery Objects–Ordinary People; Hard Drugs–Soft Drugs: Concerned Police–Members of NORMAL. The "convention" of binary oppositions was a widespread trope in late modernity, where the conditions of culture demanded *absolute other* or *absolute same*. This mix is mediated by reporter explanation, police comment, and assessments from the NORMAL group and a police spokesperson. Basically, then,

Table 5.3.

		Verbal		Visual
Anchorman	1	The police phone-in against drugs, code-name NOAH, will start on Monday, but today Adelaide's media got a look at the operation's nerve centre. At the same time, a Marijuana Law Reform group is mounting an anti-NOAH campaign, which it has called Judas. Tony Hull reports.	1	Verbal box NOAH enclosing still of leaves of marijuana and a brass hookah.
Reporter voice-over	2	NOAH stands for Narcotics, Opiates, Amphetamines, and Hashish.	2	Lounge-suited men (one woman) around a table littered with files, telephones, office equipment. Armed policemen leaning against wall, in background.
	3i	The object of the exercise is to spur the community	3i	Closeup of one of the drug officers studying papers.
	ii	out of its apathy and onto the phone. Police are hoping for	ii	Box of pill bottles
	iii	information which will lead them to those who grow, manufacture, and deal in drugs. And police are making no distinction between soft and hard drugs. Inspector Barry Moyes is leading	iii	Set-piece closeup of users' equipment. Syringe, spoon, powder, bottle of drug sticks, crusher, plastic
	iv	the operation.	iv	bags of marijuana leaves. Closeup of the inspector. Looks down all the time.
Moyes		If we get phone calls that people have a marijuana plant in their backyard, the police call, find the evidence there, quite obviously it's a short, sharp shiny matter.		
Reporter voice-over	4	He fired this broadside at NORMAL, the group who is opposed to the phone-in.	4	Repeat of shot 2.
Moyes	5	We're bitterly disappointed with their approach. I believe that they've completely missed the point; they're politically motivated and in actual fact I believe that they've done nothing but support and publicise this particular campaign.	5	Repeat of 3iv. Looks down all the time.
Reporter voice-over	6	NORMAL hits back, at their own news conferences, saying it was committed to wiping out drug abuse, and that it was the police who were on the wrong track.	6	Table with 2 men, 1 woman, as spokespeople for opposition group. Behind them, on wall, a larger poster giving phone number for legal advice, which dominates the screen.

Table 5.3. (cont.)

		Verbal		Visual
NORMAL represen- tative	7	In fact, we want a responsible attitude; this is not a responsible attitude; this is not a responsible campaign. This campaign will result in persecution of marijuana smokers only. The hard drug dealers won't be caught.	7	Closeup of spokesman.
Reporter	8	Margaret Colmer explained why Young Labour (Labour Party) had given its support to NORMAL.	8	Picture of Ms. Colmer.
Colmer	9	Young Labour's involved because we're very disappointed that the ALP (Australian Labour Party) in the state hasn't got the courage to do something about a strong decriminalisation policy. They have not got one.	9	Closeup of Miss Colmer.
Reporter Voice-over	10	She claims that there are 100,000 young South Australians smoking grass and in this International Youth Year, their opinions should be taken notice of. Tony Hull, Eyewitness News.	10i ii	Repeat shot 6. Repeat 3iii.
Anchorman		Operation NOAH, and its alternatives.		

Note: The numbers in the verbal column should be read with the corresponding numbers in the visual column.

it appears to be a helpful report on a difficult, worrisome, and far from simple social, cultural, and criminal matter.

At a deeper, connotative level, however, the report is not so balanced. Pressure is exerted upon the audience through a number of crucial visual signals, all of which cohere around potential threat to the community, to individuals, and, implicitly, to future generations. First there is the repeated visual of the set-display of drug users' equipment in the police operations room. There is no explanation offered about the collection; the items are just there, each carrying a varying weight of culture-message and moral panic. Although there is no verbal gloss the audience is assumed to be well able to understand the "grammar" of a silent picture whose "syntax" is coded by the positions-in-frame of the objects. These include a syringe, a spoon, a mound of white powder, metal crushers, pill boxes, a bottle of clear liquid, and plastic bags of marijuana leaves. The syringe is centrally placed, with the white powder and pill boxes below it, forming a triangular group; the other objects are arranged around this tableau—a structure that makes imaginary links to real or fantasized scenery.[8]

It is significant that when this visual is first used it is preceded by shots of drug-squad officers looking busy and thoughtful, with armed, uniformed policemen standing at the back of the room. The fight against drug rings might be centered around ordinary-seeming professionals, but behind and above that relaxed scene is the clear status of state power and the looming fact of controlled aggression.

The second time that the set-piece display is used is in the final visual of the report. The drug scene is the image left on the screen, as the anchorman simplistically summarizes the whole report as, "Operation Noah and its alternatives."

This verbal message, coming immediately after the drugs visual, is a travesty of accuracy and serves to confuse the already complex set of messages just transmitted. It is an opportunity for members of the audience to feel anxiety but also to try out their own stories in their heads, a cultural exchange not controlled by the news discourse. The anchorman's statement, "its alternatives," reduces the issue to another oppositional set; trying to frame a choice between a comprehensive attempt by the police to develop an information network and the actions of two groups of young people, one of which is attempting to obstruct the police scheme, the other, actively promoting the legalization of a particular drug. More than this, the anchorman's comment offers an additional binary tension: Mature Responsibility against Misguided Youth. It is a significant agenda setter because the next item, a wholly verbal segment, is structurally connected to the summarizing comment already made, highlighted by the visual of the drug tableau.

"Eyewitness News" returns to the studio and Jeremy Cordeaux, off camera, has moved into the other anchorperson's seat. He is immediately given, therefore, institutional and semiofficial status. Cordeaux, for some five years, was the top-rated midmorning radio host. His segment had been a regular on Channel Ten and confirmed the media status he possessed. His image is that of the new executive, smooth, unflustered. His persona is of the new individualism, in thrall to no group or party, that is, it bespeaks a no-nonsense, commonsensical approach to social affairs with a hint of entrepreneurial buccaneership, beneath a smooth exterior.

This new-man toughness, tempered with humanity, is well suggested by his "editorial" (for that is what his segment is), a brilliant piece of popular manipulative journalism (table 5.4). His text is delivered front-on, three-quarter closeup. Of course, there is no need for any visuals; the audience has had

Table 5.4.

Verbal	Visual
To me, the lowest form of human life is the pusher, the drug pusher. These people literally push death through a needle. On this very news service last night I saw a man in Kings Cross, in Sydney, who had been stabbed to death by, presumably, a drug-crazed addict. Behind this tragedy, make no mistake, there was a pusher, just as guilty as the man who committed that murder. Now, beginning on Monday in this state, there is a police operation called Operation NOAH. It's an important move and one designed specifically to do something about the drug problem. It's a move which should have the total support of every thinking South Australian. While I believe that everyone of us has the right to either agree or disagree, to me it is off the planet that the Young Labour Movement, the Young Democrats (Australian Democrats, the third party represented in National and State parliments); and others want to mount their own, and conflicting, phone-in. Of course, there are arguments about the links between marijuana and heroin but nevertheless the link is there, however tenuous. Drug pushers are the parasites of society with not one ounce of compassion for the half-dead kid lying in a shop doorway. Somehow I believe we have a responsibility to make Operation NOAH succeed. Our kids depend on it; the future of this State may well rely on it. Interestingly, the competition is calling its phone-in Operation Judas; the police are calling theirs Operation NOAH. Both are biblical names. Noah served the world; need I tell you what Judas did? I'm Jeremy Cordeaux.	Verbal box CORDEAUX COMMENTS behind Cordeaux, who takes the anchorman seat.

them already. In any case, Cordeaux provides vivid word-pictures that link directly to the NOAH segment and, even more immediately, to the discourse motif of controlled anxiety.

His style is not that of binary pairs but one of suggestive strings. The most vivid one is: DRUGS—PUSHER—PARASITE—DEATH—GUILT. The underpinning one is: THE STATE'S FUTURE WELL BEING—POLICE RESPONSIBILITY—COMMUNITY SUPPORT. The complementary critique is: STATUS OF OPPOSITION—IRRESPONSIBILITY—BETRAYAL.

Cordeaux skillfully ties these strings together with his word-pictures, images that reflect levels of knowledge in the audience. The first string is focused through "a drug-crazed addict." This is a probe deliberately aimed because the referent in the report is a presumption on his part that a man had been stabbed to death by an addict. It is an image that holds together both urban terror (outside normal experience) and moral thread (inside the social fabric that sustains members of the audience).

The second string is focused through the biblical reference to Noah, a sharp, shrewd gloss on the original, predictable acronym. In a largely conservative, lower-middle-class, Christian community it makes a vivid impact, which Cordeaux underlines with his own interpretive reminder of the original Noah's achievement (saving the world from destruction). The verbal metaphoric leap from prehistory to current society is breathtaking in this medium and in this form; the invitation to the audience to achieve biblical, social, and moral coherence by a single act of support for police initiative is stunning in implication and bold in the confident assertiveness of the tone in which it is made.

The third string is the critical one, which aims to undermine opposition to NOAH, focused by the vulgar "off the planet," a gross dismissive that places any disagreement to the police scheme as beyond reality. At the end of his editorial Cordeaux stretches this everyday string into more biblical knowledge and leaves it vibrating with the invitation for members of the audience to supply their own moral and cultural judgments to the allies of Judas.

The NOAH news report and the Cordeaux editorial are clearly to be "read" together. They are linked thematically; they offer constructive visual and verbal discourse frames; they both supply evidence of disruption and pain but suggest ways of controlling the damage: on the one hand, through formal agencies of state authority, and on the other, through possession of correct social attitudes.

After Cordeaux's reverberating image, virtually a climatic challenge, the program offers the audience release through the "normality" of the entertainment world. It is a happy story of expectation dashed but followed by fulfillment, as Adelaide fans are finally given the opportunity to purchase Bruce Springsteen concert tickets. This report is linked with the next item, another one in the "threat" genre, the intrusiveness of "body searches" at pop concerts, to ensure a reduction in alcohol-related misbehavior. The anchorman introduces the report as being on the "subject of concerts"—which it is—but thematically it is linked to the previous drug items. This report is about how another drug, alcohol, indirectly causes discomfort to the innocent public because of the measures that informal authority must take to ensure accept-able social behavior.

The news report itself is a "soft" one in that the threat element is cushioned by its placement next to the Springsteen item, but the links with the previous reports are there. More important, Channel Ten's disruption motif is returned to front-of-camera position after the "distanced" Springsteen interlude. Signifi-cantly, there is no verbal box headliner for the Springsteen report, an omis-sion that, at least, allows the possibility that Cordeaux's adjurations will spill over into the early moments of the next report. The agenda-setting verbal con-vention of the boxes could inhibit, momentarily, such a focus.

The illicit drug theme is very strong in this news program. After the items NOAH, CORDEAUX COMMENTS, and BODY SEARCH, relieved by HIGH LOAD, a trivial animal story (though notice the use of "high," with its drug connotation), there is a partial return to the theme in NO DOPE (table 5.5), a genuinely verbal performance by the off-camera reporter.

There is minor visual interest in the report, the novelty value of a pig sniffing out marijuana canisters. The reporter's discourse style, however, is self-conscious and literary: corny ("pig in a poke"); slightly mocking ("unlikely to find a suitcase full of cannabis in the middle of a field"); pretentious ("ol-factory maelstrom"); playful ("bring home the bacon unsmoked every time"); and, at the one disjunctive moment in the report, culturally provocative ("crazed German dope freak"—echoes of Cordeaux).

The report is an exercise in light relief after all the folk-devilry but the link is nonetheless there. It also represents a lowering of tension before the next item, the agonizing report of missing children, one that I've already suggest-ed is strong in local mythology and therefore part of Channel Ten's seeming-ly inexorable drive to place tension, pain, and threat at the forefront of new(s) knowledge.

The Maintenance of Ideology

Television news as a form adapts general entertainment conventions, and these typically cohere around dramatic tensions and climactic plateaux. However, it is clearly understood now that there are no "pure" forms of media. All media genres develop their particular conventions within ideological frames. Ideol-ogy, after all, is only a set of cultural assumptions that become "natural," taken-for-granted normality. This is why news can never present any new knowl-

Table 5.5.

		Verbal		Visual
Anchorman	1	Louise hails from West Germany where, as you're about to see, it's no longer safe to hide a bit of hashish. If you do, the pigs will get you.	1	Verbal Box NO DOPE enclosing still picture of a large pig.
Voice-over	2	Police Commissioner Werner Franke believes he's found a new ally in the fight against marijuana abuse.	2	Closeup of hands holding a canister of dope.
	3	He plants it. But he's not doing it in the hope that he's going to prevent any crazed German dope freak from ever digging it up again. After all, this is just a demonstration.	3	Franke burying canister in a field.
	4	Police Commissioner Franke's new secret weapon is—a pig named Louise. The porky porker has been trained to sniff out the drug. Other police forces round the world use dogs but Commissioner Franke reckons that's just a pig in a poke.	4	Pig on leash sniffing in field.
	5	Louise found this buried treasure without much trouble.	5	Pig digs up the canister. Franke rewards Louise with a tasty morsel.
	6	And to make the task more difficult, he then hid the cannabis in a suitcase. Quibblers might say you'd be unlikely to find a suitcase full of cannabis in the middle of a field and they'd question how Louise would perform in the olfactory maelstrom of a crowded airport lounge.	6	Closeups of pig's snout.
			7	Louise sniffs through a row of of suitcases, laid out on the grass.
	8	But as far as the commissioner is concerned, Louise is going to bring home the bacon unsmoked every time.	8	Finds correct case.

- - - - - - - - - - - - - - - - - -

Studio—medium shot of both anchormen.

Note: The numbers in the verbal column should be read with the corresponding numbers in the visual column.

edge that breaks conventional modes of general assumption. The problem is that program producers select the sets of assumptions (and control the images that mediate them) from the range of official and semi-official versions of the world that governments, trade unions, wire services, and other bodies produce, which, in total, make up the surfaces of culture.

The issue that gave scope for ideological structuring in this news program was the Defense of International Weaponry or the Western Alliance. This perennial issue in modernity's discourse of international affairs has a very limited script since the configuration of attitudes inevitably leads to the binary pair of *We* (Western Alliance) with *They* (new powers from the East) or that of defense-offense. These pairs are unexceptional because they are (re)produced as faithful reportage of official attitudes. The test case for presentation of new knowledge will be on the rare occasions when convention is threatened by the unexpected, when something erupts that threatens to undermine ideological reality.

Such an event happened on the news day of the broadcast under analysis. It is a fascinating and instructive segment of television news because it was partly created, partly reactive and spontaneous, postmodern, no less, but wholly structured in conventions. In table 5.1 the item is verbally fixed for the audience as BOMB BID.

At the surface level the report bore a distinct resemblance to classic comedy in that the discourse tone of the anchorman had no intrinsic link to the overt subject. The report told of a lone motorized hang glider manned by an antinuclear protester trying to "bomb" visiting American destroyers with dye bombs as they steamed out of Sydney harbor. The visuals (some without sound) showed young people with guitars and drums taking part in a protest on land while three elderly pro-American men waved handkerchiefs in an attempt to "counter" the demonstration.

The reporter's version continued this tone in the verbal text but the complementary visual text produced a sense of the bathetic rather than the comic:

Verbal	Visual
"An ultra-light modern aircraft appeared from nowhere to mingle with media aircraft, hovering above the departing ships. His targets were American destroyers *Buchanan* and *John Young*. But his military expertise wasn't up to the sophistication of his targets."	Paint bomb, hand-dropped harmlessly into the ocean.

The whole text bordered on the mock heroic. The reporter told of the attempted escape of the protester, who landed his aircraft mistakenly in the grounds of an Australian vessel, abandoned his orange flight suit, and temporarily eluded pursuing security personnel until he was finally cornered by naval officers. The "elevated" style of the report was consistent, regular, and pretentious, including phrases such as: "[the] landing was purely a presage of things to come"; "preferring to make good his escape on foot"; "the tide of Time and Faith was running out"; "abandoning the tell-tale orange overalls"; "the defiant protester."

The regularity and consistency suggest conscious artifice beyond the call to make journalistic sense and this was confirmed in a switch of tone in the wrapup segment of the report. This account was factual, direct, and stylistically uncluttered, a no-nonsense presentation of new information.

Taken in isolation the report can be interpreted as a quick-witted, rather flexible response to a chance event. It was a relatively accomplished way of overcoming the presentational dilemma that the unexpected aviator caused. At the outset the assignment must have appeared as a conventional action story with the potential for good coverage of demonstrations and clashes with officialdom. That possibility disappeared as soon as the nature of the protagonists became clear—a mild and youthful group of musicians confronted by a geriatric trio. Hardly the stuff of action news drama. Without hope of a land-based clash the news crew literally took to the air with the intention of filing a standard piece of visual-interest reportage of the fleet. Suddenly a glider "appeared from nowhere" and "the drama unveiled." But *what* drama? More a mockery of the archetypal news event, it turned news discourse conventions upside down and forced the medium to partake, on the protester's terms, in a satiric ritual of comic audacity.

The television reporter took the point and offered an unstressed tribute by the form of his report. What started as a potential We-They scenario was transformed into a set of valuings that made their own demonstrable point by contrast. Opposition to the fleet of destroyers was coded in guitar-strumming youthful protesters and by a bizarre act of harmless defiance, a theater spectacle representing energy and life. Such an episode uses the codes of news drama to break the chains of old knowledge. More important for the underlying argument in this chapter, the story is a postmodern instance before its time. The story is a dislocation, a definition of the discourse categories in the conventional modern narrative of ideological containment. Better still, a premodern precursor of change, the glider (an agent presaging the control of space), intruded upon a scene and orchestrated a medium (the video camcorder) that, in its current linkages with new technologies, was about to control time. In this unique news story, text and visuals revealed the ludicrousness of old ideology in the comic extremes of binary oppositions.

That is the good. Now for the bad. Our complex, threatened world cannot be negotiated as though it is a perpetual holiday. So the reporter—almost regretfully, judging by the terse matter-of-factness of his final words—reminded us of our real (i.e., mediated) reality. For the audience, he stressed that the point of the fleet's visit was not an incidental action in a comic drama but as main lead in a defense exercise between two navies. The seriousness of this joint exercise was indicated by the concluding visual text. Two sets of ships, American and Australian, were held in frame with overhead shots. The camera and therefore the audience followed in line, minor partners in a great alliance. It was a final bold visual as the ships (and our imaginations) sailed into the ocean's unknown distance, a beautifully coherent analog of the need for (particular) friends to help face a future under threat from many directions.

The news report immediately following BOMB BID is, according to the verbal box, OPERA ROW. This account told of the cancellation of a performance by Dame Joan Sutherland due to a labor union dispute. Opera fans were enraged by the cancellation since it prevented their seeing Dame Joan's last-ever appearance in *The Tales of Hoffmann* and threatened the entire season of the Australian Opera. This story has an important orientating function: from the diffused universal threat of ultimate military and political confrontation to a local, narrowly cultural tension. This diversion to the more familiar national context is a significant and regular part of the structural string that threads together the different levels of threat and anxiety. This particular switch illustrates an upsurge in tension as the spotlight simultaneously plays upon the local in space and upon the comprehensible in perception. A trade union dispute is always an ideal source of unambiguous meaning-making since the ideological boundaries are firm and impervious in the public's consciousness. In the context of Channel Ten news the opera story's conventional code was to return the audience to storymaking normality after the absurdities of BOMB BID.

The report possessed verbal and visual symbolic status. The report's text was dotted with the exaggerated tags that have developed, with overuse, into an ideological semantic. This reporter's terminology bristled with hyperbole: "sensational cancellation"; "fans were enraged" (this not supported by the visuals); "a bitter disappointment"; "a tragic folly of the highest order." These terms were the reporter's linkages to the selected individual segments of the reports, all of which pointed to the thwarting of a legitimate cultural experience by bloody-minded and greedy trade unionists.[9] It is a standard text in all popular media's perennial joustings with union power, one of which portrays the general public (although in this case it is an affluent specialized segment of it) as innocent, helpless sufferers. This media myth was given status and credibility by the comment of the well-heeled, high-status Dame Joan as she left Australia for her home in Switzerland: "As usual, it's the general public that bear the brunt of any industrial action."

One aspect of this report that emphasized the return to normal news discourse is that which assigns members of the public a role in the story. Predictably, their selected comments further hardened and confirmed the sense, already stressed, of disruption and disharmony. Their expressions of anger, defiance, and disappointment contrasted vividly with a union spokesman's rather sullen, semicoherent, and obviously truncated explanation of his members' action. Nothing was going to distract the audience from the favored culturally dominant coding for a union story.

The final piece of information offered by the reporter neatly locked the audience into a double perception. First, if union action continued then the whole of the opera season would be canceled. Second, and related, this conditional threat was yet another example of the world's disruptive news. Worse still, it lay in an unspecified future time.

Following this story of selfishness, stubbornness, and self-interest comes the contrast, a story of gratitude for an anonymous gift of the chance of life for a little girl seemingly overwhelmed by medical machinery but bravely, if wanly, struggling on. It is a simple human interest story coded in sharp contrast to OPERA ROW. The THANK YOU story had two overt intentions: one, to extol the skills of surgeons who had transplanted an adult heart into a ten-year-old girl named Nicole, Australia's youngest transplant patient, "who was momentarily dead on the operating table"; second, to announce a surgical record—the hospital's successful conclusion of two transplants in one day. An anonymous family had donated the heart after an automobile crash had killed their adult son. Nicole gains a new lease on life as does another patient, part of a surgical record set by the Sydney hospital's doctors. These workers are dedicated and hardworking, helping members of the public to a better life by their professional devotion.

This report displays the Tension-Climax-Release rhythm but the THANK YOU report has a further function in that its optimism and uplift are actually the preliminary notes to the commercial-break coda of containment, all items of which promise some sort of fulfillment, comfort, and contentment within the domestic arena. Again, the stress is upon normality and the sequence is placed as an interlude between the theme of disruption to a young life and the more radical fracture as caused by the domestic and social disruption of a prison story. The prison riot report has been coded in tension and in expectation by the anchorman's preview, "a major crackdown . . . in the face of prisoner uprising. Coming up next . . ." So, even the comfort and contentment of the commercial sequence has to be viewed with a feeling of disturbance in the exciting potential of a prison riot story, "coming up next."

A Mix of Codes

A "classic" rhetorical method that can confuse an audience is to employ a range of images, mixed metaphors, and a variety of styles within one performance or message. Television news presents a similar emphasis because stories are produced according to a very narrow range of visual conventions. The visual codes are largely predictable, lacking any pretense of naturalism, which is why so much attention should be paid to the verbal language of news reports. Nonetheless, production values demand variety and interest. A report on the Irish Republican Army in Channel Ten's news (table 5.6) illustrates one re-

Table 5.6.

		Verbal		Visual
Anchorman (2)	1	In London an Old Bailey jury has sentenced two of the IRA's top bombers to five life sentences each. Thomas Quigley and Paul Cavanagh will spend at least 35 years behind bars. Scott Chisolm reports.	1	Verbal Box JAIL encasing photographs of IRA terrorists.
Reporter	2	Thomas Quigley was one of the IRA's top planners. He chose the targets to be hit.	2	Box IRA Bombers Enlarged head shot of Thomas Quigley.
	3	Paul Cavanagh was much more dangerous. He decided how the targets would be hit and he designed the bombs.	3	Same as (2) with addition of Cavanagh's enlarged head shot.
	4	They were part of the IRA's five-man active service unit on the British mainland in 1981.	4	Same as (3) with 3 silhouettes underneath.
	5	Evelyn Glenholm is still on the run. The other two, police told the court, are no longer a threat.	5	As (4) and Glenholm's face fills one of the silhouettes.
	6	Their first target was an army barracks in Chelsea. The bomb killed two civilians who happened to be passing by. Detectives knew at once they were looking for the most professional terrorist squad ever to have infiltrated the mainland.	6	Aftermath of explosion file photos.
	7	Days later, their second bomb went off in a hamburger bar in Oxford Street.	7	Aftermath of explosion file photos.
	8	Killing the bomb disposal officer who was trying to defuse it.	8	Superimposed head shot of dead man.

Table 5.6. (cont.)

	Verbal		Visual
9	Their third bomb, outside one of London's largest department stores, was successfully defused and later analyzed.	9	Still of department store frontage.
10	A fourth explosion blew apart the bedroom of Britain's attorney general. He and his wife weren't home that night.	10	Shot of house, with policeman on guard.
11	It was here that police got their first real clue. Detectives found a fingerprint and it was Quigley's.	11	Shot of two detectives talking, outside house.
12	Here, they found more fingerprints and forensic links to the 1981 bombings. Within weeks, police had five names and after a tip-off, Quigley was arrested in Belfast and brought to London.	12	Long shot, telescoped, of forest, with police searching undergrowth.
13	Meanwhile, Special Branch officers were tailing a Rover. In it was Cavanagh and three others. The Rover led them to two more huge arms dumps hidden in forests. The first in Nottinghamshire and the second in Northamptonshire.	13	*Reconstructed visual narrative.* White Rover car traveling the original route. Pictures taken by a following camera-car, sometimes from behind, sometimes from the side as camera "overtakes" the Rover.
14	Machine guns, pistols, grenades, explosives, and timing devices were recovered. But police lost the car and its occupants. Special Branch hadn't told the anti-terrorist squad about its operation	14	Close-up shots of weapons laid out on a sheet.
15	and they now know that the ones that got away were Britain's most wanted men—the Harrod's bombers. They had them in sight, almost within reach, and let them slip away.	15	Back to reconstructed journey on roadways.
16	When they located the Rover they found traces of explosives inside and Paul Cavanagh's thumbprint on a bag in the boot [trunk]. He was traced to Belfast, arrested, and brought to London.	16	Several stills of car.
17	Tonight, Cavanagh and Quigley are on their way to two of Britain's most heavily-guarded prison cells. Meanwhile, the authorities are bracing themselves for the inevitable, the next phase in the IRA's mainland campaign. Scott Chisolm in London for Eyewitness News.	17	Reporter, talking live, to camera outside Scotland Yard.

sponse to this professional imperative and also offers an interesting variation on the containment style that I describe in this chapter.

The most interesting aspect of the report is its mix of fact and fiction, of past and present and future. Such a range in itself presents a challenge to audiences in that the mind cannot easily and naturally settle on the general narrative direction of the report. This particular story, on a theme firmly entrenched in viewers' minds as "violent" (the "current" British-Irish troubles began in 1968 and the "mediated" impact has been one of death, destruction, and religion-inspired mayhem), runs the distant risk of news overkill. The report lessens the possibility of such an impact by its "sliding panel" technique of narrative. Table 5.7 indicates the bewildering switches over time and genre type in the complete segment, a nice confirmation of postmodern conventions being utilized by this most modern medium.

The use of tenses in this report is important. In English, tense has two main functions. One, to place an event in time; two, to indicate an event's status, that is, present (verifiable), past (not necessarily verifiable), future (predictive). "Stories" are usually presented in the past tense so it is of particular interest that this largely factual report is mostly in the past tense; hence, "story"; hence, "fiction."[10]

Table 5.7. IRA Bombers

Transcript Reference Table 8	Verbal/Visual		Time Focus	General Genre Type
1	i	Verbal	Present	Fact
	ii	Verbal	Future	Fact
2	i	Verbal	Past	Fact
	ii	Visual	Past	Fact
3	i	Verbal	Past	Fact
	ii	Visual	Past	Fact
4	i	Verbal	Past	Fact
	ii	Visual	Past	Fact
5	i	Verbal	Implied future/present	Fact
	ii	Visual	Present	Fact
6–12		Verbal and visual	Past	Fact
13–16		Verbal	Past	Fact
13–16		Visual	Past	Fiction
17	i	Verbal	Present	Fact
	ii	Verbal	Future	Implied fact
	iii	Visual	Present	Fact

Of course, this represents a news confusion because the audience knows full well that the Irish issue exists and that the IRA carry out military-style operations. Consequently, the tense of the report is a kind of idealized method for organizing narrative, signposts to help us avoid historical and temporal inconvenience. But in the overall news style of Channel Ten, past tense is directly consonant with the dramatizing and sensationalizing of the stories. The overall scheme, therefore, implies created fiction even though the events come out of the world's daily experiences, which, of necessity, are largely predictable and mundane. Such ordinariness requires a gloss, one provided by this channel's transformations.

This particular report, known to be out of world fact, is given the status of news fiction by the use of a visual reconstruction (transcript reference 13–16). The vantage point for viewers is, imaginatively, that of the pursuer (the police). Therefore, the viewer has the refracted status of legal authority. This visual segment also gives a semblance of narrative pace to what has been a catalog of old news and further dims the fact that the report (and the chase) is concerned with case-hardened murderers.

The momentary vicarious excitement, the confusion of visual genres, the timelessness of the reporting are further aids toward the containment policy of Channel Ten, a policy that enables fictive excitement, factual report, and panic mongering to be held in some sort of coded balance, a balance that allows general audience involvement and individual viewer fascination without invoking fear. The foregoing analyses are sufficient for my argument since Channel Ten news employs the described repetitive structure and "tropes" ceaselessly.

Conclusion

Television news is a cultural construct generated by ideology because, as a product of a mass medium, it operates within the terrain wherein frameworks of understanding of the world are used, and it helps to produce, generate, and distribute definitions of this world.

Stuart Hall has argued that conventional critiques on ideological themes that assume "that we are dealing with a kind of rationally calculative system and figures of thought that just correspond to a rationally given economic interest does not describe the maelstrom of potential ideological subjects that are."[11] He then claims that what human beings eventually become, "in action," is not only a product of what is inside our heads (i.e., not exclusively a psychological definition) and not exclusively where we are economically positioned; rather, particular ideological mechanisms and institutions and forces can construct us into different forms of practice.[12]

Hall's comments inject a note of necessary caution into those kinds of ideological studies that assume that any message that can be glossed ideologically automatically produces ideological clones in the reception of knowledge by the audience. It is more reasonable to assume that, for individual members of audience, the surfaces of social and private life are constantly changing and that these personal repositionings produce novel intersections and overlaps in personal experience. It is likely that at some point on these crossovers some new cultural knowledge is gained and people's ideological frames resituated.

It is within the context of the flux of "knowledge" that Channel Ten's shifting structure is important. By eschewing coherence for rhythmic stress in the types of news report, and by the regularized placements of happy/unhappy, climax/release, stress/contentment narratives, the station's entertainment principle of restrained excitement and vitality can be successfully maintained. It is this implicit rhythmic coding that is the "ritual experience" of television news, but it is not a variant of classical ritual with its integrative, cathartic, or celebratory functions, which may temporarily prove uncontrollable. Rather, television news ritual is a conscious, controlled, and artful structure whose intention is to create audiences, not for the advertiser and its commercial productions, but for the vast and shifting terrain, the very human desire for exciting and arresting stories. That aching void, unfathomable, unfillable, is the ground for a certain kind of knowledge. It is a knowledge rooted in vicarious experience, structured by threat and resolved by familiar codes of entertainment.

In this sense Lewis's comment that television news discourse alienates the audience from its own history has some force. The alienation, however, is away from *official* history; from cultures' conventional realities; from audience members' placement in the structure of (non) power. People do not forget their own private histories or their roots—many tenaciously cling to both. The silences that official discourses impose *are* serious matters and television news reporting stands condemned for its complicity. But the condition of culture that such absences help to form may not be so dire. The form and narrative styles of television news are potentially varied and subtle, and what may have happened over the past twenty years is that audiences have been educated to appreciate storytelling. In the future world, where many restrictions and containments may have disappeared, the scope for the audiences' reconnection with the wider world increases. In the process, *news* becomes irrelevant. In its place, stories about the world will be told by other genres. Soap opera may deal with realities beyond those of adolescent phantasm (in Brazil, we have seen how one soap opera helped to bring down the Collor presidency). Crime may be explicated by the thriller serial ("Miami Vice" gave us more real information about the drug trade than did official stories in the media). Movies do help us to understand the corruptions of power (Oliver Stone's *J.F.K,* the BBC's *Edge of Darkness*). Novelists such as Andrew Vachs chart the hideous, hidden world of the pedophile. And audiences will be connected to these stories more firmly, and therefore with the chance of making intelligent, critical assessments, because they understand form and method much more surely than in the past. More important, stories-that-set-out-to-be-stories employ narrative styles we all know intuitively (even television news adopts traditional storytelling forms; Hero-Villain; Chase [Investigation]-Climax; Exploiter-Victim; Good-Bad Moral Universes) so that experience of new genres, which extend the familiar codes by means of connections to the unfamiliar *Real,* may gradually develop new understandings.

The future world will be a much more porous one than heretofore. With new technologies, there will be much more leakage from official stories, and many more members of the audience will be making news that will have the potential to make fissures in the discourses of power. The Rodney King trials, brought about by an amateur video camera user, were the most popularly celebrated of recent instances, and (from the modern) internet-displayed demands of the Zapatista rebel leadership placing unexpected pressure on the Mexican government's official texts (from the postmodern) are but reminders of the mix of discourses in old-new time that soon will be commonplace.

Of course, such events will place a strain on the containment structure described in the paper. But, by then, television news may be just one of many story makers that the audience consciously will use to make sense of the worlds of power.

Notes

A complete transcript of the news program is available to interested readers. Contact Mary S. Mander at her email address, msm4@psu.edu, or write to her at 129 Carnegie Bldg., Pennsylvania State University, University Park, PA 16802.

1. See R. Brunt and M. Jordin, "The Politics 'Bias': How Television Audiences View Current Affairs," in *Propaganda, Persuasion and Politics,* ed. J. Hawthorn (London: Edward Arnold, 1987); David Morley, *The "Nationwide" Audience* (London: British

Film Institute, 1980), and *Family Television* (London: CoMedia, 1986); Justin Lewis, *The Ideological Octopus* (New York: Routledge, 1991).

2. Lewis, 156.

3. Ibid., 157.

4. H. Davis and P. Walton, "Death of a Premier: Consensus and Closure in International News," in *Language, Image, Media* (London: Blackwell, 1983).

5. See, however, James Der Deriann's uncompromising and startling paper on terrorist discourses, where he argues that global terrorism's real threat is not in widespread territorial networks but in "a non-place, an electronic cyberspace that reproduces and contextualises the terrorist act for the global audience. . . . it is the interventionary power of governments, the representational practices of the media, and the conformist interpretations of the evidence that reconstitute and magnify the force of Terrorism." "The Terrorist Discourse: Signs, States and Symbols of Global Political Violence," in *World Security: Trends and Challenges at Century's End,* ed. Michael T. Klase and Daniel C. Thomas (New York: St. Martin's, 1991), 257.

6. Adelaide, capital of South Australia, has a population of 950,000 in a state population of 1.3 million.

7. This too can be explained by knowledge of recent national events. The still picture, framed, is a head-and-shoulder shot of a Sydney magistrate, arraigned on corruption charges. It had been a sensational long-running affair, enough, one would suppose, for the news producers to confidently expect recognition of the general theme of crime-justice.

8. The distorted technical iconography of drug use has respectable literary antecedents and while I would assert no link between Charles Dickens and contemporary popular imagination, his description of an opium den in the opening pages of *The Mystery of Edwin Drood* is a tantalizing cultural image possessing potency still. The drab who operates the den laments to herself, "Ah, poor me, my poor hand shakes like to drop off! I see ye coming-to, and I ses to my poor self, 'I'll have another ready for him, and he'll bear in mind the market price of opium and pay according.' O my poor head! I makes my pipe of old penny ink-bottles, ye see, deary—this one—and I fits in a mouthpiece, this way, and I takes my mixer out of this thimble with this little horn spoon, and so I fills, deary!" (London: Penguin, 1983, p. 38).

9. See Glasgow University Media Group's *Bad News* (London: Routledge, 1976); *More Bad News* (London: Routledge, 1980); and *Really Bad News* (London: Writers and Readers Cooperative, 1982).

10. In necessary contrast, the items in the commercial-break segments are in the (universal) present tense (satisfaction available now). Thus validity status, as coded through linguistic tense, is another element of containments. At regular intervals the audience is taken out of past/present/future ambiguities of the world's carnage into the certain and immediate reality of unambiguous consumption.

11. Stuart Hall, "Ideology and the Modern World," Melbourne University of Latrobe, occasional paper no. 65 (Melbourne, Australia, 1983), 2.

12. Ibid., 4.

6

Television News Narrative

Peter Dahlgren

The national evening television news programs in North America and Western Europe have been, since their inception, the flagships of television journalism. Internationally, news and current affairs programs have rapidly evolved, as we witness the emergence of relatively new genres such as "reality reconstructions" and tabloid formats. Increasingly, "infotainment" programs begin to blur the distinction between news and popular culture.[1] Older genres, such as current affairs talk shows, have gained in prominence. The evening TV newscasts have changed over the past decade or so—chiefly moving to a somewhat faster tempo and more sensational content—yet they remain at the core of television journalism.

Within media research, studies of TV news have considered its organizational and institutional structures, its audiences, and most of all, the actual programming itself. What knowledge one derives from any study is of course predicated on the kinds of questions one poses and the premises behind them. The dominant tradition of research has used a variety of social and behavioral science approaches. In studying the programming, individuals who work within this tradition use what I call an "information orientation," which is for the most part compatible with journalism's view of itself and with its discourses about itself. The focus of such research is on the transmission of messages, mapping and analyzing the factual content of the news in the light of such concerns as accuracy, impartiality, comprehension, and so on.

In the early 1970s another research tradition emerged, with theoretical roots in neo-Marxism and critical theory. Along with political-economic analysis of TV news, those working within this tradition saw as their task the elucidation of the ideological dimensions of news, underscoring the various ways the programming reproduces social relations of domination, chiefly along class lines.

About a decade later, a third direction began to appear. This research tradition might be called "culturological," though a less clumsy label is "interpretive," or hermeneutic.[2] Its intellectual origins are varied, though its indebtedness to hermeneutics is apparent.[3] Interpretive media researchers approach television programming (of all kinds) with the problematic of meaning as its key analytic concern: how meaning is produced and encoded in the programming and, beyond that, how viewers construct meaning in the process of reception, and what the societal significance might be attributed to the meanings that circulate via television.[4]

With this emphasis on the social implications of sense making, here too the critique of ideology can certainly become relevant.[5] However, in the hermeneutic tradition, all meaning is not reducible to ideology. The production and circulation of meaning, as the quintessential human activity, is seen as fundamental for the social order. Whether or not the particular meanings within a media genre or other contemporary discourse are ideological is itself an interpretive question: the text must be analyzed in relation to its societal context and the social relations into which it enters. While social order inevitably implies social conflict, there is nothing automatically ideological in the symbolic communication of either order or conflict. Ideology is seen as an ever-present possibility, and interpretive research is thus always potentially critical.

Citing the international evidence that shows that viewers are in fact left with little "information" in the strict sense,[6] researchers within the hermeneutic tradition underscore the repetitive dimensions of TV news, treating it and its formats as a recurring phenomenon in everyday life. In terms of research perspectives, the hermeneutic tradition tends to emphasize the media as cultural phenomena and as ritual.[7] While by no means denying that TV news does transfer information to its viewers, this perspective argues that the real social significance of TV news lies not so much with its presentation of fleeting facts, but rather with the relatively stable symbolic universe it presents. From the standpoint of the viewers' experience and sense making, this leans toward not only the "extra-informational" but even the "extra-rational." Indeed, the epistemic bias of the television medium itself, with its visual representation, is such that it is assumed to operate even beyond the boundaries of formal, rational cognitive activity.

It should be noted here that this rather eclectic hermeneutic tradition both incorporates elements of and partly merges into what has come to be known as cultural studies, though it is not identical to that field. While cultural studies as a field tends to be more self-conscious about its own identity, its boundaries are by no means clear.[8]

This interpretive turn in television studies—and media research generally—usually makes use of qualitative methods.[9] This is evident in the interviews and ethnographies around audiences,[10] as well as in analyses of the programming itself, where an array of methods are used, including semiotic, narratological, feminist, and psychoanalytic approaches.[11]

Hermeneutic studies often analyze TV news using the everyday epistemology of viewers as its horizon; the goal is to try to elucidate what the programs can mean for the viewers themselves and not merely to draw out some exclusive interpretation that is unique to the researcher or privileged critic. These studies thus involve in a sense a double hermeneutic: in analyzing TV news, the researcher must also take into account the interpretive practices of the viewers. Analysis with an implicit audience in mind is necessarily done with modesty. Any audience is quite heterogeneous, and at best such research can try to clarify the possible and likely trajectories of sense making among viewers. Like all "reader-oriented" text studies (some of them discussions of the tensions between researchers' and readers' interpretations),[12] such research needs to keep in touch with the qualitative audience studies that ethnographically probe viewers' production of meaning.

Meaning is ultimately not an issue of logical or empirical proof, but of intersubjectively shared sense. As such, it is always to some extent equivocal and multivalent, and it pivots on establishing a consensus with the reader. This holds true for the relationship between television and its viewers as well as between research and its readers. One possible asset the researchers of TV news have is that they can assume that most of their readers will also be TV news viewers.

Among the more useful analytic frameworks for interpretive television analysis are those of narrative and myth. These are particularly helpful in studying TV news, since the foundation of many stories in the news is some element of social conflict. Social conflict in the real world must of course be given some form of culturally accessible representation if it is to be communicated, and drama is normally an ingredient here.[13] Myth and narrative, however, are by no means neutral. They always invite certain ways of seeing the world and exclude others, with specific political implications, as many commentators have noted.[14] This hermeneutic tradition, drawing upon myth and narrative to analyze representations of social conflict, is an intellectual distant cousin to the American strand of rhetorical analysis that builds upon Kenneth Burke's dramatism.[15]

The presentation that follows probes two related themes: how certain features of the established TV news narrative convey meaning to the viewer, and how TV news, mediated via viewers' sense-making practices in everyday life, operates at a mythic level for the social order as a whole. In the text, I occasionally use the concept of "ideation," which means "the process of forming ideas or images." I find this to be a convenient, nontechnical synonym for the production of the meaning of the process of making sense, especially in regard to TV news, not least because it straddles the verbal/visual dichotomy as well as that of rational/extra-rational. My concern here is more with the process, rather than the products of meaning-making.

The discussion builds upon a study of TV news done in Sweden; hence, the examples derive from Swedish data. However, despite some variations in the forms of presentation on the TV news programs in different countries, the genre has become quite international by now and most readers should find nothing unfamiliar in my illustrations.

Narrative, Reality, and Meaning

All stories have a storyteller, be it an individual person or a collectivity. This holds true for narrative accounts about events in the real world as well as for fictional tales. Storytelling, of necessity, bears the stamp of human subjectivity; its traces cannot be totally removed. I do not say this with the debates about journalistic "objectivity" in mind—that becomes a specialized problematic within a very particular context. Rather, to underscore the inextricable component of human subjectivity and intentionality within all storytelling is to highlight once more the "constructivist" notion that *social* reality is always in part a human production, an ongoing result of cultural practices, including language use. Meaning is a construction, albeit at times fragile and elusive, and one of the archetypical practices by which we generate meaning about real-world happenings is through narrative form.

The real world "out there," the world of events, does not speak; it is mute. Events flow in a natural timeframe, that is, their own; their order and duration, to the extent that they are available to our perception, are fixed. Narrative, on the other hand, is limited by human perception and understanding. It takes a selection of events and presents them, such that the order and duration do not necessarily correspond to that of the original events. The narrative presents a sequence of events that refer to a set of events beyond itself. While this is on the surface quite obvious, the theoretical point here is that we have different levels of reality, which are bridged by human intervention. One can add that there is yet a third level, that in which the audience encounters the narrative, makes sense of it, and thus recapitulates the original natural order and duration based on what the level of narrative reality contains.

So between the real events and the audience we find narrative. But narrative does more than just link; as I suggested, it contributes to the generation of meaning. How does it do this? It would seem that meaning does not arise merely out of a chronological display of episodes. The narrative form itself "works" on the raw materials of sequential episode. Paul Ricoeur neatly captures the process by pointing to two dimensions of narrative: what he calls the episodic and the configurational. The episodic consists of precisely those features that shape the contingencies of the story's unfolding. They address the expectations of development, considering the questions "and so?" "what next?" "and then?" and others. In other words, this is simply the sequential flow, the building blocks of episode (which again do not necessarily correspond to the order of the external events).[16]

The configurational dimension consists of all the elements that "grasp together" successive events and extract a configuration, imposing a formal coherency on that which would otherwise remain a sequence of senseless happenings. The mechanics of the configurational dimension vary between genres, cultures, and historical epochs, but I think one can make a claim on some universal principle here: there is a human drive or longing for "closure" in our understanding of the real world. Since the real world does not speak to us, it always holds out the possibility of normative or moral chaos. The seemingly arbitrary nature of reality, the void of meaninglessness, is countered in general by the patterns of cultures, which give a coherence to the world. More specifically, the world is made more stable and intelligible by the narratives we encounter and (re)tell.

According to Hayden White, all narrative contains moral viewpoints, thus responding to the basic human longing that the real world should appear to us as coherent and basically just—a desire whose fulfillment remains elusive.[17] This insight, derived from a merger of literature with philosophical anthropology, suggests that a narrator, a speaker of stories, always remains in part a subject who expresses a consciousness. We can readily accept this with fiction, but with stories that relate events from the real world, this becomes culturally untenable. I am not thinking only of journalism but of all settings where narrative discourse must somehow claim legitimacy as being "objective" in some sense of the word, such as legal, medical, or social scientific contexts. My point is not in any way to argue for a pure or polarized position: that all storytelling is colored by subjectivity and thus the ideal of objectivity is meaningless. I do not think such a line is productive. One could make such a case, but the formal claim as such has little import in our lives. Instead, I think we do better simply to come to terms with a basic feature of the human condition that says that no narrator is or can be a mere funnel or mouthpiece of the real world, that events could just speak themselves through a narrator. The real world does not present itself in neat story form, with beginnings, middles, and endings. People, in their cultures, make narratives. To tell stories means we are already and always implicated in contributing to the definition and construction of meaning in social reality. By extension, we, as narrators, can never escape the responsibility that ensues with the narrative practice: we help "create" the world, even if only to a small degree. All stories contain normative and explanatory aspects, as I mentioned above. All storytellers are, in a sense, "cultural rhetoricians" who advocate particular ways of seeing the world and foster particular dispositions toward it.

Psychologically and culturally, it is of course difficult to live with this view on a daily basis, since it keeps alive the discomfiture of arbitrariness and potential chaos that the human need for order tries to counteract. Thus, particularly with repetitive and institutionalized storytelling that has a central place in our society, a considerable degree of "reification" is probably inevitable. That is, the human and social origins of the telling become lost from view or are actively displaced from our awareness. The subjective element of storytelling is occluded, thereby enhancing the aura of the narrator as a funnel of reality and undergirding his or her legitimacy.

The configurational dimensions of TV news narrative, which derive from the qualities of the medium itself as well as from the traditions of storytelling that have become established by professionalism, give shape and coherence to the story-world. They help convey the story-world, rendering it accessible and meaningful to the viewer. Let us explore some of these configurational dimensions and see how they work.

The Prime Narrator

In conversation, when we speak about "the news," there is often a double reference. On the one hand we mean the reports of the events themselves, the stories that are told. On the other hand, we may also be referring to the storyteller, the collective agency who tells us about the events, as in, for example, "What was on the news last night?" This ambiguity tacitly recognizes that the events quite obviously do not present themselves, but are told to us, by somebody. The "somebody" here is not just the newscaster per se, but rather a still more fundamental storyteller, whom I call the prime narrator.

The prime narrator is in a sense the "invisible hand" behind the programs themselves, the ensemble of unseen staff whose production efforts in selection, editing, and presentation result in the program as a whole. The prime narrator is the institution of professional TV news; it is greater than the sum of the faces of the newscasters and reporters.

The programs do not begin with news narratives; they begin with a display of the program vessel that carries the stories, which we recognize as the TV news program. The program vessel is presented by this prime narrator; this is the teller who brings us not only the events but even presents the "assistants," the newscasters and reporters we see on the screen. The disembodied presence of the prime narrator is a fundamental configurational element for the production of meaning. For the viewer, the process of ideation begins with the encounter with this prime narrator and an understanding of its identity, that is, its social location and the status of the knowledge it provides. The identity of prime narrator fosters a relationship with the viewer: the audience is situated in a subordinate relation of dependence to a storyteller that seemingly has the whole world as its terrain of knowledge and seldom reveals the methodology of its knowing or the boundaries of its knowledge. It appears Olympian.

To say this is not necessarily a critical comment; rather it is to indicate that this identity of the prime narrator, which is revealed by the symbolic displays that connote globalism, command of technical apparatus, access to the powerful, briskness, seriousness, and an aura of urgency given the time constraints— all of these attributes of identity are basic, even if taken for granted, to the configurational dimension of news narration. They provide a baseline of perceptual organization and culturally conditioned narrative intelligibility. *Who* is narrating, with the consequent trust and dependence, is foundational for the ideation process via narrative.

Moreover, the prime narrator, in bringing us the program in its entirety, creates an underlying narrative that links the episodes of the news stories into an overarching narrative at the level of the program itself. The order and duration of the stories, their juxtapositions and transitions, signify meaning by implying differences: classificatory distinctions as to the respective importance between stories, their location on the cognitive map of the prime narrator (which becomes our map) such as the typifications of "hard news," "ongoing" stories, "human interest," and so forth. The use of headlines at the start of the program, each with its graphic still image, the presentation of "important" international and national news first (in stories of relatively long duration), the potpourri of short news items (each generally thirty seconds or less and mostly unaccompanied by moving visuals, which are frequently grouped in blocks), all these kinds of production conventions help the viewer to sort and structure output.

The Voices of the News

Moving from the level of the program as a production totality with its unseen prime narrator to the people who *are* visible, we become aware of how their relative position within the story-world provides the audience with an essential footing for making sense of the narratives. This configurational aspect is conveyed by several means, and the resulting hierarchy pivots principally on the issue of whose knowledge commands more legitimacy within the logic of the narratives.

One initial distinction becomes readily apparent, and that is the general contrast between those who have and those who lack what could be called performative competence. The newscasters and journalists who appear or who are heard in the program clearly have the competence to perform within television journalism. They speak with an assurance that identifies their professional stature and commands audience attention. This competence is displayed in particular by their use of "news talk," the particular manner of speech we have come to associate with journalism. It is identified by its vocabulary, syntax, idiomatic formulations, and, not least, voice inflection. These together result in a speech that is matter-of-fact and self-assured, with little or no trace of self-doubt, emotion, or uncertainty about the material it presents. It conveys seriousness, and where appropriate, urgency and even light touches of irony. News talk is confident talk, secure in its professionalism.

Among the news actors, there are other versions of performative competence. Public figures, those who appear frequently in the news, have a competence in expressing their views and arguing their cases. They usually appear thoroughly at home in front of a camera or in the presence of interviewers. They are for the most part articulate, seldom stammering or groping for words. Rarely do they use the pauses, hesitations, or nonverbal sounds and punctuations that typify everyday speech (such as "um," "er," "well, uh, you know"). Similarly, others who have high positions, even if they are not regular faces in the news, manage by and large to speak with an assurance and level of verbal sophistication that suggests a sense of control and confidence. Corporate and union leaders, scientific experts, and high-ranking bureaucrats, for example, fall into this category. Obviously there are instances where they seem to fail in their verbal competence, which may then convey a slightly comical impression as a result of the contrast with their formal position.

Those tending to lack performative competence are frequently the address-ees of action, people from groups who are at the receiving end of a decision or are the victims of an event. Also, the marginal, the unorganized, and of-ten "average citizens" are found here. In short, they tend to be those who do *not* initiate news actions, or at least not action with high status or legitimacy (e.g., angry protesters who seemingly are on the fringes of orderly behavior often lack this performative competence). The vast majority of the popula-tion lacks performative competence; hence the compelling aura of those who display it.

Performative competence is one distinction, and here newspeople and the powerful find themselves on the same side of a boundary. But there is anoth-er, more structural dimension that tends to *separate* them. If we recall that the prime narrator is the "storyteller" who presents us with the program, we can continue down a chain of mediations, where the audience is "turned over" to yet other voices. The prime narrator, after the opening of the program, recedes in favor of the anchorperson, who then continues as the voice of the prime narrator. The difference, however, is that the audience *sees* the anchorperson, who becomes not only a master of ceremonies for the entire program but also the source of much of the news as well. For the audience, the anchorperson becomes the baseline, the "human connection," the subjectivity that serves as liaison between the viewer and the whole story-world of TV news.

This is only partly due to the familiarity the audience has with the specific individuals who rotate in the function of anchorperson. The prime factor is the position of the anchorperson vis-à-vis others in the program and vis-à-vis the viewer. The dominant pattern is as follows. The anchorperson begins a story; if it is relatively short, he or she will finish it and then begin another. If it is longer, the anchorperson not only begins it but provides an overview of the entire story, often touching on most of the narrative units that com-prise the full story. Then the anchorperson turns us over to a reporter, who may or may not be visible on the screen, and who in turn may have one or more film segments to present. In these visual segments, we often find the news actors. Then, at the end, we return to the anchorperson, who may make some wrapup statement, suggesting the implications of possible further developments that might be anticipated. Then the anchorperson begins the next story or turns us over to a commentator or, at the very end, to the weather forecaster.

That it is the anchorperson who begins, and that we return to him or her at the conclusion of each story, is significant. But it is with and through the anchorperson, above all others, that the audience relates to the stories, since no other figure directly addresses the viewers throughout the program. We the viewers align ourselves with the anchorperson's view of the world; he or she has apparent access to everything and command over the technical and personnel resources of the entire news operations. Thus, his or her knowledge is paramount over that of the others in the program; for instance, the reporters to whom the anchor turns us over are in a sense subordinates. They further expand upon the basic lines of a story that the anchor introduces.

We can understand the significance of this role by simply imagining an alternative program structure where each story is begun by a different reporter, where there is no central figure. The chances are we would feel "adrift" precisely because we had no "anchor"—no one human subjectivity who mediates and buffers the story-world by his or her commanding presence. Or even more extreme, if we were to see TV news programs without an anchorperson, where the reporters themselves were never seen on the screen—only graphics and filmed segments with voice-overs—lacking the simple (para-) social context provided by human faces, we might experience anxiety. We would wonder what (sense) to make of the stories, feeling lost without the reassurance and sense-making cues from concrete people. (This of course is a result of our cultural conditioning; with radio we have different expectations about the experience of listening.)

Among news actors, we find a rather stable hierarchy as well. This is transmitted partly by their relative performative competence, as I discussed, but also in the manner in which they are permitted to speak within the context of production conventions of the programs, their "degrees of freedom." First, it is clear that certain categories of actors have a seemingly legitimate claim to "make news"; they have access to the story-world and are relatively free to initiate news. Calling a press conference, for instance, is the classic case. Yet even within interviews we can see differences of degrees of freedom, with the interviewer permitting different actors different amounts of "space" to speak their minds. At one extreme, the interviewer respectfully presents questions that at base merely introduce topics, e.g., "What about wage controls?" This allows the news actors considerable free play. At the other extreme, the reporter tries to corner the news actor, asking pinpoint questions and steering the directions of the interview. (One can note in passing the situation where reporters, through various devices such as voice inflection or pseudo-aggressive syntax, try to create an image of a "hard-hitting" interview when in fact allowing a high degree of freedom.)

The degree of freedom permitted tends to correlate with political and economic position and thus the knowledge expressed by elite figures tends to have a built-in legitimacy. Thus, at the top, we again see the major politicians (exceptions here are if politicians find themselves in a scandal or otherwise on the defensive: reporters then tend to restrict the degrees of freedom). Also, such groups as high-ranking corporate executives, military officials, experts, and upper echelon union officials are permitted considerable freedom. As we move down the ladder, to say, workers on the factory floor, average citizens, children, and so forth, the questioning becomes more focused. Often such interviews are merely oriented to elicit predictable reactions to illustrate what has already been said within the story. Consequently, the knowledge status of such actors is low and clearly subordinate to that of other categories of actors.

High-ranking politicians are usually the initiators of action and are given much freedom in the interviews, as I have indicated. In this sense their position in the hierarchy is superior to that of the reporters, who mediate the politicians to the audience. Yet on the other hand, within the narrative logic of the programs, these actors often appear as appendages to the reporters' knowing, and by extension, the anchorperson's as well. In a news story, the anchorperson and then the reporter will tell, for example, that a particular politician has expressed his intention to initiate new tax legislation. Then we see and hear the politician doing this in film sequence, thereby becoming merely an illustration of what the journalist said. The effect is strengthened when, in the wrapup of the story, the reporter or anchorperson makes some interpretive remarks, perhaps explaining the politician's motives (e.g., "He is trying to increase his support among home owners and his proposal is aimed to help him politically in this regard"). This sets up a relationship of irony, where the reporter and the audience together know something about the politician, without his being aware that he is an object of their knowledge.

Despite the occasional tension between reporters and officials regarding whose horizons are more convincing, the hierarchy of legitimate knowledge varies little. The implicit invitation to see the world through the eyes of the different people who speak within the news program becomes a scheme for aiding the audience to achieve narrative closure—to attain some ideational resolution within the narratives. The use of visuals further provides strong clues for "preferred" meanings in the news stories.

Regarding Visuals

Like the verbal language, the use of visuals tends to draw upon a basic repertoire, the range of which is limited by convention. Here I will take up just a
few points pertaining to the discussion at hand.

As many observers have remarked, TV news is not really as "visual" as we
may commonly assume, in the sense that many stories consist simply of the
anchorperson with some still photos, maps, or graphs as accompaniment.
Further, the current state of TV news professionalism still retains strong ties
with its roots in the press and radio: narrative in TV news for the most part
is structured around a text to which visuals are added. Narrative seldom speaks
here with the visual as the prime voice, though one can occasionally notice
that some exciting visual footage has been received by the studio and run with
a minimum of verbal "story" since the facts were perhaps not yet available.
The visuals were so compelling that they *had* to be shown. It remains to be
seen whether, over the next generation, this will change. If new recruits to
the profession come increasingly from backgrounds in film or video rather
than print or radio, "visual thinking" may take new directions.

This is not to suggest that the visuals today are by any means insignificant.
Indeed, they are central to TV news as a cultural form and are integral to its
narrative dynamics. That the anchorperson appears as an animate image is
clearly crucial. Accompanying stills, such as photos of faces or buildings, maps,
graphs, or drawings add a second dimension beyond the anchorperson. Such
images serve a variety of functions, not least pedagogical, by concretizing or
capturing a theme from the text, providing added information, or evoking
culturally shared associations. Exactly how they function cognitively for the
audience varies with how they are used. In terms of narrative dynamics, however, I would suggest that their role is fundamentally ancillary to the verbal
dimension of the anchorperson's presentation.

With moving visuals, on the other hand, we move into a third experiential
domain, which is of a different order. Film theory through the years has struggled to define the exact nature of filmic narrative and the experience of watching a movie. A review of this literature is beyond my purposes here, but I would
posit that a few basic themes from film theory are pertinent to film and video
segments on TV news. First, such moving images, together with their aural
component, create the possibility of an experiential reality beyond our immediate here and now. Our coordinates of time and space thereby are expanded.
Second we can experience a co-presence with this reality beyond our own; if
theater builds upon the suspension of disbelief, film's capacity for "illusion" is

far more potent. Particularly via moving visuals, the prime narrator of TV news presents a story-world that we may perceive as "immediate." Third, through the tradition of documentary (which in turn reflects thinking that emerged with the history of the photograph), we have a culturally conditioned sense that distinguishes between the filmic narrative that presents itself as "fiction" and that which claims to be a representation of "reality."

These themes provide a background against which to understand some of the features of moving images in TV news. The variables that comprise the typical production conventions of film and video segments become relevant not only for understanding how moving images operate in general according to the themes developed by film theory. More specifically, and for our concerns here, such conventions serve as "shorthand" carriers of meaning within the story-world and thus must be seen as one set of building blocks within the process of ideation.

For example, camera work, such as the distance from a news actor, the angle and height of the camera in relation to the actor, and movement by panning or zooming, can subtly signify meaning. Understandably, certain tacit "rules" have emerged to specify camera work in various situations; these are economical ways of routinizing how camera work should proceed. Thus, as Tuchman and others have pointed out, we have become accustomed to seeing news actors who command legitimacy as being presented with a respectful medium shot, connoting conversational distance.[18] Extreme closeups tend to suggest emotionality, or some form of intensity not in keeping with the aura of rationality appropriate for public figures. Likewise, long shots distance us, rendering the figure more of an object and less of a person. A bird's-eye-view angle can increase our sense of superior knowing over the actors appearing "below" us, and so on.

From the baseline of such conventions of camera work, variations become telling. A closeup of a demonstrator, who is already angry, enhances the image of irrationality, and thereby undermines legitimacy, or credibility, or both. Consider the (unlikely) possibility of seeing all the nation's leading political figures gathered in a crowd, shot from a long distance with a bird's-eye view: the impact would be at total variance with the relationship structured by the camera work with which we are accustomed.

In a similar vein, the contextual settings of the visuals are telling. The setting of the news studio itself has an aura of "headquarters," of command over the world outside. Anyone framed by this setting tends to be accorded status; a studio interview is rarely conducted with "an average citizen." Footage recorded on location—particularly locations removed from our own everyday experiences—clearly invokes the competence of the news organization and our dependence upon it. Interviews with the powerful, set in their offices or in the "halls and corridors of power" unambiguously connote their position. Interviews also indicate the position of the news organization, which has such easy access to the powerful. Such interviews and conferences tend to be neatly arranged, with no disturbances or intrusions. The fact that they are carried out so smoothly again bespeaks the collaboration of news and the powerful. Consider a story based on a chance encounter with a minister who was strolling in a park. The question would immediately arise from the viewer: is this the way news get done? Is it *that* random? By contrast, interviews "on route," for example, at an airport, convey a sense of urgency and importance. An "at home" setting can be appropriate after a public figure has become established and recognized in the news; this can add an attractive "just folks" aura to complement the public identity.

At the other end of the scale, outdoor settings with many people tend to convey less status, though not necessarily a lack of legitimacy. A man in the street interview suggests "vox populi"—a democracy at work, showcasing the average citizen as an opinion holder. Alternatively, interviews framed by "crowds" can, depending on camera work and other variables, connote the potential irrationality of collective behavior—mob rule. Strictly speaking, such details of production conventions cannot say *nothing:* they always convey some meaning, even if such meaning often hovers below the threshold of conscious awareness. Taken together, these various conventions constitute loose codes that have become part of our cultural tools for organizing collective perception; they signal to the viewer how to interpret the visual content they frame. I say "loose" codes because we should be wary of arguing that there is a rigid grammar at work here. There is not. Such a formalist or structuralist perspective imposes an illusory exactitude on the materials and inevitably ends up saying more about its own methodological foundations than about how meaning is transmitted to the viewer.

But in simple and summary terms, I would suggest that the moving images operate within the narrative logic of TV news by accomplishing a few essential pragmatics for the viewer. Not every segment will necessarily accomplish all of the following but we can generally find several at work in any given accompaniment of moving visuals. They can

1. establish locale and typify the scene and its atmosphere;
2. identify and classify the news actors;

3. cue our existing storehouse of knowledge, associations, and dispositions;
4. mobilize our curiosity;
5. evoke affective response and involvement;
6. deflect cognitive and analytic thought;
7. confirm the story-world of TV news as reality in which to involve oneself, particularly as the images, over time, become increasingly self-referential, evoking memory of prior images, perhaps more than memory of experience within our own lived reality;
8. and camouflage their origins of production, by rendering the camera work and editing "invisible" via the aesthetics of naturalism and realism.

This last point in turn denies the subjectivity of storytelling and enhances the aura of objectivity of the programs. Objectivity is confirmed as a possibility, and the news organization is legitimated as a practitioner of this ideal. A mediated reality is transformed into an immediate reality, with the translation process lost from view. This final observation should not be read as an objection or criticism. I am not implying that the news organization should continually demonstrate how it produces visuals, or something equally absurd. Rather, I suggest it is important to understand *that* this process takes place and that it is significant for the dynamics of narrative to succeed.

Cues, Codes, and Closure

The visual cues we receive from moving images and which are somewhat systematized into codes take the audience quite far in making sense of specific stories and the story-world as a whole. The visual cues and codes, largely taken for granted by both the news organization and audiences, work toward a symmetry of meaning—that the sense derived by the audiences is the one preferred by the journalists and producers. However, this closure is never and can never be complete.

First of all, there are all the problems of comprehension, misunderstanding, and "information loss" that research has underscored over the years. Yet there is another question, which has to do with the notion of convention itself. As I have noted, the production routines invite certain ways, usually conventional, of seeing the objects in moving images. But this can backfire when there is an intention to portray action or events that are at variance with conventional perceptions, or when there is an intention to invite a new way of seeing a routine event. The reliance on conventional cues and codes can transmit a standardized interpretation that overrides the text's efforts to bring out new perspectives. A brief example will illustrate this.

A long story had to do with young people who had occupied an abandoned building in Berlin. The police had been called in, there were demonstrations and riots, and one youth died. In headlining the story, reference was made to the possibility of there appearing a whole new generation of terrorists. The visual showed fires and clashes with police, then demonstrations with a closeup of a very angry, unkempt, and somewhat inarticulate young man. There were also some shots of youngsters (actually looking quite pleasant and somewhat placid) sitting on the streets and singing. Then we cut to an office, where a lawyer is interviewed, discussing the situation. He is in a suit, and the background includes desks, books, and so on. The subtext of the visuals cues the familiar associations of rioting youth, chaos, and disturbance; the police are needed to combat anarchy. The lawyer at the end appears as the voice of reason, seemingly expressing views of the establishment, which further implies reassurance that order must and will be restored.

However, after several viewings of the story, in which we were able to listen and follow the text more carefully, something entirely different emerged. The lawyer, it turns out, is a political radical. He says that if the state continues to use violence in defense of private property, especially against youths who are economically on the margins of society, one can expect more trouble in the future, perhaps a new generation of desperate activists, terrorists (hence the headline). Moreover, the tone of the speaker text, upon careful listening, was quite sympathetic to the plight of the young people, and underscored the brutality of the Berlin police. Most of this was lost beneath the conventional visual cues, which triggered routine associations *and* dispositions.

The point here is not how a particular story could have been improved, but rather that the meaning within a story may not always be unitary. In addition, the visuals, by their cueing, may contribute to recognition and familiarity but also render the story-world of TV news more predictable than the journalists actually intend.

Finally, in regard to closure of meaning, I again stress that the interplay between the givenness of the text and the sensemaking by the audience places a wedge in the door, which makes it impossible to close. The audience's meaning-making cannot be ignored. Having thus examined some of the dynamics of TV news discourse, I turn now to a discussion of the process of ideation at the societal level.

TV News and the Social Order

It is important to recognize and acknowledge that ideation is not the movement of audio-visual images or brain waves in a social vacuum. The ideation of TV news is part of a rather stable, daily transmitted discourse that, together with the technical features of its transmission, fosters certain epistemic biases. For the viewers the ideation of TV news is an integral and inseparable aspect of the more general dynamics by which people make sense of the world and produce meaning within their everyday lives. For the social order as a whole the ideation of the TV news discourse is of prime significance for the prevailing institutional arrangements and the predominant culture. My concern here is to highlight TV news as a central mediation between the overarching societal structure and the level of daily existence.

Making Sense in Everyday Life

At the most fundamental level, the act of producing meaning structures our lives. In making sense of the world around us we create a bulwark against the terror of an infinite abyss or existential void. We generate a sense of control over potential chaos; "culture" itself can be seen as essentially stable patterns of shared meaning. But while meaning tends to drive out ambiguity and dissonance and to seek resolution, it always remains somewhat precarious. Meaning is seldom unequivocal, and the order it creates always resides in the shadow of entropy. Basic scaffoldings in our lives can change dramatically or even fall apart, wreaking havoc with the sense of our existence.

Such profound collapse of meaning is of course the exception. Normally, we are not confronted with the alternative of basic order versus rampant chaos; such pivotal moments are restricted to psychological and social crises of great magnitude. Indeed, for most people most of the time, the parameters of existence seem marked by a pervasive aura of continuity.

The primary setting in which we make sense of our realities is that of everyday life. It has an "imperative presence," as Berger and Luckmann point out, with its immediate, here-and-now familiarity.[19] Everyday life is characterized by practical activity—getting things done, taking care of all the details of daily existence; its mind set is a pretheoretic one, with knowledge judged in pragmatic terms. Knowing where to get the best vegetables, how best to deal with one's landlord, what course of action to take if a water pipe begins to leak, ad infinitum, is the knowledge of everyday life. The horizon of everyday life serves as a baseline for definitions of self and the social world.

While the unconscious can prompt a decentered subjectivity, dividing consciousness against itself, setting impulses of desire and control against each other, and so on, such experience, even if consciously recognized, is still interpreted with the "normalcy" of everyday life as the gauge.

Let us for the moment put aside the realm of the unconscious, as well as the exceptional situations where meaning in our lives becomes severely unraveled. Let us look instead to some of the dynamics of sense making. First of all, and in keeping with the quality of familiarity of everyday life, making sense is largely a *routine* process. It thus affords stability via both the familiar nature of the process and the contexts in which it occurs. In everyday life, most routine objects of our perception are greeted as unproblematic until further notice—until something induces us to examine them. At that point, reflection can take place, and definitional changes are made, if necessary, yielding new givens. This may center on purely trivial matters or even persona/ social crises. In short, I suggest that one of the central dynamics of making sense is precisely this dialectic between *taking for granted* and *questioning.*

Most of the stimuli we encounter are part of repetitive patterns; they are experienced as part of our normal world and hence taken for granted. The quality of habituation (routine) becomes dominant in everyday life. We cannot question everything all the time—this would obliterate the basic sense of order we need to experience meaning in our lives. Conversely, we simply cannot always continue to take for granted absolutely everything we carry with us from the past. Some closure would render us incompetent to deal with even minor changes in everyday life. Thus this dialectic. However, people's agility and scope in utilizing this dialectic vary considerably. Some (at least at certain times) eagerly question large areas of their existence. Others continue to take much for granted until they feel absolutely forced to question. People also vary in which areas of their own lives or of the social world they are likely to question.

What is it that is taken for granted or questioned in the process of ideation? We can extract a number of key elements:

—prior stocks of knowledge, in the form of skills, information, facts, and the like;

—affective orientations, the preexisting valences of emotional orientation, attitudes, and so on relevant to the topic at hand;

—patterns of typification, the classification schemes and categorizing devices for organizing phenomena, experience, and knowledge;

—zones of relevance, which are perceived areas of interest or concern;

—arenas of praxis, the contents and situations where the results of ideation can have potential import;

—appropriate discourses, which arise in the particular fields of our pluralistic life-worlds. (The important point here is that discourses are appropriate to the topic and contextual setting in which the ideation occurs.)

These elements are, of course, in mutual reciprocity. Stocks of knowledge can shape relevances and typifications; these in turn can influence the affective orientations and the arenas of praxis. A whole subfield of sociology can be built up around the task of mapping these relationships in various situations and expounding how ideation accordingly proceeds.

The Border Zones of Common Sense

We now consider the dynamics of making sense in everyday life. In relation of TV news, we can make a number of observations. To begin with, the *activity* of watching TV news is firmly anchored within the setting of everyday life. The viewing of TV news is inexorably tied to the general experience of watching TV. The news broadcasts are "in tune" with the overall output of television; there is no profound rupture of experience when the news transmissions begin. The perceptional framework established by television, via its discourses and overall epistemic biases, envelopes the newscasts as well. There is no practical difficulty as such in watching. Moreover, for the viewers, the broadcasts are a part of daily schedule, of habit, perhaps linked to notions of domestic togetherness, leisure, and so on. In short, for the viewer, TV news watching is a phenomenon and activity integrated within the practices of daily living.

When we turn to the story-world of the broadcasts, something curious arises. From the horizon of everyday life, most of the elements that come into play for making sense of the programs—stocks of knowledge, typifications, relevances, and so forth —derive from this story-world and its manner of presentation, not from the pragmatics of lived daily experience. The story-world is largely a *beyond*, a remote universe, impermeable to most praxis or intervention on the part of the viewer. Yet, as an experiential phenomenon, the story-world of TV news, with its particularist discourses and other features, manifests itself on a regular basis within everyday life, and thus becomes part of it.

Analytically, I would describe the viewing of TV news—the site of reception—as marking a boundary line. Television news ideation is fundamentally an interface, the result of a merger between the givenness of the programs and the active sensemaking of the audiences. This interface takes place and defines a social border zone between the experiences of everyday life—the pluralistic social life worlds of home, family, friends, jobs—and the public sphere of politics and social issues.[20] The "micro" world of private and interpersonal experience—where "commonsense" meaning production prevails—confronts and mingles with representations of and from the "macro" world of societal institutions, the economy, the state, politics, and the dominant culture; in this world, "specialized sense" prevails.

At this interface, common sense has its back against the wall. It must come to terms with and assimilate a discourse that claims not only to be of relevance to everyday life, but also to shape and determine many of its basic parameters. Common sense cannot meet this discourse on its own terms; it cannot draw upon its own experience except as it pertains to previous TV viewing, which but confirms its subordination. It is offered few, if any, potential areas of praxis, except to watch and wait. Ideation of the commonsense variety is confronted by a form of knowing that is patently superior to it and displays this superiority continually, in the recognizable and redundant story structure.

Yet common sense cannot merely capitulate or define itself as inadequate. That would undermine the stability and order of daily existence. So, what does it do? How does it respond?

In the Domain of the Mythic

One obvious answer is that common sense responds to this in a commonsense fashion, that is, in a manner that is at base a practical one from the standpoint of daily living. Common sense goes as far as it can, assimilating new inputs into its existing worldview, which for most of us is a patchwork of facts, attitudes, and inconsistent perspectives. Common sense recognizes its limits and is appropriately modest in its claims.

There is no doubt that this is in part true, but it is not the whole story, nor perhaps the main part of it. Rather, I would argue that the circumstances of this interface—between audiences and news, between the private spheres of everyday life and the public sphere of societal politics, and of course between viewers and the epistemic bias of the televisual medium itself—foster modes of ideation we traditionally do not associate with the realm of news and information. Common sense, confronted with its inadequacy and subordination, mobilizes a reinforcement that on the surface permits it to "save face" and carry on as usual, namely, the mythic domain (discussed below). But this ally that is conjured up originates from a psychic region quite removed from where common sense has its cerebral setting. Ideation now enters the realm of the cultural unconscious, of archetype and symbol, and the process of meaning production becomes qualitatively transformed. Ideation to a great extent now becomes relocated, to the extra-rational, to the mythic. Not totally, of course: the elements of rationalist ideation are retained. Indeed, the interface at the site of reception results in a force field between the rational and extra-rational; neither mode is reducible to the other. Yet with TV news, the extra-rational modes of ideation clearly dominate.

Common sense thus retains its social validity, and the order of everyday life is left intact, yet this is achieved by a "behind the scenes" ideational process that renders models of rational "information gathering" hopelessly inadequate to account for what transpires between the programs and viewers. But how is the mythic mode of ideation set in motion, and how does it operate?

TV news viewing is firmly anchored in the reality of everyday life. If everyday life is the most prominent of the multiple realities we inhabit, it is also the setting from which we make sense of phenomena that may originate *beyond* direct experience. Hence dreams, ecstasy, religious revelations, and so on gain meaning largely with reference to the everyday life with which they stand in contrast or to which they refer. So it is with news, which is interpreted by viewers in the light of their assumptions and experiences in daily living. The reception of TV news, at the site of viewing, marks a boundary between the experiences of everyday life with its provinces of meanings, and a world "out there" beyond our face-to-face encounters. In this regard, however, TV news is not unique.

All people, in all cultures, are confronted by the boundaries of their cognitive knowing and by an awareness that there are such "beyonds." These may take the form of specialized sense or "expert knowledge" (from the standpoint of a lay person), or metaphysical or theological issues. Much of what lies "beyond" may be deemed inconsequential, but there usually remains a residue of concerns for most people—an awareness of important things that we do not know about or which may even lie beyond the human capacity to know in the cognitive sense. It is this awareness with which people have to come to terms. Thus, ideation at some level must deal with the boundaries of our knowing, and with that which resides beyond these boundaries. This "other side" may not be empirical or tangible, but it is nonetheless of central concern for human existence. Following Roger Silverstone, I find it appropriate to refer to this mechanism as the "mythic." Rather than speak of myths as specific stories or narrative forms, it is more useful to focus on the mythic dimension of thought and language, or, given my discussion here, the *mythic domain,* of ideation. By this I mean those dimensions of ideation that pertain to or are of relevance for the primordial questions of life and death, origins and purpose of existence, and, not least, the social order under which we live. This can be clarified quite simply.

Since every culture must come to terms with the limits of everyday practical knowledge—common sense—as defined by that culture, there is a need for translating or bridging: between the known and the unknown, the familiar and the unfamiliar, the everyday and the transcendental, the profane and the sacred. This is universal; all cultures address themselves in some way to the larger issues beyond the pragmatic and offer meta-levels of meaning that can lend an ethos and pathos to everyday life, integrating its various provinces of meaning into more encompassing symbolic totalities. What I am referring to here is only partly accounted for by what can be called the "religious impulse." Religion can certainly fill this role, but I find it more useful for our purposes to generalize this function so that its embeddedness in the fabric of everyday life, its ubiquity, becomes abundantly apparent, even for highly secularized societies like our own. The process of making "meta-sense" of everyday life and the boundaries of human existence takes place within the domain of the mythic.

The mythic domain organizes collective cognition at the level of the cultural unconscious; it proceeds largely via extra-rational modes of ideation. It not only touches upon the basic questions of existence and enfolds the institutional social order in a symbolic mantle, but it also can put "everything in its right place." If the subliminal ideation of the mythic domain does not always refer directly to the realities of everyday life in a manner that permits practical activity and pragmatic reasoning, it still gives *sense* to those realities. We arrive here at a different order of meaning, a meta-meaning that can provide coherence to the experiences of daily living.

The Social Order and the Mythic Domain

In the mythic domain, thought patterns of the culture seek resolution to incongruities, paradoxes, and the "beyond." Cultural and psychic order is undergirded by encasing large sets of taken-for-granteds into a cosmic "nature" and removing them from conscious awareness. The mythic reduces the field of play of the dialectic of taking for granted or questioning to manageable and secure proportions.

Mythic ideation mediates *across* the boundaries between the known and the unknown and unknowable, as an active and creative "translation service" of the cultural unconscious. In this capacity it transposes, via condensation, displacement, and other mechanisms, the unfamiliar, the inaccessible, the threatening, or the reassuring. Such transpositions may have to do with the general need to assimilate messages or experience without forcing the culture significantly to alter its contours, or they may have to do with more specific and immediate concerns and experiences. What does this suggest for the social order as a whole? How does TV news provide an integrating mediation between the social order and the viewer?

If the mythic serves primarily to maintain existing patterns of cognition, by focusing, filtering, and translating, it can be deemed to have a conserving and preserving function for the social order. In this regard, its role is one of containment, a defensive posturing in the face of the arbitrary quality of existence: the mythic domain stands for "ultimate foundations" (that is, origins) against the equivocal nature of social reality. As such, it is for the most part uncritical. (The mythic is no doubt also mobilized in revolutionary contexts, but I would point that even here, too, it functions in an uncritical fashion.) The mythic domain does not inquire why things are the way they are; it only asserts that they are and tries to come to terms with them by utilizing symbolization rather than formal logical representation. The mythic is here and now, forever in and addressing the present, while at times evoking a reconstructed past or a promising future in order to provide more coherence to the immediate situation.

Drawing on the work of Fiske and Hartley,[21] I suggest that the mythic domain of TV news performs the following four basic operations on a regular basis within the broadcasts:

1. It establishes and concretizes the social order as part of our cognition. For most people, TV news is the prime medium through which the social order continually presents itself. The symbolic displays of the state—major institutions, leaders of the society, prevalent values, and so on, of the social order as a coherent totality—manifest themselves in the programs. Through concrete illustration and exemplification, the social order, or the "society," or the "nation" is made visible to the populace in the context of everyday living.

2. The mythic domain legitimates and celebrates the basic structures, functions, and leadership of the social order. One can see TV news programs as recurring advertisements for the existing social order. So it has been with the dominant media of all civilizations; any culture's basic messages to itself tend to be positive and at times even laudatory in character. Of course this should be the case, but since it is so routine, we take it as normal or neutral. It requires just a little imagination to sketch a news transmission that had decided to try to delegitimate the basic contours of the society, and to guess at the consequences of such presentations.

3. The mythic also serves to explain and interpret that which transpires which is of relevance for the social order. Thus, it monitors, surveys, and reports not least about conflict and controversy. The mythic neither denies nor camouflages social tensions. On the contrary, they are brought out and are part of the social order's dynamics. The point is, however, that they are rendered safe for the social order as a whole: the boundaries and limits of the issues, their significance, the stakes involved, and the array of perceived and reasonable options are presented, interpreted, and (usually) resolved in such a way that the contours of the social order remain intact. Here, we find the realm of symbolic cleansing and purging of "evil" via dramatic cycles of moral passion in the news.

4. For the viewer, the mythic domain integrates and implicates; it evokes identification and (for the most part) loyalty to the social order. It assures the status of membership by reference to various populations—citizens, taxpayers, the unemployed, voters, and so forth—within which the viewers can locate themselves.

Screen Rites: Ideology versus "Utopia"

This brief overview is intended to be only suggestive. The importance of the present discussion is to see that there is a basic coherence and logic to mythic ideation, which runs "parallel" to the rational, informational dimensions of the broadcasts. The mythic is of central importance for the maintenance and reproduction of the social order. This "cultural function," I would argue, far outweighs the import of the formal transmission and reception of factual messages. In this regard, it is not inappropriate to speak of TV news viewing as a form of *ritual*. Often, the word "ritual" is preceded by an adjective such as "mere" or "empty." But in TV news and its mythic domain, ritual is symbolic and compelling, uniting people in a shared project, emphasizing their commonality; it becomes a mediation between the individual and the social order. Through the ritual of TV news watching, the mythic domain allows the social order to resonate within everyday life and provides everyday life with a coherence larger than and beyond itself.

Such a conclusion has a "hermetic" ring to it and may seem to refuse to consider seriously the role of TV news in the maintenance of social power. Rather than terming it "uncritical," I would say that the type of cultural analysis presented here is "precritical." In recent years the critique of ideology has turned increasingly to the theme of making sense, treating it as prior to a critique: it must first be established *what* sense is being made, and *how*, before it can be deemed ideological (or liberatory, or whatever) within its social context. In other words, we are beginning to see just how subtle and "embedded" ideology is. In one current formulation, ideology becomes those systems of meaning that help to reproduce social relations of domination.[22] Here, the elucidation of meaning clearly becomes the methodological first step. Television news does contain many (shifting) ideological dimensions, but the broadcasts are not *just* ideology. To deny the multivalent and equivocal quality of meaning here only blurs our analytic insight.

If hermeneutics may at times align itself with critical theory, there is no fundamental reason why it should always and inevitably do so. There are different moments and concerns, as well as societal circumstances, that guide the direction of cultural analysis. If a "critical hermeneutics" approaches texts with the aim of demonstrating their ideological import, then a "positive hermeneutics" tries to search out their utopian or anticipatory dimensions. In other words, cultural texts must also be seen as expressing human longing, in particular the drive for harmony, identification, unity, and transcendence. Such cultural integration is expressed, evoked, and embodied by symbols, rituals, and cultural practices that convey shared meanings.

The mythic domain of ideation in TV news that I have highlighted here is certainly ripe for ideology critique; as such, it is an easy target. However, the mythic also expresses this "utopian" dimension. The hermeneutic task is not only to distinguish and analyze these two thrusts in TV news, but also to come to terms with the fact that both are present in the social order and within ourselves.

Notes

Work for this study was supported by a grant from the Humanities-Social Science Research Council (HSFR), Stockholm.

1. See, for instance, Peter Dahlgren and Colin Sparks, eds., *Journalism and Popular Culture* (London: Sage, 1992).

2. Examples of this tradition in television analysis include: Roger Silverstone, *The Message of Television* (London: Heinemann, 1981); E. Ann Kaplan, ed., *Regarding Television*, American Film Institute Monograph Series, vol. 2 (Frederick, Md.: University Publications of America, 1983); Willard D. Rowland and Bruce Watkins, eds., *Interpreting Television* (Beverly Hills, Calif.: Sage, 1984); James Carey, *Media, Myths, and Narrative: Television and the Press* (London: Sage, 1988); John Tulloch, *Television Drama: Agency, Audience, and Myth* (London: Routledge, 1990); John Hartley, *Teleology: Studies in Television* (London: Routledge, 1992); John Corner, *Television Form and Public Address* (London: Edward Arnold, 1995).

3. See Paul Ricoeur, *Hermeneutics and the Human Sciences,* trans. and ed. John B. Thompson (Cambridge: Cambridge University Press, 1981); idem, *Lecture on Ideology and Utopia* (New York: Columbia University Press, 1986).

4. See John Fiske, *Television Culture* (London: Routledge, 1987).

5. This line of reasoning is developed clearly in John B. Thompson, *Ideology and Modern Culture: Critical Theory in the Era of Mass Communication* (Cambridge: Polity Press, 1990).

6. See John P. Robinson and Mark R. Levy, *The Main Source: Learning from Television News* (Beverly Hills, Calif.: Sage, 1986); Barrie Gunter, *Poor Reception: Misunderstanding and Forgetting Broadcast News* (Hillsdale, N.J.: Lawrence Erlbaum, 1997).

7. See James Carey, *Communication as Culture* (London: Unwin Hyman, 1989).

8. See my discussion in Peter Dahlgren, "Cultural Studies as a Research Perspective: Themes and Tensions," in *International Media Research,* ed. John Corner, Philip Schlesinger, and Roger Silverstone (London: Routledge, 1997).

9. See Klaus Bruhn Jensen and Nicholas W. Jankowski, eds., *A Handbook of Qualitative Methods for Mass Communication Research* (London: Routledge, 1991).

10. For example, see David Morley, *Television, Audiences, and Cultural Studies* (London: Routledge, 1992).

11. A useful collection showing a broad range of interpretive strategies for television research is Robert C. Allen, ed., *Channels of Discourse, Reassembled* (London: Routledge, 1992).

12. An overview of "reader-oriented" research is found in Robert C. Holub, *Reception Theory* (London: Methuen, 1984); Umberto Eco, *Interpretation and Overinterpretation* (Cambridge: Cambridge University Press, 1992).

13. See Carey, *Media, Myths, and Narrative;* Silverstone.

14. See, for example, W. Lance Bennett and Murray Edelman, "Toward a New Political Narrative," *Journal of Communication* (Autumn 1985), 156–71.

15. Kenneth Burke, *On Symbols and Society* (Chicago: University of Chicago Press, 1989).

16. See Ricoeur, *Hermeneutics and the Human Sciences.*

17. See Hayden White, "The Value of Narrativity in the Representation of Reality," in W. J. T. Mitchell, ed., *On Narrative* (Chicago: University of Chicago Press, 1981).

18. Gaye Tuchman, *Making News* (New York: Free Press, 1978), esp. chap. 4, "Representation and the News Narrative."

19. Peter Berger and Thomas Luckmann, *The Social Construction of Reality* (London: Penguin, 1976), chapter 1, "The Reality of Everyday Life."

20. On the theme of the relationship between private and public spheres, and television's role in this regard, see my discussion in Peter Dahlgren, *Television and the Public Sphere* (London: Sage, 1995).

21. John Fiske and John Hartley, *Understanding Television* (London: Methuen, 1978).

22. Thompson, 56.

7

Toward a Pragmatic Understanding of Television Reception: Norwegian Coverage of the Summit Meeting between Reagan and Gorbachev in Moscow, 1988

Svein Østerud

Media and Social Conflict

No matter how we assess its contribution to communication studies, there is no denying that the Institute of Social Research, founded in Frankfurt am Main in 1923, made a lasting impression on this field of study. The leading researchers of the Frankfurt school soon came to the conclusion that Marxist social theory stood in need of revision if it were to understand the industrial capitalist society of the mid-twentieth century. In contradistinction to Marx they held that the historical process is not driven forward simply through social contradictions. To their way of thinking, conflicts between social classes were to an increasing extent articulated through the media, so they undertook to improve on Marxist theory by analyzing the relationship between class, ideology, and the media.

In 1947 Max Horkheimer and Theodor W. Adorno published a major work, *Dialektik der Aufklärung,* in which, in a chapter entitled "Kulturindustrie, Aufklärung als Massenbetrug," they advanced a general view of the media in contemporary society. As the title indicates, they coined the phrase "the culture industry," referring to the collective operations of the media. They demonstrated that the application of human reason within capitalism produced both positive and negative outcomes. Scientific rationality, which had proved so successful as a means of dominating nature, had also become a means of dominating people. The scientific-technical development no longer functioned as the basis of a social critique but had instead become the basis of legitimation of a dominating social order.

A mitigating element had been traditional high or bourgeois culture, the experience of which offered intimations of the human spirit free of domination by instrumental reason. But now, the Frankfurt theorists argued, even this zone of human life is being invaded by the forces of rationalization and instrumentalization through the industrialization of culture. The mass media, the American film and music industries, indeed all the components of the "culture industry," are becoming commodified as they are increasingly organized like any other commercial sector of manufacture and consumption. The culture industry supplies "substitute gratification" and favors the cult of personality and other authoritarian attitudes. Accordingly the media are regarded as part of a capitalist industrialization of culture that serves to reconcile people to a dominating social order in a totalizing way.

Inherent in the Frankfurt school theory is a tendency to reductionism. In the period of later industrial capitalist development, modern societies had become "mass societies," leaving people atomized and exposed to external influences, especially to the pressure of the mass propaganda of powerful leaders, the most effective of which were the mass media. The Frankfurt theorists adapted their speculative critique to a behaviorist empirical method, which assumed that the media had the power to "inject" a repressive ideology directly into the consciousness of the masses. They found themselves justified in establishing that mass culture suppressed "potentialities" and denied awareness of contradictions in a "one-dimensional world." In an essay on television that Adorno wrote nearly ten years later, he describes the effect of the cultural industry: "The more stereotypes become reified and rigid in the present setup of cultural industry, the less people are likely to change their preconceived ideas with the progress of their experience."[1]

Sociologically the Frankfurt theory is a naïve one, and that explains why it so grossly exaggerated the ideological and integrating power of the media. It was at the same time that social researchers started commenting upon the power of the new mass markets and media to produce new forms of social and mental life. C. Wright Mills, for example, contended that mass communication created a pseudoworld of products and services as well as the lifestyles that were inherent in buying those products and services. Moreover two American anthropologists, Horton and Wohl, called attention to the fact that television brings simulated communication into the living room.

These new insights into the intermediary social structures between media and the audience exploded the theory that the chief role of the media was to play down conflicts and contradictions and produce popular consent to the existing social order. The media could no longer be regarded simply as an instrument in the hands of the ruling class or bourgeois state to enforce social, political, and legal discipline. Another branch of research, one that has probed into the relationship between media institutions and politics, invites the same conclusion. An excellent illustration is provided by the study Lang and Lang carried out on the Watergate affair and the downfall of President Nixon.[2] This and other studies of significant societal events tell us that the mass media constitute a public institution that provides the channels, the means, and an arena for the playing-out of processes in which many actors and interests are involved, often in competition.

Perhaps it ought to be incumbent on any researcher who studies viewers' reception of TV news to find out in each case whether TV works in coalition with the authority of the state or counteracts it by inspiring opposition and popular movements. At all events this is an issue that is likely to be raised by quite a few of the people who expose themselves to modern TV institutions' coverage of national and international conflicts. Critical research on the role of the media during the Gulf war has demonstrated that those viewers who raised their voices because they suspected American television corporations of being hand in glove with military and civilian authorities were perfectly right.

In the case I selected to focus on in a reception study that I carried out in 1988, the summit meeting between Reagan and Gorbachev in Moscow in May–June of that year, the relationship between the media institutions in question and the political authorities does not seem to be such an important issue. Even if we are concerned here with the apparently irreconcilable conflict between the two superpowers, a conflict that has haunted us during the whole of the postwar period, the political aspect of the meeting was to a high degree played down in the television coverage of the meeting. As I shall argue in this essay, the TV coverage could hardly cause greater public awareness, let alone spark off a political movement, couched as it was in the format and the dramaturgy of the fiction series with which TV feeds us nowadays. It is fair to say that rhetorical features related to the increasing of polarity and intimacy have made their way into news reporting, inducing the viewers to perceive it as an experience potential rather than political news.

Bridging the Gap between Humanistic and Social Scientific Media Studies

When I embarked upon the above-mentioned empirical study of Norwegian viewers' reception of television news, audience research in Scandinavia was marred by a radical disagreement between scholars who had university training in social sciences and scholars with backgrounds in literary criticism and the humanities. The former group studied society and media behavior through the so-called "uses and gratifications" approach, a tradition rooted in behaviorist psychology, while the latter studied the message by means of semiological or hermeneutic methods of textual analysis.

It was almost unanimously accepted that these two research traditions ought to find some means for peaceful coexistence, and several universities were implementing institutional coordination of the two traditions in the shape of a joint faculty and curriculum. Moreover, attempts were being made to hammer out a theoretical basis for a holistic understanding that included an approach to communication combining the insights of the uses and gratifications tradition with those of the semiological and hermeneutic traditions.[3]

Needless to say, this turned out to be a very difficult undertaking. Scholars within the uses and gratifications tradition had contented themselves with studying the motives for media choice and the perceived uses and gratifications of media behavior and had failed to address the problems presented by the text. For instance, the authors of one of the classics in uses and gratifications research, *Television in the Lives of Our Children,* characterized television as "a great and shiny cafeteria" where the children could help themselves to the different dishes and eat what they desired at the moment.[4] But the television message can hardly be regarded as a ready-made object of gratification; rather it is a sign system from which meaning has to be constructed by the individual viewer according to his or her codes of construction. Correspondingly, the semiological and hermeneutic traditions were well adapted for uncovering meaning structures in the television text, but critics in these traditions were not in a position to determine whether or not these meaning structures were realized in actual communication acts. These traditions may be subjected to the same criticism that Robert K. Merton, in his 1946 book *Mass Persuasion,* leveled at contemporary media research.[5] Although this research purported to study the effect of media messages on the audience, he argued, it occupied itself almost exclusively with the content of the messages. It is the great virtue of contemporary media research, Merton maintained, to throw light on the "appeals and rhetorical devices, the stereotypes and emotive language which made up the propaganda materials,"[6] but this research was mistaken in drawing conclusions about the effect of the propaganda from the analysis of the materials. The semiological and hermeneutic traditions were without an understanding of the audience as active receivers, while the psychological uses and gratifications tradition lacked an understanding of the message as a sign system.

This theoretical discussion largely focused on the concept of reception analysis, whether it took the shape of a struggle for the right to define its meaning or aimed at rallying media scholars around a common definition. One of my own ambitions in the present essay is to contribute to giving the concept of reception analysis a holistic meaning that takes care of the best from both traditions.

Stuart Hall's Encoding/Decoding Model—and a Critique

Hardly any community of researchers has been more inclined toward the development of a holistic understanding of communication than the Centre for Contemporary Cultural Studies at the University of Birmingham. Therefore it seems appropriate to take the seminal article "Encoding and Decoding in the Television Discourse," written by Stuart Hall, one of the most prominent spokespersons of the so-called Birmingham school,[7] as the starting point for an analysis of the concept of media reception.

On the model of Marx's distinction in the *Grundrisse* and *Capital* between separate stages in the circulation of commodities, Hall describes communication as a circulation of messages, a circulation that comprises corresponding stages, namely, production, distribution, and consumption. The meaningful content that is produced at one end of the chain of circulation can be transmitted only through a form that consists of linguistic signs and is organized by means of linguistic codes and conventions. Like all other messages of communication, it is given a discursive form that is determined not only by the material tools (that is, the media technology), but also by the conditions of production (that is, the organization of media practice). It is in this discursive form that the message is transmitted to the receivers at the other end of the chain of circulation. At this stage the discourse will have to be translated again and transformed into social practice, if the circulation is to be completed. Until the "meaning" is produced at the receiving end, one cannot, to Hall's way of thinking, speak of any consumption. And unless the meaning is articulated in practice, it can have no effect.

Hall's key contribution to a holistic understanding of communication consists in describing the different stages of the circulation as integral parts of an entirety. Each stage is more or less autonomous and cannot fully vouch for the next stage of the circulation. Thus coding and decoding may be said to have separate modalities and separate conditions of existence. Both are decisive stages, even if they are relatively autonomous in relation to the communication process as a whole. Each stage may constitute an interruption or a disturbance of the efficient flow of discursive forms. Inasmuch as it is *to* the discursive form that the sender encodes a meaningful content and it is *from* the discursive form that the receiver decodes a meaningful content, this occupies a central position in the flow. The transformations to and from the discursive form are related stages, without being identical ones: "Production and reception of the television message are not, therefore, identical, but they are related: they are differentiated moments within the totality formed by the social relations of the communicative process as a whole."[8]

In separating encoding and decoding as relatively autonomous stages in the process of communication and pointing out that there need not be symmetry between them, Hall paves the way for a novel paradigm of audience or reception research. In the first place this is a paradigm that dismisses positivistic behaviorist traditions of any kind, whether it is the old effects-oriented approach or the more recent uses and gratifications approach. Second, it is a paradigm that extends the semiological approach to include not only the encoding but also the decoding, that is, not only the production but also the reception of messages.

No matter how justified it is to dismiss the behaviorist paradigm that for so long dominated communication research, it seems to be this very dismissal that induced Hall to establish a sharp distinction between the decoding of the message and the use of it: "Before this message can have an 'effect' (however defined), satisfy a 'need' or be put to a 'use,' it must first be appropriated as a meaningful discourse and be meaningfully decoded. It is this set of decoded meanings which 'have an effect,' influence, entertain, instruct or persuade, with very complex perceptual, cognitive, emotional, ideological or behavioural consequences."[9]

Here the aspect of *use* is understood as a secondary phenomenon. It is described as the "perceptual, cognitive, emotional, ideological or behavioural consequences" of a preceding appropriation of the meaning of the message. But in practice it may be difficult to operate with such a sharp distinction between an intellectual appropriation of its meaning and a behavioral use of it. These processes often merge in such a way that it is impossible to determine what is the prelude and what is the sequel.

Allow me to try to throw light on this by introducing John Dewey's epoch-making article from 1896, "The Reflex Arc Concept in Psychology."[10] In this article Dewey questions the distinction between sensation and movement as stimulus and response, respectively. According to Dewey the older dualism of body and soul finds a distinct echo in the current dualism of stimulus and response. We tend to understand the sensory-motor circuit from our preconceived ideas of rigid distinctions between sensations, thoughts, and acts. Dewey criticizes the prevailing concept of the reflex arc, namely, that it "is not a comprehensive, or organic unity, but a patchwork of disjointed parts, a mechanical conjunction of unallied processes."[11] He shows that sensory stimulus, central connections, and motor responses should be viewed, not as separate and complete entities in themselves, but as divisions of labor within the single concrete whole. Stimulus and response are "not distinctions of existence, but teleological distinctions, that is, distinctions of function, or part played, with reference to reaching or maintaining an end."[12] To Dewey's way of thinking the ordinary concept of the reflex arc is a survival of the metaphysical dualism, first formulated by Plato. Dewey's own reflex arc formulation "is neither physical (or physiological) nor psychological; it is a mixed materialistic-spiritualistic assumption."[13]

This pragmatic reorientation of epistemology is summarized in the following dictum from Dewey's later work *Democracy and Education,* published in 1916: "The material of thinking is not thoughts, but acts, facts, events and the relation between things."[14] Hall, instead of taking advantage of the insights produced by Dewey and his copragmatists, Charles Sanders Peirce and William James, pursues the dualism between meaning and use, between thinking and acting.

Hall restores the concept of "ideology" and describes how the media "make things mean" through the active work of "selecting and presenting, of structuring and shaping."[15] His preoccupation is with the way in which the media do their best to create credibility, legitimacy, and taken-for-grantedness, and in doing so impose a delimited or "preferred" range of meanings on the audience. In his article on encoding and decoding, Hall discusses linguistic phenomena such as denotation and connotation, polysemy, misunderstanding and selective perception, phenomena primarily related to the sign and the coding of signs. On the other hand, there is in his article only a very rudimentary account of the social context of linguistic signs, that is, how they are embedded in the social practice of the user. This is no doubt a consequence of the fact that Hall's theory of signification may be diagnosed as an amalgamation of structural linguistic theory in the vein of Saussure and Barthes, and Marxist-inspired social thinking à la Gramsci and Althusser. None of these allows of empirical studies of individual and concrete acts of communication, structural linguistics for being too abstract and focused on linguistic structure (*langue*) rather than concrete speech acts (*parole*), and Marxist social thinking for being too macro-oriented to the neglect of individual communicative acts.

Insofar as the researcher assumes the task of carrying out microsociological studies of acts of communication, he or she will have to supplement Hall's theory of signification with some kind of *discourse analysis* that obliterates the distinction between words and deeds and treats signs as speech acts. Discourse analysis, whether it draws its inspiration from the psycholinguistic theories of Roman Jakobson or Karl Bühler, or from the late Wittgenstein-initiated speech act theory developed by Austin and Searle, conceives of the discourse as a regulating device between system and process. In discourse analysis, words are not maps of reality; rather, they gain their meaning through their use in social interchange, within the "language game" of the culture. Both the psycholinguistic theories and the speech act theory concern themselves with the way in which our linguistic utterances act on reality, the former differentiating between their various potential functions, and the latter analyzing them as performative of action in the world.

Discourses are power relations. Accordingly, discourse analysis may also include the study of the conflict, or rather negotiation, between the discourses of a TV program and the discourses that each individual viewer will bring to bear upon it to make it into a text that bears meanings for him or her. In order to distinguish this kind of discourse analysis from the more familiar kind that exclusively occupies itself either with the production of signs or with signifying products, I propose to call it *sociological discourse analysis.* Decisive for the outcome of this conflict or negotiation is the social position of the individual viewer. So the object of the sociological discourse analysis will, for one thing, be to identify the discourses or frames of interpretation that the individual viewers carry with them to the various cultural arenas.

Television Reception Is Behavioral

Notwithstanding their frequent references to Marxism, the key figures in English cultural studies came originally from backgrounds in literary criticism and the humanities. This goes a long way to explaining the widespread failure to incorporate socioeconomic insights into cultural studies analyses.[16] However, in the group of researchers belonging to the Centre for Contemporary Cultural Studies there is one significant exception, David Morley, who was initially trained as a sociologist.

Morley was the first to put Hall's semiological and cultural theory through an empirical investigation, reported in *The "Nationwide" Audience* from 1980. Drawing on a basic model from Parkin's political sociology (adapted to communication studies by Hall), Morley suggests that there are three broad frames within which decoders may position themselves in relation to media texts. The first is the *dominant,* wherein decoding is aligned with the dominant encodings or interpretative frameworks of the message itself. Second is the *negotiated,* in which "decoders may take the meaning broadly as encoded; but by relating the message to some concrete, located or situational context which reflects their position and interests they may modify or partly inflect the meaning."[17] Third is the *oppositional,* wherein the decoder recognizes the dominant encoding, but interprets it in an oppositional way.

Morley's empirical research on the potential for "differential decoding" of TV programs clears new ground in communication studies, even though Merton's "differential analysis" in the forties may be regarded as a predecessor. Whereas critical-theory-guided researchers had tended to argue that the ideology in the structure of the text works almost irresistibly to position and construct the subjectivity of the viewer, Morley frees the text from complete ideological closure, shifting the site of meaning away from the text and toward the viewer. As Morley says:

> Thus the meaning of the text must be thought of in terms of which set of discourses it encounters in any particular set of circumstances, and how this encounter may restructure both the meaning of the text and the discourses which it meets. The meaning of the text will be constructed differently according to the discourses (knowledges, prejudices, resistances, etc.) brought to bear on the text by the reader and the crucial factor in the encounter of audience/subject and text will be the range of discourses at the disposal of the audience.[18]

But in liberating viewers from the ideological power of the text, trying to reestablish them as social subjects, Morley lands them in another situation of structural determinacy. He tends to reduce viewers to little more than embodiments of ideological positions. Surely, Morley falls victim to the same sociologism for which he blames Parkin, namely, converting social classes into "meaning-systems," that is, ideological positions, and then taking viewers to be impersonations of these meaning-systems. On the whole there is in Morley's analyses a mechanistic linking of socioeconomic base and ideological superstructure that prevents him from doing justice to the complexity of his research project.

In later works, *Family Television* (1986) and *Television, Audiences and Cultural Studies* (1992), Morley examines critically his own analyses in The *"Nationwide" Audience* and points to the usefulness of Pierre Bourdieu's concept of "habitus" as a way of grasping the subtle interplay between structure and action, between social determinants and individual initiative.[19] There are, in fact, increasing numbers of media scholars who advocate using Bourdieu's concepts of "habitus" and "cultural capital" in empirical investigations,[20] but so far very few have suited the action to the word.

To some extent my own audience research is an attempt to try out the usefulness of Bourdieu's concepts of "habitus" and "capital." Before giving an account of the empirical component of my research, I feel bound to offer a definition of these concepts. *Habitus,* first, is a Latin word that Bourdieu renders sometimes with "disposition," sometimes with "competence." It was preceded by another word in Bourdieu's early writing, the Greek *ethos,* which meant "habit" and figured as an equivalent technical term in his first report on the Kabyle society in Algeria.[21] However, rather than denoting what we ordinarily understand by "habit," habitus denotes a moral code that is internalized in the agent and intimately associated with his self-esteem. It is not a moral obligation that the agent is fully conscious of, but rather a practical logic that he has appropriated through learning processes. This practical logic or disposition is, in other words, a product of his being socialized into a specific culture, for example, the Kabyle culture, and it has, so to speak, located itself in his body. Bourdieu compares this bodily disposition with the Aristotelian concept of *hexis,* which he defines as follows: "Bodily *hexis* is political mythology realized, *embodied,* turned into a permanent disposition, a durable manner of standing, speaking, and thereby of *feeling* and *thinking.*"[22]

Bourdieu himself calls attention to the parallel between these unconscious dispositions and Chomsky's generative grammar, which denotes language users' ability to produce an unlimited number of correct sentences. Chomsky, too, is concerned with inherent principles or structures that generate practice in every language user without his or her awareness. But in contrast with Chomsky's generative grammar, Bourdieu's habitus is not innate in humans; it is rather a socially and culturally developed competence. Habitus represents a system of generative schemes completely adapted to the objective conditions under which they are developed, and capable of generating all the thoughts, perceptions, and actions that correspond with these conditions, and no others.

What Bourdieu tries to capture through the concept of habitus is the rationality or rather the practical logic that unfolds in concrete situations where relations between members of society are established. Bourdieu also speaks of this practical logic as a *modus operandi* in an account of Panofsky's art history, where he introduces a distinction between *modus operandi* and *opus operatum.* Art historians like Panofsky are prone to extracting from the *opus operatum,* that is, the art product, the supposed principles of its production, thereby undermining the understanding of the logic of practice in the very moment in which they try to offer it. They repress the question of artistic production under the concept of the "objective intention" of the work.

In adopting Bourdieu's concept of habitus we have placed ourselves in a position to overcome what may be regarded as the major flaws in Morley's reductionist audience studies. First, habitus helps us to bridge the gap between the interpretive and the behavioral aspects of media reception, between "questions of interpretation and questions of use."[23] Second, habitus enables us to transcend the dichotomy between action and social structure, between the individual and the social class. Instead of making the individual the impersonation of his or her class-specific ideology, as Morley tends to do, Bourdieu insists on the relative autonomy of the individual. According to Bourdieu there is a relation of *homology* between the singular worldviews of the different members of the same class. Each individual habitus or system of dispositions may be seen as a structural variant of the group or class habitus. In the same breath, Bourdieu speaks of the harmonization or orchestration of group or class habitus that results from the homogeneity of the conditions of existence. He seems to be elaborating this metaphor drawn from the realm of music when he describes action as "regulated improvisation": it is in the power of each agent to improvise on the group or class habitus that his conditions of existence have inculcated in him.

While habitus is the generative schemes that enable each of us to generate thoughts, perceptions, and actions, *cultural capital* is the objectivation of the generative schemes. It is the volume of capital (including not only the cultural, but also the economic and social capital) each of us has appropriated to oneself that determines one's position in the social space. In contrast with Marx, who saw class differences as a reflection of differential access to the means of production and what was produced, Bourdieu argues that cultural capital should be considered as playing a similar role to that of economic capital in the production of social inequalities.[24] Thus the conceptual space within which Bourdieu defines class is not that of production, but that of social relations in general. Rogers Brubaker describes his conceptualization of social class as follows: "Class divisions are defined not by differing relations to the means of production, but by differing conditions of existence, differing systems of dispositions produced by differential conditioning, and differing endowments of power or capital."[25] To put it differently, homogeneous conditions of existence produce homogeneous systems of dispositions capable of generating similar practices and tastes.

The Encoding of the Television Text

In the wake of Roland Barthes's ingenious study of French popular culture, *Mythologies,* from 1972, there has been an animated discussion among media scholars as to whether media texts are "open" to any and all interpretations that readers wish to make of them. Stuart Hall's "preferred reading" model may be regarded as an alternative to the once widely held view that audiences see only what they want to see. Hall's model is in fact a corrective to the prevalent tendencies entirely to dissolve the text into its readings, and hence to dispense with formal analysis of media texts altogether.

But even if we accept Hall's idea of the ideological closure of the television text we do not have to endorse the amplification that there is *one dominant reading* that all viewers will have to relate to. There are, in fact, directive closures encoded in the message, but they can hardly be said to direct the viewers toward a single dominant or preferred reading. Rather these directive closures establish the boundaries of the arena within which the struggle for meaning can occur.[26]

Moreover, I would argue that "struggle for meaning" is not an accurate description of the processes of negotiation between text and audience. The "reading" in which the encounter between a particular text and an individual recipient results should rather be regarded as a way of putting the text to use, or as an actualization of one (or several) of its potential functions. Media texts or programs are in fact not only polysemantic but also *multifunctional.* Norman Fairclough is right in criticizing news discourse analysis for overlooking this point and for adopting too narrow a focus on the interplay between text and audience: "First, the focus is on representations; social relations and identities in news discourse—and the interpersonal function of language—receive little attention. Second, texts are analyzed linguistically, but not intertextually, in terms of their constitution through configurations of discourses and genres."[27] Fairclough's distinction between three main categories of function, *ideational, interpersonal,* and *textual,* helps us toward a better grasp of the complexity of news communication.[28] However, even more helpful in my own research has been the subtle functional theory of the linguist Roman Jakobson. This is as much a theory of communication as a linguistic theory. Even though Jakobson's theory is developed on the basis of analyses of everyday verbal language, it seems well adapted for elucidating television functions insofar as they are dependent upon and defined by the functions performed by speech in general. Of course, television is a semiotic system that goes beyond mere words—but much of its visual content takes a form of "paralinguistic" signs derived ultimately from pretelevisual linguistic codes.

Jakobson has isolated six discrete functions, all of which can be observed at work on television:

1. *The referential function* is the most familiar function of language, where the relationship between a sign and its *referent* or object is dominant. Jakobson also calls it the "denotative" or "cognitive" function.

2. *The emotive function* focuses on the relationship between a sign and its *encoder* or addresser; it aims at a direct expression of his attitude toward the subject of the message (for example, "it's been a long day" communicates the speaker's attitude toward the day, and does not refer to its timespan).

3. *The conative function* concerns the relationship between the sign and its *decoder.* Imperative commands are messages where the conative function is most clearly dominant. It finds its purest grammatical expression in the imperative and vocative.

4. *The poetic function* is primarily the concern of the message with *itself.* It is not confined to poetry but applies to the reference of any message to its own textuality, its structure and conventions (for example, the political slogan "I like Ike"). On the other hand, the linguistic scrutiny of poetry cannot limit itself to the poetic function.

5. *The phatic function* of the message is mainly to stress the *act of communication* between parties involved. Fixed expressions of greeting and remarks about the weather are its classic examples. Television programs use it frequently, perhaps because of, rather than in spite of, the "remote" relationship between broadcaster and viewer.

6. *The metalinguistic function* of language is to communicate a message *about language.* Literary criticism is all metalanguage, the present essay being an instance of it.[29]

According to Jakobson the act of communication consists of six different factors, each of which underlies one of the above-mentioned functions. The *emitter* sends a *message* to the *receiver.* In order for the message to function it is dependent on a *context* to refer to, a *code* that is entirely or partially common to emitter and receiver, and finally a *contact,* that is, a physical channel or a psychological connection between them that enables them to initiate and proceed with an act of communication. These factors can all be paired with each other in varying combinations, defining different functions.

Jakobson's theoretical model may be regarded as a repertoire of the textual functions to which the television audience will have to relate, each member selecting from the repertoire his or her own reading according to his or her discursive capacity. Hence, for an analyst who assumes that reading is an interplay between the potentialities of the text and the capacity of the individual spectator, this is a more suitable model than the various uses and gratifications models, originating from the reductionist functional theory of communication that prevailed in the previous decades.

Program Analysis of Coverage of the 1988 Moscow Summit

The focus of my interview with Norwegian viewers about their media habits in general and their news consumption in particular was a summary of the coverage by the NRK Television News Department, *Dagsrevyen,* of the summit meeting between Reagan and Gorbachev in Moscow, 29 May–2 June 1988. The summary contained passages from Reagan's arrival at Moscow airport and his drive through the main streets of Moscow to the accompaniment of a military parade; from speeches of welcome and official visits to a special school and to the monastery of Danilov; from meetings and exchanges of documents; from addresses to dissidents, writers, and students; from correspondent reports about the acrimonious conflict between Gorbachev and Yeltsin; from press conferences and an official dinner in the Kremlin. It also contained a glimpse of Reagan and Gorbachev strolling on Red Square, and an abstract of a panel discussion in a magazine program, *Fredagsforum,* between some people generally recognized as experts on foreign policy.

This summit meeting was the third in a series of meetings between Reagan and Gorbachev, and this series of meetings was to prove instrumental in making Gorbachev put a brake on the arms race and tear down the Berlin Wall. However, when I singled out this program for the focus of my investigations, it was not only for its political importance, but also because it epitomizes the format and discursive form of the modern television news report.

The coverage of the Moscow meeting should be regarded as an installment of a serial drama inasmuch as it harks back to television coverage of previous summit meetings.[30] First, it picks up and develops the theme of an antagonistic relationship between the two leaders and hence between their peoples, a theme that was so strongly articulated in the report from the closing of the Reykjavik meeting. Second, it endeavors to revive the state of suspense in which the reporters plunged us in the hours before the concluding press conference of the Washington summit meeting.

No doubt we are here dealing with what Jakobson called *the poetic function,* alluding to the relationship between the message and itself. The message is no longer an instrument of communication but is now the object of communication. In modern television news there is a growing tendency partly to supplant the world to which the programs refer with the world they represent. This allows some viewers to be more involved in the stylizations of the news discourse and its familiar motifs and devices than in the extratextual reality. In an empirical study of how a fiction program, more precisely "Dallas," was perceived by viewers in different cultures, Katz and Liebes found that it was read *referentially* by some, and more *poetically* by others.[31] Some non-American ethnic groups read "Dallas" referentially, as a representation of the American way of life, whereas others read it more poetically, as a structure of narrative conventions, characterization, and dramatic conflict. American ethnic groups, on the other hand, were more flexible, showing signs of reading it both referentially and poetically. It is fair to say that referential readings foreground the representational qualities of the text and poetic readings foreground its discursivity. In a study of news reception Peter Dahlgren used the same distinction to explain a difference of reading practice among viewers. He comments that for some viewers of the news, "the reference to outer reality may appear weak, and meaning may be embodied more in the message's self-reference, fostering aesthetic involvement of some form. In Roman Jakobson's terms, the 'referential function' may at times be subordinate to the 'poetic function.'"[32]

There is, no doubt, a similarity between reading the news and reading fiction, and the TV coverage of the Moscow meeting can hardly be reckoned among those programs that try to counteract the tendency in current TV production to combine fictional and nonfictional components in a new mode of narration, namely, the documentary-drama or the drama-documentary.[33] The summit meeting series has in common with fiction series that it works on a sense of perpetual tension between individuals. The two adversaries encounter different incidents that reach some kind of resolution in each episode or, to be more correct, each meeting. Nevertheless, both the Reykjavik meeting and the Washington meeting may be said to end in what one, in a fictional mode of narration, would call a cliff-hanging question: for the Reykjavik meeting, whether the two adversaries would ever be in a position to speak to one another again; and for the Washington meeting, whether they would be able to clear away the last obstacle to true and lasting friendship. Generally speaking the summit meeting series gathers together segments to form patterns of repetition. The repetition is both of situation, that is, of a basic problematic, and of characters, that is, of reporters, presenters, expert commentators, families, publicity managers, interpreters, and the rest of the staff. The series tends to present itself as a kind of continuous update, since TV itself offers an immediacy at the level of the image and the experience of viewing. Its movement is one of beginning in the immediate past and returning to the present.

This form of narration proposes a particular kind of position of viewing inasmuch as it provokes the aesthetic sensibility of the viewer: his or her feeling for suspense, drama, and adventure. There will always be viewers (and there were some in my own sample) who are quite prepared to use these discursive resources and read TV news poetically. But the more common audience response will surely be to negotiate with, and make meaning of, news messages on the assumption that they *refer to* outer reality. This is all the more natural because news reports generally set out to be realistic representations of this reality. There is one segment of the summary presented to the respondents that very effectively bears out its claim to be a "window on the world," as if the glass of the screen can provide an innocent vision of the world. That is when, in a TV interview, a journalist from one of Norway's leading newspapers, *Dagbladet,* observes that "the Russians are faster than the Americans when it comes to spreading news," implying that when it comes to efficiency and speed the Russian press service has now caught up with their American colleagues. Together with the report from the press center, which was set up in the Hotel Rossia for five thousand members of the press, this statement suggests that modern information technology and information services work for efficient and dependable news transmission.

However, revealing to the audience the massive technical paraphernalia installed in the press center and the hectic rush of people to and fro should not be seen as an unequivocal invitation to read the news programs referentially. For some viewers this very passage may function as *metalanguage,* indicating that the transmission of information from the summit meeting is a cultural product produced through systems that include the increasingly sophisticated and converging technologies of information and communication—the screens, satellites, fiber optics, computers. It may, in other words, remind us that television is part of a complex cultural and industrial whole rather than some neutral instrument for mirroring the world.

To approach the three remaining functions in Jakobson's theory, namely, the emotive, the conative, and the phatic function, is to dip deep into the sphere of rhetoric. Jakobson allows these functions to correspond with the following three decisive factors in the communicative act: *communicator, re-*

cipient, and *contact,* respectively. When analyzing TV communication, as is the case here, we must be aware that the role of communicator is shared between those who appear on the screen and those who produce the program. Often the analyst will be hard put to draw a sharp distinction between the influence of the persons on the screen and that of the producers of the program. As we will see, this is the case in the particular episode that, in what follows, will be taken up for examination to exemplify the above-mentioned functions.

One of the passages of the summary shown to my twenty interviewees is concerned with Reagan's and Gorbachev's allegedly impromptu stroll on Red Square in Moscow on 31 May. This episode, which attracted so much attention from the media, may be regarded as an acid test of Gorbachev's novel policy of *glasnost.* Unlike his predecessors, Gorbachev had set himself to transform Soviet society into a democracy on the model of the most advanced Western democracies. This is explicitly stated in the book *Perestroika,* where he formulates his reform policy:

> Our socialist society, which has resolutely embarked on the road of democratic renewal, has a vital stake in active participation by every citizen—every worker, every collective farmer, every scientist and every professional—in both the discussion of our plans and their implementation. And the mass media are playing and will continue to play a tremendous role in this. Naturally, they are not the only channel for expressing the people's will, for reflecting their views and moods. But they are the most representative and massive rostrum of glasnost. The Party wants every citizen to voice his opinion confidently from that rostrum; the voice of citizens should not only make known the discussions that are taking place in the country but also be a guarantor of democratic control over the correctness of decisions and their conformity with the interests and requirements of the masses, and, at the next stage, over the fulfillment of the decisions.[34]

On the strength of the glasnost policy, Gorbachev aims at pulling the Soviet citizen into the public sphere, making him a participant in a democratic process of resolution. The prerequisite for such democratization is that each citizen is not only kept informed about current political decisions but is also allowed freely to express his or her opinion about them. A major role in this democratization is intended for the mass media.

Both the political program enunciated by Gorbachev in his book and the public dialogue in which he engaged the Moscow citizens gathered in Red Square for the occasion had their roots in the political proceedings that took place in the Greek city states of antiquity. The public negotiations that were conducted in the marketplace, the so-called *agora,* in the city state of Athens in the fifth century B.C., are often presented as a prototype and a standard for democracy. It is, no doubt, a standard of this kind Gorbachev had in mind when, before an audience of Moscow inhabitants, he enjoined that the discussions between himself and Reagan should observe the following rules: "The truth comes out in dialogue. The proverb has a sequel: If the discussion reaches the boiling point, the truth evaporates." This corresponds to the way in which Jürgen Habermas, in *The Structural Transformation of the Public Sphere,* describes the ideal coordination of action in the public sphere: the interlocutors should commit themselves to seek truth and to argue rationally without having recourse to emotional appeals.[35]

The premise of Habermas's definition of the public sphere is the distinction between private and public, which he traces back to the distinction drawn by the ancient Greek city states between the *oikos*-sphere and *polis*-sphere. The polis-sphere, which was common to all free citizens, was sharply divided from the oikos-sphere, which was the sphere of each individual. The public sphere was constituted in discussion (*lexis*), which could also assume the forms of consultation and legal proceedings, as well as in common action (*praxis*) such as warfare and athletic games. This was a sphere of freedom and independence where the citizens could make resolutions without being forced to worry about their own and their families' sustenance. Entitled to take part in the negotiations in the agora were only those who were freeholders and could provide for themselves and any family. In other words, their status in polis was based on their position as oikos-owners.

The Greek model of the public sphere as sharply divided from the private still obtains in Western civilization, a fact that will no doubt dispose many recipients to take Gorbachev's words at face value and interpret the episode on Red Square as an attempt on his part to introduce a more democratic practice in Soviet policy. However, the episode also permits another interpretation. It bears a certain resemblance to an episode that occurred during the previous summit meeting, the one that took place in Washington in 1987. On that occasion Gorbachev unexpectedly stopped the airport limousine that was transporting him to the White House and took a walk along a suburban Washington street, shaking hands with spectators gathered along the route. This gesture was in sharp contrast to the demeanor of his predecessors in the Soviet leadership and must be understood as a pure public relations campaign, an attempt at ingratiating himself with the American people.

Should the two leaders' stroll on Red Square be interpreted, then, as a prolongation of Gorbachev's PR campaign, this time with the Soviet Russian people as his target? There is one particular intermezzo that speaks in favor of such an interpretation, namely, when Gorbachev takes a little boy on his arm and urges him to shake hands with President Reagan. At the very moment when Reagan grasps the hand of the little boy on Gorbachev's arm, the role of father, which they both hold in their private lives, blends with their roles as political leaders. The implicit message is that our common future, in the person of the little boy, is secure in the hands of the two elder statesmen. They have been endowed with the ability to govern and to make decisions on our behalf, and it only remains for us to hand over our power of decision to them.

In political terms, we have here a perforation of the line of demarcation between the public and the private spheres. This fusion of the public and the private spheres is of course one of the characteristic features of the current transformation of the public sphere, as it has been diagnosed by Habermas. In linguistic, or rather rhetorical, terms, this is an example of a metaphorical redefinition of a situation. The relation between the two heads of state and the people is converted into a father-child relation. It seems fair to say that both the crowd assembled on Red Square and the audience watching the program on the screen are put under the guardianship of the two elder statesmen.

In situations of this kind it will always be difficult to determine whether one is faced with deliberate manipulation by the politician concerned, or only with a manifestation of his or her well-developed social sensibility. In this case, however, we do know that the whole intermezzo was arranged beforehand, the Moscow citizens assembled on Red Square being assigned special roles for the occasion, and the space where it unfolded being closed. It is, in other words, a theatrical performance, but not street theater inasmuch as the citizens on Red Square, including the little boy, should be regarded as actors rather than spectators. Jointly with Reagan and Gorbachev, they may be said to have put on a TV play in front of viewers all over the world.

It would be interesting to know whether TV producers who transmitted the summit meeting to audiences in the United States and Western Europe were in on this political strategy or rather innocently rendered what the politicians offered them. But this question cannot be settled on the basis of a program analysis; it can only be fully elucidated through an analysis of the institutional conditions for the production of these programs.

If we interpret the communicative potential of this program in the way suggested above, the language—whether verbal or pictorial—should be analyzed in terms of the triad *emotive, conative,* and *phatic functions* rather than in terms of *referential function,* to keep to Jakobson's terminology. In the first place the communicator, in this case Gorbachev (and to a lesser degree Reagan), seems to carry more weight than the message he communicates. Accordingly Gorbachev's character, his *ethos,* to use the language of Aristotle, may exert more influence on members of the audience than his words. If the communicator possesses charisma (and that seems to be the case here), he can make spectators disregard any critical attitudes and adopt the image he draws of himself.

So far we have been concerned with what Jakobson called the emotive function of the language, where language is expressive of the communicator's emotional state. Like gestures—and they are abundant in this intermezzo—linguistic expressions are symptoms of the communicator's state of mind. Here Jakobson revives from the thirties Karl Bühler's theory of the *symptom function* of language, where the linguistic expression has a set direction toward the communicator.

There are cases where it is hard to determine whether the emotive or the phatic function is predominant, and this intermezzo is one of them. According to Jakobson, we are confronted with a phatic function when the linguistic expression primarily serves "to establish, to prolong or to discontinue communication, to check whether the channel works, to attract the attention of the interlocutor or to confirm his continued attention."[36] In the intermezzo on Red Square the informative value of the verbal communication is next to none, the words of the two leaders barely carrying any more meaning than their gestures. The whole intermezzo is composed of more or less ritualized acts, similar to Gorbachev's shaking hands with American citizens in the suburbs of Washington the previous year. What Gorbachev (and Reagan), in fact, does is to establish communication partly with the people gathered on Red Square, and partly with the TV viewers watching from their individual living rooms.

Among viewers who are sensitive to these kinds of rhetorical device, there is a strong tendency to restrict their critical questioning of the program to one single question: Do the emotional expressions of the two leaders come from the bottom of their hearts, or are they just put on? In other words, can we trust that their manifest behavior corresponds to their inner being, that they are authentic persons? In the case of those viewers who are taken in by the two charismatic leaders, the intermezzo may be said to have a strong *conative* function. As already suggested, it may be understood as an exhortation to the viewers to give up their authority as political subjects and allow the leaders to make decisions for the future on their behalf.

The setting of the intermezzo consisting, in front, of a long row of people queuing up along the Kremlin wall, and of St. Basil's Cathedral in the background, becomes on this interpretation mere scenery around the performing main actors. Only viewers who are not seduced by the momentary fascination of the two leaders, and who have preserved a sense of history, will be able to read the program as a compound textual structure, where different components of meaning sometimes contradict one another and sometimes merge into a complex whole. The latter viewers will be in a position to understand that Gorbachev's road to democracy in the Soviet Union will be a thorny one, taking into consideration the strong authoritarian tradition attested by all these citizens queuing up to pay Lenin their respects and the oppression of religious communities recalled to us by the chiming bells of St. Basil's.

Some Reflections on the Method

In order to establish how the messages analyzed above had in fact been received and interpreted by sections of the media audience in different structural positions, I initiated field research by interview. The aim of the project was, in other words, to construct a typology of the range of decodings made, and to analyze how and why they vary. As a framework for analysis I used, as already suggested, Bourdieu's theory of practice, formulated through the concept of *habitus*. Accordingly, I assumed that there is a correspondence between class, that is, socioeconomic position, and cultural and interpretative codes or competencies among the viewers.

I attempted to construct a sample of people who might be expected to vary from the most "doxic" mode through intermediate modes to the most sophisticated mode of decoding. With this sample I aimed primarily to identify the key points of difference between the classes, but without playing down the points at which the interpretations of the different classes might overlap. The sample consisted of twenty individuals, all drawn from Oslo or its immediate surroundings. Even if these persons' position in social space—their class positions—cannot be regarded as identical with their occupational position, occupation is a good economic indicator of position in social space.[37] Occupation does in fact normally reflect economic situation and educational level, although there are cases where an occupation may be obtained by a person who does not have the required educational background. This may cause difficulties in a research project where people are selected for interviews on the basis of their occupation.

I was, in fact, faced with such difficulties as I used my circle of acquaintances to help me find persons to fill the occupational roles that I wanted to be represented in my sample. In most cases I was able to circumvent these difficulties by making further inquiries about my respondents before we met for the interview. However, in one case I discovered only during the interview that the person in front of me possessed a cultural capital that greatly surpassed the number of years of his formal education.

With a view to bringing out a few basic ideal-typical decodings I chose to use the sampling strategy that is termed *stratified purposeful sampling.*[38] Needless to say, the basic parameters in my sample were cultural and economic capital, but other sociodemographic factors, such as position in the structures of age and sex, were also taken into account. The sample details are set out in table 7.1.

As suggested in the table, we have here four different groups, each consisting of persons with approximately the same volume of economic and cultural capital. On the one hand, this classification largely corresponds with the scale of competencies devised by the Norwegian Office of Population and Census Statistics (Statistisk Sentralbyrå) for occupational classification. On the other, it shares much in common with more theory-based classifications, like the one developed by Bourdieu, where classes represent occupational

Table 7.1. Sample Details

Occupation	Sex	Age (years)	Education (years)	Income (kroner)
Upper secondary pupil	F	17	11.0	n.a.
Farmer	M	57	11.5	175,000
Housewife	F	51	8.5	50,000
Mobile library driver	M	49	8.0	120,000
Head duty officer	F	59	13.0	145,000
Physiotherapist (intern)	M	27	16.0	85,000
Advertising designer	M	43	12.0	650,000
Small shopkeeper	F	48	14.5	289,000
Political secretary (part-time)	M	23	14.0	90,000
Securities broker	M	28	16.0	450,000
Member of Parliament	F	49	12.0	220,000
Director of cultural affairs	M	52	18.0	300,000
Headmistress (retired)	F	74	18.0	200,000
Principal	M	53	18.0	240,000
Newspaper editor	M	37	17.0	395,000
Research officer	M	42	> 18.0	400,000
Director general (research foundation)	F	39	> 18.0	300,000
Professor (retired)	M	73	> 18.0	300,000
Director general (public administration)	F	48	16.0	600,000
Author	M	44	16.0	270,000

aggregates. As will appear from the table, my sample population is divided into four levels or classes: semiskilled and unskilled working class, lower middle class, middle class, and upper middle class. The first-mentioned class consists of farmers and manual workers, supervisors of manual workers, and lower-grade technicians. In the second class we find employees in administration and commerce, rank-and-file employees in services, and small proprietors. To the third class belong lower-grade professionals, administrators and officials, higher-grade technicians, managers in small business and industrial establishments, supervisors of nonmanual employees. Finally, the upper class is composed of higher-grade professionals, administrators and officials, managers in large industrial establishments, and major proprietors.

Each person in my sample was shown the summary of NRK's TV coverage of the Moscow meeting and interviewed in depth about how he or she interpreted the program and understood the role of television in his or her overall leisure activities. Each person (with one or two exceptions) was interviewed in his or her home during the week of 3–10 June 1988. The interviews, which lasted between one and two hours, were tape recorded and then transcribed for analysis.

I used a structured interviewing method but designed it to allow a fair degree of probing. On points of significance, I returned the conversation to the same theme at different stages in the interview, and from different angles. This implies that anyone "having me on"—consciously or unconsciously—by representing themselves through an artificial or stereotyped persona that did not correspond to their "real" activities would have to be able to sustain their adopted persona through quite a complex form of interrogation. Nonetheless, it remains true that I was dealing ultimately with respondents' own accounts of how they deal with television. But, as already indicated, my interviewing technique had some built-in safeguards against the possibility of respondents presenting entirely disingenuous accounts of their viewing behavior.

Focusing Data

My own entry to the analysis of the data was provided by a metaphor that came to my mind even while I was in the process of finalizing the interview guide, a metaphor originating from Roman mythology. In ancient Rome, the entrance to a house was believed to be guarded by the god *Janus*. His name is related to the Latin word for door, *janua*. In the northwestern corner of the Forum Romanum there was a double gate that was consecrated to Janus, and in the middle there was a bronze image of the god with the two faces, one looking east and the other looking west. According to popular religion, the vigilant god was able to look both forward and backward, both in space and time. Just as Janus was the god of entry in a spatial sense, he was also the god of every entry or beginning in time. The first month of the year, *Januarius,* was named after him, and the first day of each month was consecrated to him. To the Romans, Janus seems to have been a symbol that they used not only to orientate themselves in time and space, but also to signal their relationship to the outside world. Whenever the Romans were at war with neighboring states, the leaves of the double gate were left open, but in times of peace they were shut.

Throughout the project the two-faced Janus functioned as a metaphor and a sensitizing concept for my investigation.[39] The TV screen may be compared with the two-faced Janus inasmuch as one side of it faces the living room of the viewer, while the other faces the outside world. The actual television box is situated so to speak on the door sill, that is, on the threshold between the private and the public spheres. Home is of course the site of that part of our lives which we do not want to expose to the public, whereas the space outside is accessible to all, and therefore the arena for affairs that the citizens must deal with jointly. The television box is part of the inventory of our private homes, and the images we receive on the screen are incorporated in the cultural milieu we create in our living rooms. On the other hand, the images on the screen point to the public sphere, to the world beyond the private home of the individual viewer, enticing him or her to undertake imaginary journeys to unknown places and countries.

The location of television on the threshold between interior and exterior, between the private and the public spheres, gives rise to a fundamental ambiguity in its way of functioning. Like Janus's double gate on the Forum Romanum, television can shut the outside world out, with the consequence that the images on the screen are reduced to decorative and entertaining elements in the home milieu of the viewers. On the other hand it can also be kept open to the outside world and give the viewers the feeling of being transported to arenas where the political discussions take place, in the case of both domestic and foreign affairs. However, the recent modernization of program production blurs the boundaries between these two spheres. This leads to an interweaving of the two functions of television, counteracting any attempts made by viewers to keep the private and the public spheres strictly apart.

A similar understanding of the function of television is to be found in Roger Silverstone's book *Television and Everyday Life,* where he places television between opposing tendencies, represented by "home" and "reach":

Television and other media are part of home—part of its idealization, part of its reality. The dimension of home that involves positive feelings of security and belonging is both challenged and reinforced by a medium that brings the world into the interior. New media or unacceptable images are threatening, and television is something that has to be controlled, if only on behalf of the children. Yet the "box in the corner" is, in our dependence on it, a crucial link to a shared or shareable world of community and nation, and, as such, acts to extend the boundaries of home beyond the front door.[40]

This is an elaboration of Joshua Meyrowitz's seminal discussion of television's contribution to changing the relationship between home and reach.[41] Exploiting a notion derived from the linguist André Martinet, Silverstone specifies this as the "double articulation" of television in domestic culture: television is articulated into the household both as an object and as a medium: "As an object it is bought and incorporated into the culture of the household for its aesthetic and functional characteristics. . . . As a medium, through the structure and contents of its programming as well as through the mediation of public and private spheres more broadly, it draws the members of the household into a world of public and shared meanings."[42] To elucidate in all its aspects the incorporation of television into our domestic culture Silverstone resorts to a metaphor: the "domestication" of the medium. Literally, domestication involves bringing objects in from the wild. Here, it refers to "the transition, which is also a translation, of objects across the boundaries that separate public and private spaces."[43] But even if the viewers are always in the process of "taming" the medium both as object and as meanings, television remains, at least potentially, "savage." It has the capacity to offer new horizons and new opportunities and provides the means for fundamental transformations in our relationship to time and space.[44]

To bring out the double articulation or the double face of television is to reproduce one of the crucial insights of Marshall McLuhan, an insight that Jean Baudrillard in an early work makes use of when arguing that televisual consumption is class-differentiated: "There are those for whom TV is an object, there are those for whom it is a cultural exercise: on this radical opposition a cultural class privilege is established that is registered in an essential social privilege."[45] Even if this is a rather axiomatic statement, it contains a core of truth: that television can mean different things to different people, and that variation between them in the pattern of consumption somehow reflects differences in their social status.

Looking for Themes in the Data

This initial stage of my dealings with the data may be characterized as one of sociological imagination. It included not only a perusal of theoretical litera-ture in search of sensitizing metaphors and concepts but also a thoroughgo-ing familiarization with the data. Two themes emerged from the outset, name-ly, *time* and *space,* themes that were inherent in the Janus metaphor and at the same time cut across the individual interviews.

Time and space are of course also the main constituents of our everyday life-world, as it is described by Alfred Schutz and Thomas Luckmann in their life-world sociology.[46] They speak of both a "spatial" and a "temporal" arrange-ment of everyday life. The world of daily life is given to us in a taken-for-granted way. Spatially it is partitioned in a primary zone of operation, that is, "the world within actual reach," and a secondary zone of operation, or "the world within potential reach." The former is described as follows: "The place in which I find myself, my actual 'here,' is the starting point for my orienta-tion in space. It is the zero-point of the system of coordinates within which the dimensions of orientation, the distances and perspectives of objects, be-come determined in the field that surrounds me. Relative to my animate organism, I classify the elements of my surroundings under the categories right, left, above, below, in front of, behind, near, far, etc."[47] About the latter Schutz and Luckmann state:

> The fundamental expectation that I can bring whatever sectors of the world I please into my reach is empirically arranged not only according to *subjective de-grees of probability* but also according to *grades of ability* that are physical, tech-nical, etc. My position in a particular time and society is part of the latter limi-tation. (A citizen of the Middle Ages could travel to China only with the greatest difficulties and with the greatest loss of time. Today I can fly to Hong Kong in a day. My children may be able to take a trip to the moon.)[48]

To this spatial arrangement of the life-world corresponds a temporal one. What is in a person's "actual reach" is also in his or her "present reach": the "here" corresponds to a "now," and to transcend the world as extension is also to transcend it as duration. According to Schutz and Luckmann the struc-ture of life-worldly time is built up where *the subjective time* of the stream of consciousness intersects with *the world time or the calendar time.* We all re-construct our everyday life by grappling with the incongruence of the vari-ous temporal dimensions. However, what Schutz and Luckmann did not anticipate, or at least failed to specify, is that in late modernity, television was to become the principal arena for our temporal articulations. Nor did they conceive of television as a medium that more efficiently than any previous technology enables us to transcend spatial bounds, even if it only allows of imaginary travels.

Anthony Giddens is a modern sociologist who also understands the reproduction of social life in terms of our organization of time-space. In his theory of structuration he explains social conduct as an interchange between *social integration* and *system integration*.[49] Social integration has to do with interaction between actors in contexts of copresence, whereas system integration has to do with interaction between actors or collectivities who are physically absent in time and space. In contrast to the work of Schutz and Luckmann, which is chiefly a contribution to the theory of consciousness, Giddens's work belongs to the theory of communication tradition. However, his interest in this work does not stop at communication or social interaction, it also embraces communication technology and the impact technological development can have on social life.

Of special relevance to the interpretation of my data is his pair of concepts "time-space routinization" and "time-space distanciation." These are concepts that Giddens plays upon when explaining how social life is constituted in different social systems. The organization of social time and space belongs to what he calls the authoritative resources of the social system, and these resources will vary according to the technological level of the social system in question. Accordingly, "time-space routinization," that is, relations between people who are copresent in time and space, tended to control social life in traditional societies. As a consequence of the advent of modern communication technology, social life increasingly depends on interactions with others who are absent in time and space. Yet the continuity of everyday life is still largely maintained by routinized interactions between people who are copresent in time and space. But in late modernity we have at our disposal the technological ability to indulge in greater "time-space distanciation," or—to quote Giddens—to transcend the limitations of individual "presence" by the "stretching of social relations across time and space."[50]

In late modernity we are all caught up in this oscillation between "time-space routinization" and "time-space distanciation," between social integration and system integration. Within the framework of this polarity we form our individual life-paths, and this is a process that to a growing extent is enacted in front of the television screen. Accordingly it was possible to extract from my own interview data a whole gamut of individual life-paths or lifetime biographies. The individuals ranged from those who simply made TV viewing part of their routine activities, taking their own interaction with TV and its talking heads to be precious little different from ordinary face-to-face talk in their own living room, to those who coordinate, in a deliberate way, daily activities and spells of TV viewing in order to obtain the opportunity to make imaginary "travels" and to "communicate" with people living in remote places and times.

As suggested, time and space were the first themes to emerge from the data (theme 1 and theme 2). But these were soon to be followed by another theme, the arrangement of the social world (theme 3), which may be compared with a life-world constituent in Schutz and Luckmann's account. In their analysis, we all have an immediate experience of other beings "like me," and they end up with assuming the intersubjectivity of the world taken for granted. In my own data, on the other hand, the immediate experience of the social arrangement was one of hierarchy and difference rather than likeness and intersubjectivity. My respondents seemed to be aware that power is unequally distributed in society and had no hesitation in placing themselves in the social and political order. There were those who regarded themselves as incompetent to perform in the public sphere, leaving it to those in power to make decisions for them on their behalf. And there were those who availed themselves of what Giddens calls authoritative resources, including modern communication technology, to take part in political discussions and assert themselves in the public sphere.

Finally, a fourth theme may be extracted from the data, namely, the understanding of the TV medium (theme 4). This theme is constructed mainly on the basis of the answers given by my respondents to the question: "Do you feel that the TV coverage gives a true picture of what happened during the summit meeting?" For some of the respondents television seemed to constitute a "window on the world," as if the glass on the screen provided a vision of the world uncontaminated by the politics of representation. At the opposite end of the scale, there were respondents who were fully aware of the complexities involved in the process of technically mediating reality. Even if these respondents were able to see that reality, as it is rendered by television, is a construction, a joint product of human and technical intervention, they knew how to make use of television both to orient themselves in reality and to make themselves felt in that reality.[51]

From Sensitizing Metaphor to Definitive Concepts

After these four themes had been identified, partly generated by the Janus metaphor, the time had come to explore the possibility of developing a typology of viewer responses to TV news. The first step in this procedure would be to redefine the themes as parameters, a step that has already been anticipated in the preceding presentation of the themes. The next would be to examine the material carefully in order to determine each respondent's position or value on all four parameters. During this examination a high degree of covariation emerged between the individual respondents' values on the different parameters, and it seemed appropriate to set up a matrix describing the relationship between themes and values on the corresponding parameters.

On the basis of this matrix I outlined a tentative typology capable of grouping together respondents with almost equal values on all the parameters. I ended up with four groups or ideal-types—to borrow an expression from Weber. These ideal-types could not easily be denominated by what Van Maanen called "first-order concepts," that is, concepts derived from the material itself.[52] To characterize them I felt compelled to resort to "second-order concepts," "notions used by the researcher to explain the patterning of the first-order concepts." As I was here confronted with variation between different behavioral and discursive modes, it was appropriate to take advantage of Bourdieu's theory of practice reported earlier in this chapter. His concept of *habitus* seemed eminently suitable for handling the complexities of viewing behavior in my sample.

It was more challenging, however, to invent labeling concepts that could bring out the specificity of each of the four ideal-types and at the same time take good care of their common denominator. Again I turned to Bourdieu, drawing three epistemological concepts, *doxa, orthodoxy,* and *heterodoxy,* from a chapter of his book *Outline of a Theory of Practice,* where his real purpose is to distinguish between different social formations.[53] To characterize different patterns of viewing behavior by epistemological concepts is of course somewhat inaccurate, for viewing behavior cannot simply be equated with epistemology. Nevertheless, epistemology is an important aspect of our everyday conduct, including TV viewing, and at least one of the themes that I was able to identify in the interview data has a direct bearing on epistemology, namely, *the understanding of the TV medium.* In dealing with this theme the respondents revealed how they understood the mediation process: whether they understood the TV medium as transparent, allowing the viewer directly to observe the "facts" of the world, or as an interfering factor supplying us only with multiple constructions of reality.

It was this variation in epistemological orientation among the respondents that I tried to capture through the concepts *doxa, orthodoxy,* and *heterodoxy.* In Bourdieu's theory, *doxa* refers to an "immediate adherence to the world of tradition experienced as a 'natural world,' and taken for granted."[54] To people who adopt the doxic mode of thought, the social world is self-evident and undisputed. They fail, in other words, to see that there can be any rival or antagonistic principle to the prevailing classification of the world. The way in which the concept of doxa is explained here, it also borders on another of the four themes of in my data, *the arrangement of the social world.* The doxic mode implies endorsing the established political order, entrusting the power of decision to the political authorities and renouncing one's own political rights.

Now I was ready to start the final coding by connecting empirical indicators, drawn from the interview data, to what I began to regard as *definitive concepts.* The first concept (concept A) was doxa, and the relevant doxa indicator pertaining to theme 4 (the understanding of the TV medium) seemed to be:

A.4 Adherence to a naïve realism: TV reflects reality, the images function as a guarantee of truth.

And the doxa indicator for theme 3 (the arrangement of the social world) was:

A.3 Faith in politicians: openness to their charismatic influence.

Another two doxa indicators soon emerged, indicators related to the themes of time and space. The one related to space may be defined as:

A.2 TV's "talking heads" function as pseudo-Gemeinschaft for the viewers, who cherish them and identify with them.

And the one related to time:

A.1 Ritualized contact with the medium: TV viewing integrated in a regular, cyclic time rhythm.

The coding procedure followed the same pattern for the next definitive concept, *orthodoxy* (concept B). In order to home in on this concept I once more consulted Bourdieu, who offers an instructive account of the transition from a doxic to an orthodox mode of thought. According to Bourdieu, the transition presupposes a critique that brings the undiscussed into discussion, the unformulated into formulation, in this way destroying the self-evidence of "the field of doxa." In other words, "the field of doxa" is substituted by "the field of opinion" as the locus of the confrontation of rival understandings or "competing possibles."

Hence, an indicator in my data pertaining to the understanding of the TV

medium and at the same time capable of accommodating Bourdieu's definition of the orthodox mode would be:

B.4 Full confidence in the NRK reporters, as opposed to distrust of the
    TV medium ("TV can lie").

Similarly the orthodoxy indicator for the arrangement of the social world
seemed to be:

B.3 Dependence on authoritative experts for the interpretation of the
    political messages, inasmuch as politicians and politics are taken to
    function as, respectively, actors and media show.

This agrees well with the etymology of the word *orthodoxy*, meaning the
"straight" or "right" opinion, that is, the generally accepted ways of thinking
and speaking the natural and social world. The corresponding indicator pertaining to space is:

B.2 Confusion about the location of the television between "home"
    and "reach," and with respect to the ensuing ambivalence of the
    medium.

And to time:

B.1 Collision between the daily routine of the respondents and the
    timetable of television, provoking stress and interpersonal conflicts.

Next in turn for the coding procedure was *heterodoxy* or *the heterodox mode*
(concept C). On this point Bourdieu is less explicit. However, it would be
an extension of his way of thinking to define the transition from orthodoxy
to heterodoxy as a change from naïve adherence to the authorized or dominant discourse to a fully developed political consciousness, with an ability to
frame an autonomous discourse based on one's own experiences. The corresponding indicator in my data seemed to be:

C.4 Understanding of news reports as rational and informative, provid-
    ed that reporters comply with "public service" norms of objectivity,
    balance, and neutrality.

The heterodoxy indicator for the arrangement of the social world is:

C.3 Understanding of politics as a rational, objective public sphere that
    ought to remain uncontaminated by the private sphere.

The same rationalistic and moralizing bent marks the space/time indicators of the heterodox mode:

C.2 Efforts to separate the public sphere from the private sphere, information from entertainment.

And:

C.1 Carefully regulated and controlled use of television based on an absolute distinction between spells of learning and spells of relaxation, between informative programs and entertaining programs.

For the fourth ideal-type, no designation was immediately available in Bourdieu's theory. However, in another context Bourdieu introduces a cognate concept that may help us to continue this reasoning, namely, *the paradox.* Hence I propose that the fourth ideal-type should be called *the paradoxical mode* (concept D). As the name intimates, this is a mode of thought that can keep opposite perspectives in mind at the same time. In this particular case it means knowing that TV can give no objective description of social reality and yet constantly being dependent on it for one's information about that reality. The corresponding indicator in my data seemed to be:

D.4 Awareness that viewers' perception of reality is a social construct: a product of their own framework of interpretation and the media's staged description.

The indicator for the arrangement of the social world runs in the same direction:

D.3 Understanding of politics as symbol production and role play: to get under its surface demands probing into the logic of the game or the dramaturgy of political actions.

The space/time indicators of the paradoxical mode appeared thus:

D.2 Adoption of a pragmatic attitude: since the public and the private spheres have merged, and TV newscasts provide information and entertainment at the same time, the viewer has to accept the one with the other.

And:

D.1 The viewer will practice strategic and flexible contact with the TV medium: find ways of combining TV viewing with various other tasks.

The Four Habitus Profiles Presented and Explained

After I had completed these steps of comparing indicator to indicator, of confronting similarities and differences among categories of respondents, the following taxonomy of habitus profiles emerged, a taxonomy that seemed to fit very well with the data in table 7.2.

There was a very close correspondence between this habitus taxonomy and the distribution of economic and cultural capital in my sample. Yet there were both differences within each individual category or habitus profile and over-lappings between habitus profiles that are partly concealed in table 7.2.

The doxic mode of thought can be traced in the four persons who may be said to constitute the lowest class in my sample, the upper secondary pupil, the farmer, the housewife, the mobile library driver, and the head duty officer. However, the data seemed to provide a basis for distinguishing between two different versions of the doxic mode. Among those who were employed in, or had close relations with, primary industries, the TV consumption seemed to vary according to the seasons: they tended to fit their spells of TV viewing into their working routine, which was more or less determined by the cyclic rhythm of nature. On the other hand, those who were engaged in service industries and had regular working hours were inclined to allow the timetable of television to determine the rhythm of their leisure time. One of them, the mobile library driver, regarded watching TV almost as a basic need; only sleep could keep him from watching the afternoon and evening programs. Among the members of this class there was a certain reluctance to voice their opinion publicly unless in matters of local politics, in which one of them was actually involved.

The orthodox mode of thought characterized the second class in my sample, represented by the physiotherapist, the advertising designer, the small shopkeeper, the political secretary, and the securities broker. In Bourdieu's hierarchy, all these professions would come under the lower middle class. As pointed out above, among these viewers an ambivalent attitude to the TV medium prevailed. But this ambivalence was managed differently by the different viewers. The small shopkeeper, who may be said to belong to the old lower middle class, experienced a feeling of being drawn between a sense of obligation to keep informed about the state of affairs and a sense of fascination with the visual impressions provided by the medium. This dilemma made her skeptical about TV news altogether and prompted her to seek information through the newspapers instead.

A corresponding ethical attitude to the TV medium was to be found in

Table 7.2. The Four Habitus Profiles

Theme	Profile 1	Profile 2
Organization of time	The viewers arrange their TV viewing in a regular, indeed cyclic time rhythm. They exercise a predominantly ritualised contact with the medium: the medium functions as a means of maintaining norms and values, of creating "ontological security" among the viewers.	The viewers experience a collision between their own daily routine and that of TV. This results in stress and conflicts: they are caught between "home" and "reach," between socio-oriented and concept-oriented viewing. Attempts are often made to reconcile their ambivalence to the medium through different combination strategies: some seek excitement in "live" news, others use the news broadcasts as the stimulus for conversation in the company of others.
Organization of space	The "talking heads" on the screen produce spatial proximity, form a "pseudo-Gemeinschaft" for the viewers, and become the object of their empathy. Certain viewers experience para-social interaction, i.e., face-to-face contact with the people on the screen.	This ambivalence, which is connected with the spatial location of the TV screen between "home" and "reach," assumes various forms: some people are torn between the duty to be informed and the desire to be entertained; others between interest in the content (politics) and fascination by the form (aesthetics). There is a tendency among the viewers to attempt to circumvent this ambivalence by indulging in the hybrid genre "faction."
Arrangement of the social world	Faith in politicians: the viewers lay themselves open to the charismatic influence of politicians, even though they are fully aware of this influence. They meet politicians wanting to get close to them, to shake their hands, to be photographed together with them. They do not distinguish between the politician and the private individual, and have no objection to political discussions assuming the form of "public private conversations."	Distrust of politics and politicians: the viewers see through the politicians' charismatic ability to influence and regard them as actors, and their politics as a "media show" or "big act." They see themselves as being uninfluenced by them. The viewers have no reservations about appearing in the media to give their own opinions, but they actually borrow ideas from, or seek confirmation of their opinions from, experts with great authority.
Understanding of the medium	Realism: TV reflects reality; the TV images function for the viewers as a guaranty of truth. In their eyes the TV medium records objectively, while journalists often comment subjectively.	The TV medium can lie: in the viewers' eyes the reality in the TV pictures is staged. However the viewers have reason to trust NRK's reporters, who are responsible for the staging.

Table 7.2. (cont.)

Profile 3	Profile 4
The viewers practice regulated and controlled use of TV: viewing is fitted into a carefully thought-out timetable that is based on an absolute distinction between "home" and "reach." For them viewing the news is concept-oriented: it demands peace and quiet and full concentration. (One viewer goes to the extreme of *listening* to TV news without the picture because she experiences the picture as a distracting factor.)	The viewers practice strategic and flexible contact with the TV medium: they combine viewing with various other tasks. Thus for these people the distinction between "home" and "reach," between socio-oriented and concept-oriented TV use is partly obliterated.
The viewers adopt the norms of the bourgeois public: "home" (the private sphere) is kept totally separate from "reach" (the public sphere); entertainment is distinguished from information, distracting image from informative speech, the aesthetic packaging from the historical and political reality, the emotional appeal from the rational description. The viewers are skeptical about TV as a source of information; newspapers are preferred.	The viewers acknowledge a pragmatic motive for viewing. The traditional demand for objectivity is replaced by a demand that news presentation must *function* for the viewer. This goes hand in hand with an acknowledgement of the fact that the public sphere and the private sphere merge into each other, and that TV newscasts provide information and excitement at one and the same time. This in turn opens the way for the form of the news to be ascribed significance on an equal footing with the content.
The viewers define politics as rational and objective debate, as negotiations between sincere actors. They believe themselves capable of distinguishing between authentic politics and courting the public, between the politician's political orientation and the private individual's charisma, between sincere and false politicians. They adopt an ethical, not to say moralizing, perspective to politics, and see themselves as independent in a broad sense: able on their own to form opinions and take part in democratic decision-making processes completely on their own terms.	The viewers define politics as symbol production and role-play, and see TV as an important contributor to role formation. Understanding politics is thus for them understanding the logic of the game or the dramaturgy of the political actions. TV-mediated politics is in other words also a form of aesthetics. Among some of the viewers there are leanings towards a sociological point of view on their own knowledge process; they perceive their own interpretations as being formed in confrontation with those of others and at the same time as being determined by the interpreter's own position in society.
The truth must be understood as a whole, which can only be grasped through rational considerations. The prerequisite for true acknowledgement of reality is that the media, which communicate it to the viewers, live up to the "public service" norms of objectivity, balance, neutrality and keeping to the point. Reality does in fact allow itself to be communicated neutrally and without influence from the mediating body.	The truth appears to the viewers as fragmentary, as "separate realities": the viewers' perception of it is a social construct, i.e., a product of their own framework of interpretation and the media's staged descriptions of reality. News broadcasts cannot claim objectivity in any form: the staging turns the content into a product partly of the medium itself and partly of genre-specific features.

the physiotherapist, even though his profession must be said to be among those that constitute the new lower middle class. In the other representatives of the lower middle class, the advertising designer, the political secretary, and the securities broker, a much more sympathetic, even enthusiastic, attitude to the TV medium was noticeable. These persons attempted to circumvent their ambivalence by indulging in the hybrid genre "faction." Generally speaking they seemed to be more dependent on the new media in their work and were more aesthetically oriented than the representatives of the old lower middle class, who have already been described as ethically oriented.

The heterodox mode proved to be characteristic of four of the five persons I had selected to represent the middle class or what Bourdieu calls the bourgeoisie, namely, the member of Parliament, the director of cultural affairs, the headmistress, and the principal. The fifth person, the editor, turned out to possess a much higher degree of cultural capital than anticipated. Like all the other persons in my sample, he was selected initially on the basis of his occupational position and next on the basis of his educational background. However, before the interview had proceeded far I realized that his cultural competence surpassed by far the level of his formal education, and that he ought to be ranked with the persons in my last class, who belong to the elite of society.

The other four members of this class were persons who knew how to exploit the news reports on TV to widen their intellectual horizon and frame their own opinions. But in order to achieve this they deemed it necessary to keep to news reports that were uncontaminated by elements of entertainment. The member of Parliament even went to the length of switching off the pictures while listening to TV news reports, fearing that the pictures might distract her from the content of the news items.

These are persons who assert themselves in the public sphere, persons who regard television as a medium for their own performance on the arena of politics and for the maintenance of the public sphere. Bourdieu says that they have "the sense of distinction." His classical example of bourgeois "distinction" is the claim that there is a "disinterested" or "pure taste" in the Kantian sense. The mark of "distinction" in my sample seemed to be the adherence to the "public service" purpose of NRK combined with the demand that news reports should live up to the norms of objectivity, balance, and neutrality.

However, it is a question whether these traditional norms are fully practicable in the present situation of competition between different television channels and between different media. One may even ask whether it is not an illusion to believe that television can offer a true-to-life picture of reality. This was in fact called into question by three of the persons in the fourth and last group, which contained representatives of the cultural and economic elite of society. The research officer, the author, and the director general of a research foundation (and I could also add the editor from the third class) demonstrated *a paradoxical mode* of thought that corresponds with what Bourdieu, in his article "Le paradoxe du sociologue," calls sociological insight or reflexivity.[55] The sociologist is bound to give an objective description of social reality, knowing at the same time that the description he makes is determined by his position in the social hierarchy. That is his particular insight or reflexivity.

As suggested, the research officer, the author, the director general of a research foundation, and the editor were conscious of the fact that television can offer no objective picture of reality, and that they nevertheless were dependent on it for being well informed. That seemed to be their paradoxical mode. Moreover, they had a notion that in their attempt to obtain information they would be under the influence of expert commentaries, and that their own understanding of reality was determined by their own position in society.

It is, of course, no surprise that these people have high positions in our society, and that these are positions that presuppose more cultural than economic capital. An exception was constituted by the director general in public administration, whose economic and social capital were superior to her cultural capital. She did not question the ability of television to offer a true-to-life picture of reality but contented herself with stating the fact that it can only give us a segment of reality. However, by giving ear to the journalists and commentators whom she trusted, she felt able to get a true and complete picture of reality. On the whole she seemed to possess much of the same orthodoxy or "cultural goodwill"—to use another term from Bourdieu—that I found in the lower middle class.

Like the director general in public administration, the retired professor argued that television can give us only a segment of reality, giving away that he used to supplement TV viewing with reading a fair number of newspapers and periodicals to be well informed. He too seemed fundamentally not to doubt television's ability to mirror reality. More than any of the other respondents he played down the specificity of the TV medium. He was the only one I could not persuade to watch the video with the summary of NRK's coverage of the Moscow meeting. To his way of thinking it would have been a waste of time since he had already seen most of the programs and remembered them very well. To him television was not qualitatively different from other media, it was simply an instrument for the collection of information and knowledge. His diverging TV habitus may perhaps be explained by the fact that he grew up with other media and had already established a relationship with the radio, newspapers, and periodicals when TV came along. At age seventy-three he was by far the oldest person in this class, and the difference between his own attitude to TV and that of the other persons in the class may be interpreted as one of generation.

As it appears from this typology, there is no authority for believing that television can be instrumental in a process of democratization. Persons who already possess a high cultural capital will be able to take advantage of the medium both to increase their cultural capital and to a growing extent to make themselves felt on the public arena. Persons with little cultural and economic capital on the other hand are likely to fall victim partly to the rhetoric displayed in the medium itself, and partly to the expert commentators who have emerged in the wake of television.

Notes

1. Theodor Adorno, "Television and the Patterns of Mass Culture," *Quarterly of Film, Radio and Television* 8 (1954), 229.

2. Gladys Engel Lang and Kurt Lang, *The Battle for Public Opinion: The President, the Press, and the Polls during Watergate,* (New York: Columbia University Press, 1983).

3. See Kim C. Schrøder, "Convergence of Antagonistic Traditions?" *European Journal of Communication* 2:1 (1987), 7–31; Klaus Bruhn Jensen and Karl E. Rosengren, "Five Traditions in Search of the Audience," *European Journal of Communication* 5:2/3 (1990), 207–38; Daniel Dayan and Elihu Katz, *Media Events: The Live Broadcasting of History* (Cambridge, Mass.: Harvard University Press, 1992), state that "the rich theorizing of the humanist and the careful empiricism of the social scientist are only now being combined in the analysis of television" (235).

4. Wilbur Schramm, Jack Lyle, and Edwin B. Parker, *Television in the Lives of Our Children* (Stanford: Stanford University Press, 1961), 2.

5. Robert K. Merton, *Mass Persuasion: The Social Psychology of a War Bond Drive* (New York: Harper, 1946), 1ff.

6. Ibid., xii.

7. Stuart Hall, "Encoding and Decoding in the Television Discourse," *Education and Culture* 6 (1975); later published under the title of "Encoding and Decoding," in *Culture, Media, Language,* ed. Stuart Hall, Dorothy Hobson, Andrew Lowe, and Paul Willis (London: Hutchinson, 1980), 128–38.

8. Ibid., 130.

9. Ibid.

10. The article was first published in *Psychological Review* 3 (July 1896), 357–70.

11. Ibid., 358.

12. Ibid., 365.

13. Ibid.

14. Quotes from John Dewey, *Democracy and Education* (New York: Free Press, 1966), 156.

15. Stuart Hall, "The Rediscovery of 'Ideology': Return of the Repressed in Media Studies," in *Culture, Society and the Media,* ed. Michael Gurevitch, Tony Bennett, James Curran, and Janet Woollacott (London: Methuen, 1985), 56–90 (quote, 64).

16. Cf. Graham Murdock, "Cultural Studies: Missing Links," *Critical Studies in Mass Communications* 6:4 (1989), 436.

17. David Morley, "Cultural Transformations: The Politics of Resistance" in *Language, Image, Media,* ed. Howard Davis and Paul Walton (Oxford: Blackwell, 1983), 109–110.

18. David Morley, *The "Nationwide" Audience* (London: British Film Institute, 1980), 18. See V. N. Volosinov, *Marxism and the Philosophy of Language* (New York: Seminar Press, 1973); he argues that reading is not a garnering of meanings from the text but is a dialogue between text and the socially situated reader.

19. In *Television, Audiences and Cultural Studies* (London: Routledge, 1992), 125, Morley says: "That the task of investigating the complex pattern of relations between structural factors and cultural practices is one which the *Nationwide* audience study only scratches the surface of, I would agree—for a much more developed account of such relations based on a much stronger corpus of empirical data, see the work of Bourdieu."

20. Advocates of Bourdieu's theories are, in addition to Morley, Graham Murdock, "Critical Inquiry and Audience Activity," in *Rethinking Communication,* vol. 2, ed. Brenda Dervin et al. (Newbury Park, Calif.: Sage, 1989), 243; John Fiske, *Television Culture* (London: Methuen, 1987), 13; Denis McQuail, *Mass Communication Theory* (London: Sage, 1994), 41; Roger Silverstone, *Television and Everyday Life* (London: Routledge, 1994), 107; and Jostein Gripsrud, *The Dynasty Years: Hollywood Television and Critical Media Studies* (London: Routledge, 1995), 122.

21. Pierre Bourdieu, "The Sentiment of Honour in Kabyle Society," in *Honour and Shame: The Values of Mediterranean Society,* ed. J. G. Peristiany (London: Weidenfeld and Nicholson, 1965), 191–241.

22. Pierre Bourdieu, *Outline of a Theory of Practice* (Cambridge: Cambridge University Press, 1977), 93f.

23. In his Introduction to David Morley, *Family Television: Cultural Power and Domestic Leisure* (London: Routledge, 1986), 9, Stuart Hall summarizes Morley's purpose as follows: "In this way, Morley very suggestively brings together two lines of critical inquiry which have tended to be kept in strict isolation—'questions of interpretation and questions of use.'" Viewing, he insists, has to be seen as a constitutive part of the "'familial or domestic relations through which we construct our lives.'"

24. For an evaluation of Bourdieu's contribution to the development of class analysis, see Rosemary Crompton, *Class and Stratification: An Introduction to Current Debates* (Cambridge: Polity Press, 1993), 173ff.

25. R. Brubaker, "Rethinking Classical Theory," *Theory and Society* 14 (1985), 745–73 (quote, 761).

26. Attempts to model the way in which a text can allow for a multiplicity of meanings within boundaries that its structure sets are to be found in Roland Barthes, *S/Z* (London: Cape, 1975), where he characterizes the narrative as a "limited plurality," and in Morley, *"Nationwide" Audience,* 10, where he describes a text as "structured polysemy."

27. Norman Fairclough, *Media Discourse* (London: Ewald Arnold, 1995), 30.

28. Ibid., 58.

29. Roman Jakobson, "Closing Statement: Linguistics and Poetics," in *Style in Language,* ed. Thomas A. Sebeok (Cambridge, Mass.: MIT Press, 1960), 350–77.

30. See John Ellis, *Visible Fictions: Cinema, Television, Video* (London: Routledge and Kegan Paul, 1982), 159, where he states: "There is no real difference in narrational form between news and soap opera. The distinction is at another level: that of source of material."

31. Elihu Katz and Tamar Liebes, "Mutual Aid in the Decoding of *Dallas:* Preliminary Notes from a Cross-Cultural Study," in *Television in Transition,* ed. Phillip Drummond and Richard Paterson (London: British Film Institute Publishing, 1985), 187–98.

32. Peter Dahlgren, "The Modes of Reception: For a Hermeneutics of TV News," in Drummond and Paterson, *Television in Transition,* 235–49 (quote, p. 238).

33. See Ellis, 146.

34. Mikhail Gorbachev, *Perestroika: New Thinking for Our Country and the World* (New York: Harper and Row, 1988), 62f.

35. Jürgen Habermas, *The Structural Transformation of the Public Sphere* (Cambridge: Polity Press, 1989), 1ff.; see also Hannah Arendt, *The Human Condition* (Chicago: University of Chicago Press, 1958), 28ff.

36. Jakobson, 355.

37. See Rosemary Crompton, *Class and Stratification: An Introduction to Current Debates* (Cambridge: Polity Press, 1993), 10, who maintains that "a very common basis for classification in modern societies is occupation"; and Frank Parkin, *Class Inequality and Political Order* (London: Paladin, 1972), 18, who asserts that: "The backbone of the class structure, and indeed of the entire reward system of modern Western society, is the occupational order."

38. See Michael Quinn Patton, *Qualitative Evaluation and Research Methods* (Newbury Park, Calif.: Sage, 1990), 174.

39. See the account of the use of metaphor in field research by John Lofland and Lyn H. Lofland, *Analyzing Social Settings: A Guide to Qualitative Observation and Analysis* (Belmont, Calif.: Wadsworth, 1984), 122f. Herbert Blumer, "What Is Wrong with Social Theory?" *American Sociological Review* 19 (1954), 3–10, gives a definition of the related analytical instrument, that is, "sensitizing concepts," where he contrasts it with

"definitive concepts" (7): "Instead, it gives the user a general sense of reference and guidance in approaching empirical instances. Where definitive concepts provide prescriptions of what to see, sensitizing concepts merely suggest directions along which to look."

40. Silverstone, 29.

41. Joshua Meyrowitz, *No Sense of Place: The Impact of Electronic Media on Social Behavior* (Oxford: Oxford University Press, 1985) spells out the cultural consequences of the fact that television perforates the boundary between the private and the public spheres.

42. Silverstone, 83.

43. Ibid., 98.

44. A related distinction, although it focuses on families' and family members' mode of communication rather than on their orientation in space, is to be found in James Lull, *Inside Family Viewing: Ethnographic Research on Television's Audiences* (London: Routledge, 1990), 49ff., where the author distinguishes between "socio-oriented" and "concept-oriented" families.

45. Jean Baudrillard, *For a Critique of the Political Economy of the Sign* (St. Louis, Mo.: Telos Press, 1981), 57.

46. Alfred Schutz and Thomas Luckmann, *The Structures of the Life-World* (London: Heinemann, 1974), 36–44.

47. Ibid., 36f. Schutz and Luckmann (41f.) give G. H. Mead credit for having analyzed the reality structure of physical objects in relation to human action. What Mead termed "the manipulative zone" is referred to as a precedent to their term "the world within reach."

48. Ibid., 39.

49. See Anthony Giddens, *The Constitution of Society: Outline of the Theory of Structuration* (Cambridge: Polity Press, 1984).

50. Ibid., 35.

51. The three first-mentioned themes—space, time, and the social arrangement of the life-world—may be compared with the "super-themes" that Klaus Bruhn Jensen identified in the interview data from a study of Danish viewers' reception of television news reported in Klaus Bruhn Jensen, "News as Social Resource," *European Journal of Communication* 3:3 (1988), 275–301. In his book *The Social Semiotics of Mass Communication* (London: Sage, 1995), 156, Jensen resumes this topic, arguing that "these super-themes apparently served as a common denominator for the universe of television news and the respondents' universe of everyday experience."

52. See John Van Maanen, "The Fact of Fiction in Organizational Ethnography," in *Qualitative Methodology*, ed. Van Maanen (Beverly Hills, Calif.: Sage, 1979), 37–55.

53. Bourdieu, *Outline*, 164 ff.

54. Ibid., 164.

55. Pierre Bourdieu, "Le paradoxe du sociologue," *Sociologie et société* 11 (1979), 85–94.

8

"Through Me You'll Live": Impasse vs. Identification in Hostage Negotiation

Connie Fletcher

A key question in the social sciences is how to discover, interpret, and represent the significant elements of another culture. Cultures may be inaccessible, geographically or psychologically. Aspects of a culture may be deliberately hidden from outsiders, veiled by a code of silence that punishes members of the culture who speak the truth. Researchers may be barred from understanding a culture by their own biases, their unwillingness to fully participate in all that is necessary to understand the culture, and even by their own research methods, which may inadvertently set up roadblocks between researcher and subject. Both the research method and the skillfulness of the written representation determine how accurately and responsibly the culture is brought to others.

Ethnography, "writing about culture," has been used in the field by cultural anthropologists such as Mead, Malinowski, Geertz, Clifford, Marcus, and Tyler in this century and has been adopted more and more by researchers in other disciplines in the last two decades. Ethnography offers an alternative model for gaining profound insights into other cultures. Ethnographic research turns standard research practice on its head: instead of engaging in detached, objective collecting and recording of data, ethnographers go into the field, become involved in their subjects' lives and stories, and render impressionistic accounts of what they've witnessed and participated in. Ethnography is known as a "whole person," or holistic, research method.

Ethnography relies on two basic research methods: interviewing and participant observation. Ethnographers approach interviewing differently than do most research interviewers. Instead of following the standard research interview format in which the interviewer dominates the interaction and the questions follow a "stimulus-response" format, ethnographers follow the lead of their sources, letting them determine the pace and content of the interview. In a standard research interview, the source is known as the "subject"; in the ethnographic interview, the source is known as the "informant."[1]

Ethnographers also use the methodology of participant observation in order to research "here and now" interactions in living cultures: "The world of everyday life is for the methodology of participant observation the ordinary, usual, typical, routine, or natural environment of human existence. This world stands in contrast to environments created and manipulated by researchers, as illustrated by experiments and surveys."[2]

The primary rule of procedure for participant observation is that the researcher ("reporter") does not operate from any theory or hypothesis but strives to discover the realities of the culture as it is actually lived. In so doing, the ethnographer is able to gain what Geertz calls "thick description,"[3] which is analysis based on a wealth of cultural signs and symbols, obtained only through close observation.

Other rules governing participant observation are that the researcher observes *while* participating and that field notes (including the researcher's own impressions, questions, doubts, and fears) be kept throughout the research.

The paradigm for ethnographic research is that of "empowerment." The experts in the field are not the researchers; the researchers are the people whose lives the experts are exploring in an effort to truly represent their culture. The concept of empowerment should govern every aspect of the enthnographer's research, from establishing relationships, to giving interviewees the power to determine the course and content of the interview, to devising a way to participate in and observe the culture. It recognizes that people are experts in their own lives; the researcher's job is to enable them to tell their own stories their own ways.

Ethnography is still a qualitative, experimental research method. Both the beauty and the curse of this method is that it depends almost entirely upon the skill and ethics of the individual researcher. The questions that surround the efficacy of ethnographic research concern how well the researcher is able to discern the complexities of a culture, how able he or she is to participate in a culture without losing his or her analytical bent, and how fully and responsibly the ethnographer is able to write about this culture.[4] Ethical questions include what purpose the research serves and how it may affect the ethnographer's informants.

My ethnographic research grew out of my interest in American police, a closed society to which I gained access after my sister became a Chicago police officer in 1981. My research followed the ethnographic model of interviewing and participant observation. In police culture, telling stories is an important part of the way the officers exchange information and make sense out of their experiences. I was able to interview and to participate in police culture as I collected these stories police told each other in groups.

The following analysis is an extension of research I conducted for an oral history called *Pure Cop* (Random House, 1991) and for a future book on hostage negotiation, based on interviews with Chicago Police Department hostage negotiators and SWAT team members. In the present chapter, these people report on their own observations as participants in the fluid culture of hostage-takers.

Hostage Negotiation

The hostage situation is an open-ended drama starting in chaos and skidding toward tragedy. What happens in this drama is complicated and, often, contaminated by its spectators/actors.

> What we do when we first get involved in these things, if the person inside doesn't have a phone, we throw them a field phone. Many times, we have people who have torn the phone out of the wall in a rage, or they're in a place that doesn't have a phone, like a garage.
>
> So we've got what we call a "throw phone," a military phone. It's in a canvas bag with a big zipper across the top. And you open it up and you get down to this black, heavy-duty plastic combat phone. It's got a crank on the side. You go, crank-crank-crank-crank-crank-crank-crank. And you then talk over this thing and you feel like Lee Marvin in an old war movie.
>
> So finally we decided—here we're trying to have empathy with the guy inside and say stuff like "I'm your buddy" and "Let's talk this over"—and we're throwing in a combat phone. Wrong message. So we changed.
>
> What we have now is a baby-blue Princess phone. Now, instead of going crank-crank-crank on the old combat phone, the guy has a little Princess. We tried to get a pink one, because that's supposed to be the best color. But our Vice Control Section got this baby-blue one on a gambling raid, so we went with that. We put a "SMILE—HAVE A NICE DAY" sticker on it.[5]

The spectators and participants include the media, who watch, report, and may affect the negotiation itself; the police, negotiators, and SWAT team members, whose monitoring determines their decision to keep negotiating or to move to assault; and the hostage taker, whose reading of the police and the situation may be overlaid by the media's own text, as delivered in broadcast reports the hostage taker is monitoring.

The entire drama may be played out, by both hostage taker and police, according to fantasies scripted by the media and Hollywood. Prior to the introduction of formal training programs in hostage negotiation in the United States in the late 1970s, fictive dramas produced by movies, television, and radio played a considerable role in the response of police to actual hostage/barricade situations. These fantasies deeply affected the expectations and actions of police officers. According to Lt. John Kennedy, founder of the Chicago Police Department's Hostage/Barricaded/Terrorist (HBT) Program and adviser to the U.S. State Department's Office of Diplomatic Security on Counterterrorist Programs:

> Before there was HBT training, how did police know what to do in a hostage situation? You could go through your whole career without getting one. So all of a sudden, you get a call, and there's a hostage situation. How did the police know what to do? *Hollywood* told them what to do.
>
> Somebody would make a movie and make things up and police would go see the movie and at some point be confronted with a hostage situation and think, "What do I do?" And what the police officer had seen before in the movies would click in—"Oh, yeah. I remember—Get a priest. Get the mother. Get the father. Put them all on the phone. Leave my gun outside. Go in. Exchange myself for the kid." All these things, which are the *worst* things to do in a hostage situation, the things that got people killed, is what, traditionally, police would do.
>
> Then somebody would come out from Hollywood and do some research. They wanted to accurately portray what cops really did in hostage situations. And the Hollywood guy would see, oh, this is what police are doing and Hollywood would then make movies showing police doing things in hostage situations that were based on what police had seen *Hollywood* doing. It was a real vicious circle, a real Catch-22.[6]

Fully realized and scripted fantasies revolving around hostage taking and negotiation can have pernicious effects upon actual negotiation. Even the clichés of media reporting of hostage situations can enfeeble negotiation attempts. For example, the reporting media regularly rely upon the formulaic description of the hostage situation as a "standoff" or "impasse" between the hostage taker and police. The hostage taker is characterized as "holding the police at bay." This use of language empowers actual and potential hostage takers, since "standoff" and "holding at bay" clearly imply that one person is holding off an entire police force, while "impasse" conjures up a drama that only some extraordinary means, a *deus ex machina* such as an entering SWAT team, can resolve. With all three reporting formulas, the media reduce the hostage situation to a conflict that can be broken only by forcible entry or violence, a reduction that distorts the dynamic, fluid nature of the negotiation into a static waiting game.

Complicating police negotiations with hostage takers still further is the presence of the electronic media at hostage events. To what extent is the hostage taker playing to the media? The potential for this seems considerable. The media—including the reporting and fantasy-generating genres—may create and escalate conflict in hostage situations through their very presence and their desire to come up with "a good story."

Statement of Problem and Method

This chapter will focus on the ways in which police specialists in hostage situations surmount the potentially dangerous media misrepresentations of these conflicts. The identification of the ways in which police use both discursive and physical tactics in hostage negotiation could also reveal some new paths for the formal study of negotiation. As cross-cultural negotiation specialist P. H. Gulliver acknowledges, this "is still in the formative stage of tentative conceptualization and hypothesis, with a paucity of specifically directed data collection and analysis."[7]

Both media theory and media reporting suffer from source silence. The most important actors in the hostage drama, the police hostage negotiators and SWAT team members, have been almost universally mute on the subject of what they actually do throughout the course of a negotiation. The reporting and scholarship on hostage negotiation is over-reliant on applications of theory[8] or upon the rare source willing to give a glimpse into negotiation. This has resulted in distortions regarding the SWAT team's role in negotiation, skewing all negotiation study to wholly discursive models. As Donohue comments, negotiation study has been too long hampered by a tendency to "focus almost exclusively on the content dimension" of tactics in negotiation.[9]

I was able to gain rare access to both hostage negotiators and SWAT team members in the Chicago Police Department through my work of assembling an oral history of police. The information presented here, which concerns the ways in which hostage negotiators and SWAT team members work to resolve a hostage situation, was gathered through interviews with seven hostage negotiators and six containment officers (the Chicago Police Department's equivalent of SWAT team members), all assigned to the Chicago Police Department's Hostage/Barricaded/Terrorist Unit. The officers I interviewed were promised anonymity for the published collection of their narratives; I will honor that anonymity here as well, identifying only Lieutenant Kennedy, by agreement. The other men and women will be referred to solely as hostage negotiators and containment officers. The interviews I conducted with these men and women, who use rhetoric to counter threatened homicide and suicide, demonstrated how rational discourse can be used to order chaos and avert or transcend tragedy.

I discovered that police have replaced the standard media model of hostage negotiation as impasse with a model of identification. Within this model, every action (whether it's a speech act or physical act such as ringing the hostage taker's doorbell or throwing a rock through the window to get him to respond) is considered tactical. As one negotiator puts it: "Anything you do can be tactical. If he's hungry, say, and you want to get something out of him, you might munch on a sandwich while you talk to him. If he's saying he's hungry and he wants some food, well, of course, you never let him have something for nothing. You might very well chew on a sandwich. Or pop a can near enough to the phone so he can hear it. Light a cigarette. Get him to give you what you want. It might be anything from a hostage to one bullet."[10]

Both hostage negotiators and containment officers work as tacticians, enhancing one another's overall effect on the negotiation, as exemplified in this description of tactics by a containment officer: "You want to wear him down so he recognizes the futility of staying barricaded in there. Turn on the power. Turn off the power, the water, the electric, the gas. If it's wintertime and it's one of those twenty-below zero days and you shut down his gas and his electric, he can't watch himself on TV and pretty soon he gets real cold in there. You break out a few windows and he gets a lot colder much quicker. You might fool around with the lighting, with noises. You bring him up and down."[11]

The Hostage/Barricaded/Terrorist unit is called up when a domestic dispute, a man-with-a-gun call, or a crime crosses over from what district police can handle into a dangerous, seemingly out-of-control standoff. A CPD hostage negotiator describes the typical HBT scene: "Every HBT situation is a homicide-in-progress. That's exactly what it is. Even if it's a barricaded person threatening suicide, the potential for homicide is still high. Homicide and suicide are two sides of the same coin. The person who has decided life is meaningless may decide to take other people on the trip with him."[12]

When the HBT unit arrives at the scene, where there may be a hostage taker or a barricaded person (considered equally dangerous because he or she may shoot anyone who gets near, or may have concealed hostages), the negotiators divide into three-person teams comprised of an intelligence gatherer, a relayer of information, and a primary negotiator. Containment officers surround the hostage taker or barricaded person in an effort to keep the person, and his or her homicidal motives, confined to as small an area as possible. As one officer reports: "The first thing you do is, you've got to contain the guy so he doesn't come running out. You've got to secure the scene. You can't let it get out-of-hand, or get any bigger than it is. And then you condense it down. If he has the run of the whole floor in a hotel, you want to get him into one wing, one set of rooms, one floor."[13]

Containment works more broadly than simply keeping the offender confined. Containment serves to place the offender's "scene-act ratio" within another "scene-act ratio," that created by the police. This is an embodiment of Burke's tenet that "the choice of circumference for the scene in terms of which a given act is to be located will have a corresponding effect upon the interpretation of the act itself."[14] Containment effectively creates a play-within-a-play, in which the hostage taker or barricaded person's motives are not unbounded but must continually come up against those of the larger agency.

The first step that containment officers take toward surmounting the model of impasse is to free the scene of media contaminants, that is, members of the media and reminders of the media script. The police shut the media out of the process by establishing inner and outer perimeters radiating out from the hostage taker. The "kill zone" is outlined by the first perimeter, the radius in which the hostage taker may shoot and kill. The second perimeter is that of the outermost limits of the scene, where negotiation teams place the media. The police also shut out the media by cutting off the electricity inside, so that the hostage taker is not responding to media messages regarding the event. Throughout the event, containment officers back up negotiators by controlling the environment of the hostage taker, freeing it from media messages and stereotypes of what actions to follow. According to Lieutenant Kennedy, "What HBT does is change the script. It keeps both responding officers and the person inside from acting according to Hollywood fantasies."[15]

Controlling the audience at the hostage/barricade scene is an integral part of clearing the hostage-negotiation scene of media involvement and neutralizing expectations concerning the hostage drama that were culled from mass-media fantasies. To an extent, the hostage taker's struggles to realize his goals are controlled and his motives changed by limiting and controlling the persons allowed on the scene, for such persons become the hostage taker's audience. According to Lieutenant Kennedy, the HBT unit of the Chicago Police never allows "the priest, the minister, the rabbi, the wife, the husband, the girlfriend, anyone who might become the suicide audience" on scene.[16]

In effect, the police-mediated hostage negotiation creates a biosphere or a "play-within-a-play" in which the hostage situation is placed within the scope of police manipulation. This is Burke's "administrative rhetoric," which he explained is best exemplified by Theodore Roosevelt's "Walk softly and carry a big stick" political philosophy.[17] In the hostage situation this is played out in alleys, in hallways, on rooftops, where both sides may carry "big sticks" in the form of assault weapons to back up their speech act/intentions and where both sides recognize that the failure of negotiation can result in death. The rest of this chapter will sketch this technique and follow the course of a hostage negotiation that exemplifies it.

Analysis

A close analysis of what happens in hostage negotiation reveals its dramatic base: tragedy is avoided through the transformation of the hostage taker's "motive"; the hostage drama headed for tragedy may end in "transformation," that is, the surrender of the hostage taker or barricaded person and/or the release of hostages. Hostage negotiation has as its primary goal changing the motive of the hostage taker or barricaded person, and in so changing the motive, changing the final outcome.

The hostage taker/barricaded person has cut himself off, segregated himself, placed himself in a divided state. Once the area has been contained, cut off from media involvement in fact or fantasy, the first act of the HBT unit is to establish identification with the negotiator by getting the hostage taker to respond to another human voice, whether through shouting, use of the bullhorn, or, preferably, talking over the phone. As one hostage negotiator explains, "It's hard to sound compassionate over a bullhorn." This illustrates the applicability of Burke's central tenet that "identification is compensatory to division."[18]

The person who has excluded himself from society may reenter by identifying with just one other person within that society. Hostage negotiation hinges on making individual human contact, laying the groundwork of identification. As one officer put it:

When we first get there, it's chaos; it's a circus. In the initial confrontation, shots may be fired, things are all confused, stress levels hit the ceiling.

The offender's inside, looking around—he's hearing the sirens, he's hearing the police radios squawking, he's hearing the officers yelling back and forth, he's hearing them running back and forth.

The guy's in a panic. He thinks Rambo and three SWAT teams are about to come swinging through the window. That's when he's going to make a mistake—he's going to start firing shots out the window; he's going to shoot a hostage; he's going to do something desperate. The police are in a panic, too. They're running around. They don't know what the hell's going on.

What we try to do, right from the start, is reduce the threat level of the new environment. The situation will start off—the offender has three hostages on the ground and he's telling them, "Move and I'll shoot you in the head." And he means it. The phone rings. He picks it up. Here's a voice that represents that entity out here. And it's a calm voice. He starts calming down. Just by getting one of our guys to get the bad guy on the phone solves half our problems.[19]

The identification strategy called "common ground"[20] is the most crucial negotiation method. It must be established at the outset, since it can reconnect the offender with the "commonsense" world he or she has abandoned through a desperate act. A hostage negotiator describes the beginning of hostage negotiation and the importance of establishing common ground:

Once they agree to talk, then you play off what they tell you and all you have to do is adjust to what they say.

"What's your name?"

"Tony."

"Tony, is it. You're not Italian?"

You phrase it like that instead of saying, "Are you Italian" or "That's Italian." And why? Because if he *is* Italian and he likes it, "Yes, I am." Then you can say, "Hey, really? Me too." If he's *not* Italian and he hates Italians, you've already said he's not Italian. So he's not mad at you. You give him an out immediately from the statement you've made.

"You're not Italian, are you?"

"What's wrong with Italians?"

"Oh, I *like* Italians."

Or it could go:

"I *hate* Italians."

"Yeah. I do too. I didn't think you were Italian."

You look for any kind of hook that'll get them going. You play with that.[21]

Where the negotiation process goes after the initial attempt at establishing common ground depends upon how accurately police at the scene can determine the hostage taker/barricaded person's true motive. Negotiators gather intelligence on the person so they can anticipate what he or she will do, by what means, and for what purpose, while containment officers seek to control the scene.

The offender's own scope of operations is, in Burkean terms, the "scene-act ratio," meaning the physical scope used by the actor, which, in turn, acts upon him; in police terms, it is the "kill zone." Once that scope has been constrained, the next step is to manipulate the offender's physical environment so that he is less comfortable being segregated from the community and identifies more with the voice of the hostage negotiator. That voice becomes the offender's one constant in a scene that is constantly changing. The importance of a deft application of the "scene-act" ratio to the hostage situation is suggested by a hostage negotiator: "As far as knowing the containment is out there, we don't like them [the hostage takers] to see containment officers because if they see them and they're armed, they might shoot. But we certainly want them to know they're [the containment officers] there. So, a lot of the times, a fellow will say, 'I see those guys. I don't want to see them.' We tell them, 'Of course there are police. Do they bother you? We'll tell them to stay back.' And then we tell the police, 'Just try to keep down, guys.'"[22]

A containment officer talks about controlling the "scene-act ratio," or environment, of the hostage taker: "We want to totally control the environment of the hostage taker: the electricity, the gas, the air conditioning, the heating, no matter what it is, we want control of it. If you can pull these resources away, then they're negotiable items, and we can negotiate them back for the release of the hostages. After a while, he comes back into reason."[23]

This application of administrative rhetoric intensifies identification by making the hostage taker/barricaded person more dependent upon the hostage negotiator. The identification strategy that Cheney terms "antithesis," through which a common enemy is faced,[24] grows out of the constant danger presented by the containment officers. At any moment these officers can become the assault team. The negotiator capitalizes on this, using what Cheney calls the "transcendent we,"[25] by reminding the offender that he or she has the option of ending the conflict without assault, through surrender or the release of hostages: "If he thinks the SWAT team's coming in, then he's gonna get real excited. 'They're at the door. I hear them coming in. They're breaking windows,' he'll say. 'Wait a minute. Slow down. Relax,' you'll say. 'Why don't we just end this?'"[26]

The negotiator's rhetoric suggests to the offender that only the negotiator can get him out of this uncomfortable, dangerous situation. This brings into play Burke's "representative anecdote."[27] As one officer explains, "You talk about anything to make it more human, less police, less criminal. You talk about the weather; you talk about sports; you talk about the wall. You're trying to establish a rapport with him. You're trying to gain his confidence. You want him to trust you—'You're in this awful situation, but I want to help you.' You're his anchor. It's sort of like, 'Through me, you'll live.'"[28]

In a successful hostage negotiation, the offender identifies with the negotiator and the hostages identify with the offender against the police, a phenomenon known as the "Stockholm syndrome." This term grew out of a bank robbery in Stockholm, Sweden, during which two men held three women hostages in a bank vault for a week. Following the incident, none of the women would testify against the bank robbers. Two of the women subsequently married two of the robbers.

The Stockholm syndrome fits the "antithesis" principle in uniting hostage taker and hostages against what is perceived as the "common enemy," the police. According to Lieutenant Kennedy, this identification can save hostages' lives:

> If you're taken hostage, what you don't want to do is isolate yourself away from the hostage-taker. You want to interact with this person, because it's easy to kill a stranger, but it's harder to kill somebody you know.
>
> You want to be responsive, that you understand their situation, maybe they're right and the police are wrong, and what can you do to help him.
>
> What will normally happen, even without you intending it, is you *will* become more responsive, you *will* identify with the hostage-taker, you will swing over to him—"What's wrong with the authorities? This guy says do this or he's going to kill me and they're not doing what he wants. What's *wrong* with these people? This guy—this guy did have a couple good points in what he was saying. And he's not that bad a guy." That's the Stockholm syndrome.[29]

The fluid, dynamic process of establishing and maintaining identification in hostage negotiations can best be seen in case studies of police-mediated hostage situations. What follows are two contrasting cases as related by CPD hostage negotiators. The first situation was contaminated by outside intervention, with a tragic outcome. The second exemplifies negotiator control over scene and audience, with a successful resolution.

A hostage negotiator reported on a barricade scene on a flight of back stairs outside an apartment building. A man had just shot his wife. He was on the landing above; the body of his wife on the landing below. A priest had arrived at the scene before HBT and remained throughout the negotiation. At one point, the priest thought the negotiator, who was letting the man cry, had run out of things to say. The priest said to the man: "It's okay to cry. Men cry sometimes. Get it all out. Get it over with." According to the negotiator, this statement gave the man permission to commit suicide:

> The next sound you heard was a roar. The next thing I felt were various parts of this man from above his neck. When the priest said the words, "Get it over with," the man took the four-word remark totally out-of-context and did what he had intended to do all along.[30]

Another negotiator gives the details of a successfully manipulated situation:

> A guy stabbed the shit out of his father-in-law, thirty, forty times. Now here's what happened. He's fighting with his wife, who's pregnant; he's got two kids—they're not his kids—they're her kids.
> She's pregnant with his baby.
> He's fighting with her a lot. He's an abuser, a beater. They live with her father. The father, who knows that there's a problem on this particular day, [is] trying to protect the daughter from further abuse at this particular moment—he's not banning the guy from the house; he's not throwing him out; he's trying to defuse this moment—he locks him out of the house.
> The son-in-law crashes a window. He tries to climb in through the window. The father-in-law therefore hits him with a baseball bat. The son-in-law gets a knife, a genuine, a real butcher knife—a real one!—a real butcher knife, stabs the father-in-law [numerous times], I think, in the thirties, in the high thirties.
> He knows he screwed up. He grabs the two children, goes down the basement stairs, and holds them at knifepoint. The father-in-law had already called the police, the police are coming, the father-in-law is dead when they get there.
> Two policemen from the Twentieth District arrive. They had known the son-in-law from domestic disturbances before. So now they're standing there, at the doorway, looking down into the basement. And they're standing there talking to this guy who's got this butcher knife and he's got both of these little children, four and five years old, I think. . . . And we get there and one of the cops, I'll never forget, he's got this look in his face, and he was so scared.
> I was scared, too.
> We got this cop's partner away and then he and I traded places. Before this, I was writing him (the cop) notes, things to say. Finally, I realized this isn't working. I wrote him a note: "Tell him you gotta check on something. A friend of mine is here. Let him talk to you a minute."
> So then I start talking to the guy in the basement. I'm standing in the doorjamb. The cop starts to go. I couldn't tell him, "You gotta stay with me," but I'm trying to let him know he shouldn't go anywhere because I don't know anything about this guy. There's gotta be things we don't know. First, I don't know

if the father-in-law's dead or alive. I don't know if they said to the guy, "Well, you killed him, but it's okay." It turned out he *didn't* know the father-in-law was dead.

I'm looking at the two kids the stepfather's holding. The little girl was real fidgety. The little boy was okay. You could tell with the boy. He didn't understand. He wasn't scared; he just didn't understand why his dad had this big knife and won't let him go.

The bond is there between the father and the little boy. You could tell. "It's okay. It's okay," he keeps telling the boy. But the bond isn't there with the girl. He's not saying anything to her. So right away, you're fearful for the little girl. Nobody else could sense that and nobody could see it because of my position. And unbeknownst to me, next door, there was a containment guy, a sniper, and the position I was standing in kept blocking their view of everything. But I just found the position I was comfortable in, and once in a while I'd move, but I kept coming back to that position I was comfortable in. It was my comfort zone.

The other police are right next to me, but the guy in the basement can't see them. He only sees me. There are containment officers in the next building, looking down. The police inside don't communicate with me verbally; they write me notes. On occasion, I'd lean across and look at a note. One time, I put my cheek on the doorjamb like I was resting and they stuck an earphone in my ear.

The guy downstairs knows I'm a detective. "Where's your gun?" he says. I had already taken my gun from my ankle holster, put it in my back waistband, because if he's gonna ask me about my gun, I can show him, *voila,* an empty holster, right?

I said, "Listen, I don't have a gun anywhere." I leaned to the left, up against the jamb, and fortunately, the guy who was standing next to me had the presence of mind to reach around, without being seen, and take the gun out of my waistband. So now I can do a pirouette, I can pull my shirt out, I open my pants and show him my underwear and I do everything possible to show him that I'm not armed, to take away what he thought was a threat.

The problem was, if he started cutting the kids, there's nothing I could do. My job is not to shoot. In that case, the only people that were in a position to do anything aggressive if necessary were the guys across the way and I didn't know they were there.

Anyway, we got to talking. I convinced him that his father-in-law wasn't dead. I convinced him that his father-in-law was the offender—"He beat you with a baseball bat."

Fortunately, somebody picked up on what I was saying, and in about four minutes, there was a case report brought to the scene that had him listed as the victim. "The Offender: father-in-law's name. Information reveals that: Victim was trying to see his wife and was attacked." I mean, we had a police report that said that this man, who had just gotten done stabbing the shit out of his father-in-law, was a victim.

I could see the little girl was scared. So I talked to her. "How to you feel?" "Oh, okay." "Are you sick to your stomach?" I kept returning to her. "How do you feel? Is your stomach bothering you? Your throat is real dry, isn't it?" I talked the kid into being sick. Pretty soon, she got dry heaves. This poor little girl.

And now the stepfather starts to feel for her. I say, "Pat, she's gotta go to the bathroom" "Well, she can go in the sewer." I said, "Pat, she's not gonna want to do that. Would you want to do that, if you were a little girl, go to the bathroom in front of your father? Let her come upstairs."

And here's the thing that I'll be criticized for the rest of my life. "If I let her come up, do you promise that she'll come back?" "I promise." Without hesitation, I said, "I promise." He's got a kid that he can cut the head off if I don't get the girl back. . . . (But) I know the bond—nobody else could see the bond between the guy and the boy. There were a lot of little things, but one thing convinced me the bond was really there with the little boy. At one point, the stepfather took the butcher knife and scratched the little girl's cheek with it. And he scratched the little boy's throat. He told *her,* "Stand still or I'll do it again," but he said to the little boy, "I'm sorry."

So we get the little girl up the stairs and they take her off and she goes to the bathroom, she threw up, she was sick. Now—*they're bringing her back.* And they've got her where I can see her. And I'm starting to think, "She's not going back there. Wait a minute." And one of the bosses comes running to me, and he's standing there—see, after a while you get to know the routine. You lean on the doorjamb whenever you want information. And the boss says, "That girl's not going back there." I kind of looked at him and then I said something to the guy in the basement so that I could respond, "What the fuck do you think I am? Stupid?" I said it to Pat, but I meant it for the boss.

I could see that Pat was nervous. He's got the knife at the kid's throat. What if he says, "Bring her down right now or I'll kill him?" What do you do?

Now the case report's here. So I say, "We've got the case report. I'll show it to you." Now he says the magic words, "I believe you."

Now he says, "What should I do, Tom?"

"We should take care of this."

"How do we do that?"

Now I've got him, but I don't know I've got him because he's still got this kid at knifepoint. For several hours, he'd been holding the kids like that. He had one or the other with a knife to their throat for hours.

I say, "Well, let me tell you this, Pat. Let me see if we can get a complaint together. So you know and because you trust me, I want you to sign a complaint, against your father-in-law. Battery."

I can hear people scrambling, so now they're looking for complaints and they're filling them out. In a few minutes, it's done. "Pat, here's the complaint. Here's what I want you to do. I'm gonna give you this complaint. I'll put it on the stairs." We'd already done that. I would put cigarettes on the stairs. I'd go down the stairs and come back up. And he'd come up one stair, holding the little boy by the collar. We went through this elaborate passing system on the twelve stairs.

"So, I'll get the complaint down the stairs."

"No, you don't have to do that."

"No, I want you to see it."

"You don't have to do that."

"Well, okay. All right."

"Tom, I think I'm gonna give up."

"All right. Let me put the complaint on the stairway. Why don't you put the knife on the stairway, take the complaint, read it, and if everything is exactly what I told you, then you go back to the bottom of the stairs, and leave the knife right there."

"Okay."

I went down three stairs. And the next thing I see is this guy coming up the stairs with the knife. He's got his arm extended and the knife's pointed right at me. He left the little boy at the bottom of the stairs. And I'm thinking, "This isn't healthy. Where do we go from here?"

If he had the little boy with him, I probably would have retreated. He didn't have the little boy and I'm thinking, "Do I run? Do I break up what we had going? Do I endanger the little boy? Do I want open heart surgery?" And all this is happening in just a second. And all of a sudden, he took the knife, turned it around, and turned the handle toward me.[31]

These two cases illustrate the importance of creating a self-contained world in which identification strategies can proceed without interference from outside agencies. The first case shows what can happen when this delicate dance is interrupted by a representative (in the person of the priest, a heavily symbolic figure) from beyond the negotiation group. In the second case, the negotiator was able to use the resources just beyond the hostage taker's view to alter reality as part of the identification process.

When hostage negotiation is successful, it is because the key was found to changing the motive behind the act. Sometimes this is discovered by accident, but generally it is revealed through a combination of identification and administrative rhetorical strategies.

When the person who has segregated himself from the world retreats even further, when the offender is immune to rhetoric, to rational discourse, the ties of identification are severed and an assault is made. In cases handled through the Chicago HBT program, in effect since July 1980, no hostage situation has ended in deadly assault. Contrary to the media belief that assault is the only possible conclusion to "impasse," trained negotiators avoid assault. As one negotiator points out, "Assault comes when all other known avenues of approach are exhausted. You've done everything you can dream of. You've done everything known to man. Assault is all that's left."[32]

Conclusion

Hostage negotiation is the art of maintaining human ties, however tenuous. It is a difficult art, due to the explosiveness of the hostage situation. It is made more difficult and dangerous by the overlay of expectations established by Hollywood, television, and the reporting media, which can contaminate hostage situations.

Police-mediated hostage negotiation has three overlapping goals: to contain the situation itself, reducing the danger to police and people in the immediate area and making it part of a police operation, rather than following the script inherited from Hollywood or TV; to transcend, in the negotiation itself, any traces of media contamination; and to transform the motive of the hostage taker from homicide/suicide to surrender.

The primary means of realizing these goals is through the model of identification. This model unites physical and discursive tactics in police-mediated hostage negotiation, offering a pathway out of the media-dictated, dangerous model of impasse.

Notes

1. See Elliot G. Mishler, *Research Interviewing* (Cambridge, Mass.: Harvard University Press, 1986).

2. Danny L. Jorgensen, *Participant Observation: A Methodology for Human Studies* (Newbury Park, Calif.: Sage, 1989), 15.

3. See Clifford Geertz, *The Interpretation of Cultures* (New York: Basic Books, 1973).

4. See John Van Maanen, *Tales of the Field: On Writing Ethnography* (Chicago: University of Chicago Press, 1988), for explorations of the pros and cons of various narrative choices open to ethnographers.

5. Connie Fletcher, *Pure Cop: Cop Talk from the Street through the Specialized Units* (New York: Random House, 1991), 214.

6. Ibid., 202–3.

7. See P. H. Gulliver, *Disputes and Negotiations: A Cross-Cultural Perspective* (New York: Academic Press, 1979), 179–207.

8. See I. W. Zartman, ed., *The Fifty Percent Solution* (Garden City, N.Y.: Doubleday, 1976); and A. Strauss, *Negotiations: Varieties, Contexts, Processes, and Social Order* (San Francisco: Jossey-Bass, 1987).

9. W. A. Donohue, "Development of a Model of Rule Use in Negotiation Interaction," *Communication Monographs* 48 (September 1981), 106.

10. Fletcher, 230–1.

11. Ibid., 230.

12. Ibid., 205.

13. Ibid., 212–13.

14. See Kenneth Burke, *A Grammar of Motives* (Berkeley: University of California Press, 1969), and *Language as Symbolic Action* (Berkeley: University of California Press, 1966).

15. Fletcher, 204.

16. Ibid., 218.

17. Burke, *Language as Symbolic Action,* 301.

18. Burke, *A Rhetoric of Motives* (Berkeley: University of California Press, 1969), 22.

19. Fletcher, 212.

20. G. Cheney, "The Rhetoric of Identification and the Study of Organizational Communication," *Quarterly Journal of Speech* 69 (# 2, 1983), 148.

21. Fletcher, 217.

22. Ibid., 214.

23. Ibid., 230.

24. Cheney, 148.

25. Ibid.

26. Fletcher, 230.

27. Burke, *A Grammar of Motives,* 59–61.

28. Fletcher, 218.

29. Ibid., 210–11.

30. Ibid., 218–21.

31. Ibid., 222–26.

32. Ibid., 236.

Contributors

ROBERT A. BAUKUS is Associate Professor of Communication in the Advertising/ PR Program, College of Communications, Pennsylvania State University, University Park. His research interests cover all sorts of message designs, approached through integrated marketing communications. He has published several groundbreaking articles on communication argumentativeness and verbal aggression in such publications as *Communications Education* and *Communications Research Reports*. His work on political communications has appeared in the *American Behavioral Scientist* and *Political Communication and Persuasion*. He does consulting in the area of marketing communications and message design for public and private corporations. His e-mail address is rab18@psu.edu.

RONALD BETTIG is Associate Professor of Communications in the Media Studies Program, Pennsylvania State University, University Park. His most recent publication is *Copyrighting Culture: The Political Economy of Intellectual Property* (1996). He has also published work in the area of internet copyright. His research interests focus on international communications and the political economy of communications. His e-mail address is rvb3@psu.edu.

PETER DAHLGREN is Professor of Media and Communication Studies, Lund University, Sweden. His work is wide ranging, addressing issues related to media, democracy, the public sphere, citizens, cultural theory, and identity processes. He is the author of *Journalism and Popular Culture* (1992) and *Television and the Public Sphere* (1995). His e-mail address is peter.dahlgren@soc.lu.se.

CONNIE FLETCHER is Associate Professor of Communications at Loyola University, Chicago. Her most widely read work involves police studies. She also is interested in negotiation and narrative. Her books include *What Cops Know* (1991), *Pure Cop* (1992), and *Breaking and Entering* (1995). Her e-mail address is cfletch@luc.edu.

MARY S. MANDER is Associate Professor of Communications in the Media Studies Program, College of Communications, Pennsylvania State University, University Park. A postmodern cultural historian, she has published several articles on war correspondents in the United States. Her research interests include postmodern cultural theory, the media and the public sphere, and the social consequences of implementing communications technologies. Her e-mail address is msm4@psu.edu.

PETER D. MOSS does systems analysis for the Department of Information Technology at the Adelaide Institute in South Australia. His research interests focus primarily on media discourses. He has published papers on aspects of radio discourse (in *Media, Culture and Society*). He is the coauthor, with C. S. Higgins, of *Sounds Real: Radio in Everyday Life* (1982) and contributed several chapters to the book *Language and the Nuclear Arms Debate: Nukespeak Today* (ed. Chilton, 1985). His e-mail address is pmoss@adel.tafe.sa.edu.au.

SVEIN ØSTERUD is Professor at the University of Oslo, Norway. His work explores news media and their audiences, media education, and the relationship between media and the public sphere, as well as media events such as the Gulf war and the death of King Olaf V. He published *The Concept of Society in Sophocles* in 1976; more recently he contributed a chapter to the forthcoming book *Consuming Audiences* (ed. Wasko and Hagen). His e-mail address is svein.osterud@ped.uio.no.

SUSAN M. STROHM is Assistant Professor of Communications in the Advertising/PR Program and Director of the Schreyer University Scholars, both in the College of Communications, Pennsylvania State University, University Park. Her research interests include mass media and social change, the role of mass communication and interpersonal communication in health-related cognitive, attitudinal, and behavioral changes. She has published articles in such academic journals as *Communication Educator*. Her primary work is in developing health education campaigns for corporate and nonprofit groups. Her e-mail address is sms14@psu.edu.

PHILLIP J. TICHENOR, GEORGE A. DONOHUE, and CLARICE N. OLIEN are all now retired from the University of Minnesota. Their pioneering work involving the knowledge-gap hypothesis appeared originally in 1970 and was elaborated in their book *Community Conflict and the Press* (1980). Here they presented empirical evidence clarifying the media's role in the context of the larger social system, at a time when such evidence was scarce. Dr. Tichenor was Professor of Journalism and Mass Communications. His work centered on media and public opinion. Dr. Donohue was Professor of Sociology. His area of specialization was social theory and community development. Dr. Olien was Professor in the Department of Rural Sociology. Her research revolved around community organization, youth development, and mass communication.

Index